# Our Literary Heritage

# Our Literary Heritage

A Pictorial History of the Writer in America

by

VAN WYCK BROOKS

and

OTTO L. BETTMANN

E. P. DUTTON & COMPANY, INC., NEW YORK

*Library of Congress Catalog Card Number: 56-8325*
*Lithographed by The Murray Printing Company, Wakefield, Mass.*

# Contents

INTRODUCTION                                                                  vii

BOOK ONE

*THE WORLD OF WASHINGTON IRVING*                                               1

Philadelphia in 1800. * The Land of Yankees. * The Dutch along
the Hudson. * Washington Irving. * Irving and Scott. * James
Fenimore Cooper. * Later Knickerbockers. * The West. * Frontier Life Contributes to National Literature. * The South. * Edgar
Allan Poe. * William Cullen Bryant. * Painters and Writers.

BOOK TWO

*THE FLOWERING OF NEW ENGLAND*                                               40

Boston and Cambridge. * New England Minds Lead the Nation.
Widening Horizons. * New England Historians Fulfill Vital Func-
tion. * The Hour had Struck for Poets. * Young Boston Goes to
Sea. * Transcendentalism Explores the Inner Life. * The Sage of
Concord. * Henry Thoreau. * Intellectual Whirlpools. * Brook
Farm. * The Alcott Family. * Nathaniel Hawthorne. * The Anti-
Slavery Writers. * Whittier, Poet-Laureate of New England. * Un-
cle Tom's Cabin. * James Russell Lowell. * Literary Boston.
Oliver Wendell Holmes. * The Saturday Club. * Epilogue.

BOOK THREE

*THE TIMES OF MELVILLE AND WHITMAN*                                          102

New York in the Fifties. * Tales of the Travellers. * Herman Mel-
ville. * Melville's Moby Dick. * Melville and Whitman. * Leaves
of Grass. * Walt Whitman: The Image of the Poet. * The Far
West. * The World of Bret Harte * Cowboys Bandits and Books.
The Midwest. * Sidney Lanier. * Negro Folklore Charms the
Nation. * Regional Writing. * George W. Cable. * Mark Twain.

# Contents

BOOK FOUR

*NEW ENGLAND: INDIAN SUMMER*  150

Henry Adams. ✳ Practicality Triumphant. ✳ The Rise of Realism. Writers Strive for a Better World. ✳ The Problem of Europe in American Breasts. ✳ Henry James. ✳ Emily Dickinson. ✳ Women Writers Gain in Influence. ✳ Poetry in Decline.

BOOK FIVE

*THE CONFIDENT YEARS*  180

The Ghetto a School for Writers. ✳ Stephen Crane. ✳ Reformers-Reporters-Writers. ✳ O. Henry. ✳ New York High Society. ✳ Chicago. ✳ The West's New Voices. ✳ Theodore Dreiser. ✳ Small Town. ✳ Willa Cather. ✳ Saving the Cowboy from Oblivion. ✳ San Francisco in the Nineties. ✳ Jack London. ✳ Ellen Glasgow. ✳ The Southwest. ✳ Gertrude Stein. ✳ Mencken of Baltimore. ✳ Sinclair Lewis.   The Imagists.   Eugene O'Neill.   Poetic Renaissance Epilogue.

*Acknowledgements.*  239

*Index.*  241

# Introduction

This book is based on the five volumes of my *Makers and Finders: a History of the Writer in America, 1800-1915*. The volumes in question are *The World of Washington Irving; The Flowering of New England; The Times of Melville and Whitman; New England: Indian Summer;* and *The Confident Years, 1885-1915*. In each case the main theme is preserved in the following pages.

My literary historical series was the work of twenty years, and I have tried to explain at length what my purpose was in still another book, *The Writer in America*. Meanwhile, Dr. Otto Bettmann suggested that he would like to make an abridgment of my series with illustrations, and this proposal interested me all the more because I could not have undertaken any such task. I could not have had the necessary detachment of mind to abbreviate my own writing in this fashion, and, besides, it is difficult for a writer to alter or condense his work when it has once passed out of the molten state. No doubt an abridgment is always better when it is made by someone who comes as a stranger to the work in question, who sees it from the outside objectively and freshly and who is not too familiar with the subject. As a cultivated newcomer from Europe, Dr. Bettmann approached my books with a kind of alert curiosity that is rare or unknown among native American students or ordinary readers, and he felt for my theme an enthusiasm that could be possible only in one who is discovering it for himself. Mature and unbiased as he was, he had enjoyed exposing himself to the stimulus of a new environment, and all this helps to explain the success with which, as it seems to me, he has carried through the present undertaking.

Dr. Bettmann has recast my work in quite a new form, cutting the narrative down to less than one-sixth of the original text while largely retaining its continuity and flow. This required some rearranging and much more condensing, but Dr. Bettmann has succeeded in keeping the thread and the core of the work without too many visible seams or harsh transitions. His object was to preserve the essential movements and the principal figures, and at the same time he has assembled the pictures that give this work an independent value. Of these there are more than five hundred, gathered from all quarters. Dr. Bettmann personally searched museums in the South for new material on Poe and other Southern writers, and he made several trips to New England looking for new pictures of the literary figures of this region. He sought out scores of museums and libraries and the families of great writers in quest of illustrations that were not previously published. To speak of one case, he wished to bring into sharper focus the remote and evasive figure of Henry Adams, of whom very few pictures are generally known. Searching in Boston, Quincy and Washington, he brought to light six additional photographs, some of them taken by Mrs. Henry Adams. These pictures covered the historian's entire career. Then he compiled, to choose two examples, entirely novel pictorial biographies of Walt Whitman and Theodore Dreiser. In several other cases, he has used illustrations not to give merely the writer himself and his milieu but rather to conjure up the mood of an important spot or the essential features of a literary movement. He has done this to represent regionalism, or the setting of Poe's tales, or Chicago as a momentary focus of literary talent.

Dr. Bettmann has called my work "a history of American life seen through the literary window," and my intention was from the beginning to show the interaction of American life and letters. I had primarily in mind the American writers of our day and what I conceived to be the interest for them of a living sense of the immediate tradition behind them. I mean that part of the world tradition of which our national tradition is, in Walt Whitman's phrase, an "evolutionary outcome," the part that represents our own peculiar experience and that is properly seen as a gateway to the rest. As for the sense of tradition itself, one may say that in all the arts it "assures the continuity of creation," as Stravinsky puts it; and it seems to me that we can best connect ourselves with the great tradition by way of the tradition that we know. Or that we *should* know, as one has to say it, for until quite lately we have had no collective memory, no sense of a continuous development in our literature and art. "In America no man and no thing endures for more than a generation," one of our novelists said a few years ago; and, moreover, the most influential critic of the last age, Mencken, was bent on "liquidating" the American past. This, at least in literature, was mainly a nineteenth-century past, and the nineteenth century was the *bête noire* of the first world-war mind that was determined to "kill" it, as Gertrude Stein remarked. Naturally, the younger writers have had little sense of our tradition. As for others, countless Americans of the old stock were growing up without any of the inherited knowledge of the history of their forbears which the older Americans seemed to have had from birth, while millions of foreign-born citizens and children of the foreign-born were unaware that America had a past. Many of these were the "cultural tramps" of whom Ole Rölvaag spoke,

## Introduction

the new Americans who had lost their old-world cultural heritage and could not find another in their new-world setting. So it seemed to me important to show in all its concrete fullness the largely unexplored range of our cultural tradition. This was my general purpose in writing the series.

I should like to add a few personal words about my collaborator. Otto Bettmann was born in 1903 in Leipzig, the ancient and still active centre of the German book-trade. His special interests as a student were social history and the history of art and in these subjects he did post-graduate work in Italy, England and France. He then became the curator of the rare book department of the State Art Library in Berlin, and there he discovered the value and importance of works of art as a means of documenting social history. He had noted in Vienna, in Breughel's "Harvest Festival," twenty separate details that visualized social history for him, illustrating, to mention three, the manners of the time and its eating habits, together with its social stratification. Presently, as an avocation, he started a file of illustrative prints, especially dealing with the field of medicine, and this was the nucleus of the Bettmann Archive, which he brought to New York in 1935. He doubted at first that the Archive would sustain him, but this was a time of great activity in the world of graphic documentation and he soon found that his services were useful to magazine editors and publishers. Meanwhile, fascinated by American history in all its aspects, he read Vernon Parrington and Charles A. Beard, and, as an expert in the graphic representation of history, he began to plan a pictorial volume to accompany my *Makers and Finders*. With the aid of the skilful book-designer, Atkinson Dymock, this has now happily developed into the present blending of pictures and text.

VAN WYCK BROOKS

Book One

# The
# World of Washington Irving

*American Authors of the Nineteenth Century. Left: first row seated, Miss Sedgwick, Mrs. Sigourney, Mrs. Southworth, Longfellow, Bryant, Halleck, Irving, R. H. Dana,*

Margaret Fuller, Channing, Mrs. Stowe, Mrs. Kirkland, Whittier. Second Row, standing, Kennedy, Holmes, Willis, Mitchell, Morris, Poe, Tuckerman, Hawthorne, Simms, P. Pendleton Cooke, Hoffman, Cooper, Prescott, Bancroft, Parke Godwin, Motley, Beecher, Curtis, Emerson, Lowell, Boker, Bayard Taylor, Saxe. Left staircase, Mrs. Mowatt Ritchie, Prentice, Alice Cary, G. W. Kendall. Right staircase, Cozzens, Gallagher, Stoddard, Mrs. Amelia Welby.

*His autobiography, clear and short ...*
*the first American literary classic.*

# Philadelphia in 1800

*...the new literary centre of*
*America where leading minds*
*found both focus and forum.*

In 1800 the many-sided mind of Franklin still brooded over Philadelphia. As a bookseller, he had introduced all the great works of the time before he drew light from the clouds with his kite-string and key; and, while organizing a hospital, a police-force and a fire-company, he had brought in the first Scotch cabbage and the first kohlrabi. He had added three fables to Aesop, and, perfecting the musical glasses, for which Mozart and Beethoven wrote compositions, he had all but invented as well the American republic. There were those who also felt that he had invented American literature, for his *Autobiography,* written to prove that writing should be "smooth, clear and short," was the first American book that was certainly a classic.

In the Philosophical Society, Franklin had brought together all the leading figures of the colonies. Largely by means of this society, the American mind had found itself and knew it was no longer the New England mind or the Southern mind but the mind of one proud new nation.

During the ensuing decades the publisher Mathew Carey justified the name of Philadelphia as the literary centre of the country. A friend of every aspiring author, he had subscribers in most of the states, and in many European countries. His general publishing interests spread far and wide; and, while Philadelphia ceased to be the capital in 1800, it remained, largely through him, the centre of light. Some of this light radiated to the provinces through the efforts of the inimitable Reverend Mason Locke Weems.

For thirty years this "Livy of the common people" plodded up and down the Southern roads as Mathew Carey's vagabond bookhawker, — as a vagabond author as well. Nothing in the way of an anecdote ever escaped him. Weems was one of Carey's most profitable authors. His images were bold and even Homeric, and, along with his unblushing fabrications in the lives he wrote of Washington, Franklin and General Francis Marion, much of his writing abounded in life and truth.

Parson Weems was a familiar figure on the roads of the South. With his ruddy visage and the locks that flowed over his clerical coat, one saw him

*Many Washington anecdotes gained circulation*
*through Parson Weems's biographical tracts.*
*He hawked these, unimpeded by*
*"roads horrid — suns torrid."*

4

bumping along in his Jersey wagon, a portable bookcase behind and a fiddle beside him. A little ink-horn hung from one of his lapels, and he carried a quill pen stuck in his hat. Now and then he stopped at a pond or a stream to wash his shirt and take a bath, suspending his linen to dry on the frame of the wagon.

Already Philadelphia had the finest American theatre as well as the best and for years the only museum. This was Peale's Museum. It was the creation of Charles Willson Peale. An enthusiast for natural history, he established his museum in the purest Philadelphia spirit of science, in order to exhibit specimens of the three kingdoms of nature in the classical order of Linnæus. It was he who originated the habitat-arrangement that Audubon developed years later.

*Peale's Museum — the seventh American wonder. Later it became a freak show and Barnum bought some of the exhibits.*

❋

Another well-known naturalist lived, just outside the town, on the five acres of his Botanic Garden. This was William Bartram, who had written the *Travels* and whose big stone dwelling stood on the banks of the Schuylkill. It was this book that largely suggested to Coleridge and Southey their plan of emigrating to the Susquehanna.

Bartram's Garden was a haunt of all the illuminati, and Charles Brockden Brown was often there, — the Philadelphia Quaker novelist who had something in common with Bartram, for both were ardent believers in the natural man.

Charles Brockden Brown had had an unhappy love affair with a young girl from Connecticut. She had played the harpsichord, he the flute, and his letters overflowed with Wertherian sorrows and the sentiments now of Richardson, now of Rousseau. His Gothic fancy was filled with ruined castles, secret vaults, sounds of horror and desperate villains. At the turn of the century Brown was publishing the novels in which Keats, like Shelley, discovered a "powerful genius."

Hastily written as they were, the novels of Charles Brockden Brown were singularly original, poetic and impressive, dim as they seemed to readers of the far-away future. Much of their machinery was hollow and factitious, though the forest scenes and the descriptions of spots in Philadelphia were graphic enough.

He added a third dimension to the Gothic novel. Analyzing human emotions after the manner of Richardson, he further explored the inner world of man. He was a precursor, in more than one respect, of Poe, Melville, Hawthorne and Henry James. Brown represented, in other words, the native American wild stock that produced these splendid blossoms in the course of time.

*Charles Brockden Brown: his Gothic fancy was filled with ruined castles, sounds of horror.*

5

# The Land of the Yankees

*famed for the stones in their*

*fields, for their schools and*

*their stiff necks.*

*The people of New England were* the most literate of all the Americans. They were the toughest-minded and the most contentious, and they had the cleverest fingers and the sharpest wits. Rebels and dissenters, inclined to "differ from all the world, and from one another and shortly from themselves," they were profounder students than others, restless, ambitious, lovers of perfection, given to improving themselves and improving others.

They had produced three men of literary genius, Cotton Mather, Jonathan Edwards and Franklin. But while there was in the region still a measure of intellectual life, the prevailing tone of mind was conservative and sterile. What Charles Francis

Charlotte Temple, *written by Susanna Rowson, a New England schoolmarm, to warn her girls against the seducer who lurked in the scarlet coat.*

Adams, a century later, called the "ice-age" of Massachusetts, retained its grip, — Connecticut was almost as cold; and the thirty years 1790 to 1820 were singularly barren and dark. Men like Fisher Ames could not believe that America was coming to much, or anything at all, in literature; the "American Burke" seemed almost to take a savage joy in denying the possibility of American writers. Every advance towards democracy meant for him an intellectual decline. As a prophet, Fisher Ames was a forerunner of Henry Adams, for whom there was not a ray in the encircling gloom.

There were, however, a few writers in New England. Who had not read *The Coquette,* the work of a lady of Boston, and who did not know *Charlotte Temple?* Susanna Rowson, the author of this popular classic, had lived at Nantasket as a child. She turned to the region of Boston, where she conducted a well-known school for young ladies, and she wrote *Charlotte Temple* to warn her dear girls against the seducer who lurked in the scarlet coat.

Connecticut could boast of some poets whom everyone knew, Timothy Dwight, Joel Barlow and John Trumbull. Poetry possessed a public function, in the years round 1800, that was unparalleled in the days of better poets. No bridge was opened without an ode, and the Fourth of July resounded with poems. The newsboys on New Year's day saluted their patrons in doggerel lines, a custom that was maintained for another generation.

Joel Barlow had first gone abroad in 1788. He was welcomed by the French thinkers and writers. He was one of the Girondist circle that included

Paine, and he was made a citizen of France and asked to stand for election to represent Savoy. It was there, in a Savoyard inn, that he wrote his best poem *The Hasty Pudding,* one of the first good American poems, so natural and fresh it was in both form and feeling. The Savoyard scene reminded him of his own Connecticut country, and the mush that passed for pudding at the inn recalled the Indian corn that his bones were made of. But the *Columbiad* was the great task of his life, and he constantly enlarged and recomposed it, celebrating liberty, reason and the glory of his country, its history, its present and its prospects. Barlow foresaw the triumph of American ideas, a republic of all mankind and a congress of nations.

Meanwhile, the other Connecticut poets were, in two or three cases at least, writers of parts, patriots, honest, gifted and sometimes witty. The most famous of these Hartford Wits, as they called themselves collectively, was John Trumbull, the lawyer who spent forty-five years in Hartford. His burlesque epic *McFingal* on the battles of the Whigs and Tories brought back memories of the Revolution and its agitations, the liberty-poles, the town-meetings. It was known and read in all the American regions and passed through thirty-two or more editions.

Over all Connecticut writers, obscure or famous, Timothy Dwight was paramount, as poet, theologian, traveller and president of Yale. A strictly home-grown Connecticut man he had established professional schools at Yale. He discovered Benjamin Silliman, the man who took the black art of chemistry out of the hands of the necromancers and planted it squarely in the schoolbooks. If not exactly a golden age, it was at Yale that a new age began at least for American science — though in other respects Connecticut and its citadel of orthodoxy remained aloof from the fertilizing thought of the world. The currents of world thought and feeling that so naturally spread on the eastern seaboard were diverted before they reached New Haven, while they found a favourable harbour in Boston and Cambridge. There the humanities were at home, and there, in days to come, was to spring a true literary movement, the flowering of New England.

*Joel Barlow's* The Hasty Pudding *was one of the first good American poems, fresh in form and feeling. He wrote it in a Savoyard inn in France.*

*Barber-shop client damns authors for their affected writing. The Connecticut wits fought for a simple style. From the* Echo, *Hartford, 1807.*

# The Dutch Along the Hudson...

*their towns, embosomed in orchards, suggested a sturdy and stable life.*

*All around New York the Dutch* note was dense and strong, as it was along the Hudson. To the verdant declivities of this peaceful stream still clung many smiling Dutch farms. The little white towns embosomed in orchards suggested a stable and immemorial life. Innkeepers, lighting their guests to bed, first pulled off their boots in order to show their respect for the clean chambers; and Dutch was spoken in all these towns, at least as much as English, which had been quite recently only a sort of court language.

In New York itself there were still many Dutch-built houses, with gables facing the street and crow-stepped roofs, especially in the Bowery, a dusty country road that was lined with Dutch farmhouses.

For all these reminders, and small as it was, — a twenty minutes walk from end to end, — New York was cosmopolitan and had always been so. In its intellectual interest, the little brick town at the foot of the island was less advanced than Philadelphia. The Dutch, as compared with the Yankees and even the Quakers, had had small regard for education, and, while Columbia College ranked with the best, the atmosphere of New York was distinctly commercial. As Washington Irving was to say, "Happily for New Amsterdam . . . the very words of learning, education, taste and talents were unheard of; a bright genius was an animal unknown and a blue-stocking lady would have been regarded with as much wonder as a horned frog or a fiery dragon."

But in 1800 literature was represented in two or three clubs, at which the members read papers and acclaimed their favourite compositions, passages from Addison, Shakespeare and especially Pope. Men talked in the eighteenth-century way, they sighed as they discussed the good old times and mourned over the ruins of ancient virtue.

The town had no professional authors until Washington Irving began to write, and the most interesting things that were written, outside the political sphere, were diaries and letters that never reached the public.

Meanwhile, the Hudson River valley and all the country about New York teemed with the legends of the Dutch. At Hell Gate, a black man, known as the Pirate's Spook, whom Stuyvesant had shot with a silver bullet, was often seen in stormy weather in a three-cornered hat, in the stern of a

jolly-boat, or so it was said; and from Tappan Zee to Albany, especially in the Highlands, every crag and cove had its story. The Donderberg and Sugar Loaf, Storm King and Anthony's Nose bristled with legends from a far-away past.

All these legends had long been current when Washington Irving, in 1800, made his first voyage up the Hudson. Irving, a boy of seventeen, sailed up the river to visit his sisters, who were living west of Albany. Sailing up to Albany was like going to Europe, and friends and relatives assembled on the wharf to speed the adventurous voyager with handkerchiefs and tears. On board the long days lent themselves to story-telling, and the captains were renowned for their yarns.

Young Irving steeped himself in the poetry of the old Dutch life. He knew every spot that was famous in history or fable, and he listened, ascending the river, while an Indian trader told him legends of the Hudson.

"It was not Irving who invested the Hudson with romance, but the Hudson that inspired Irving," T. W. Higginson wrote later. "Ichabod Crane and Rip Van Winkle or their prototypes were already on the spot waiting for biographers . . . What was needed was self-confidence and a strong literary desire to take the materials at hand."

In the twentieth century Spuyten Duyvil Creek was to become a ship canal linking the Harlem River with the Hudson; but the name recalls a far from prosaic legend recorded by Washington Irving. When the British threatened Manhattan

in 1664, Governor Stuyvesant sent his trumpeter Anthony Van Corlaer to rouse the Dutch colonists on their farms to the north. The creek was swollen by heavy rains, but Anthony swore he would cross it "in spite of the devil." The devil seized his leg and pulled him under, but not before his trumpet had done its work.

*The river valley bristled with legends and so did the places close by: Hell-gate, Tappan Zee, Storm King, Pirate's Spook, Anthony's Nose, Spuyten Duyvil.*

# Washington Irving

*the first high literary talent*

*that the country had known.*

*Washington Irving drawn by Vanderlyn, 1805.*

*Washington Irving, the son* of a Scottish merchant who had settled in New York some time before the Revolution, was one of a large and flourishing family that lived in William Street, with a garden full of apricot and plum trees. He was a law student and a very attractive young man, good-looking, sweet-tempered, affectionate, humorous and gay, a favourite of his older brothers, who had prospered in various ways and liked to make things easy and pleasant for him.

While Irving was moody and had occasional fits of depression, he was high-spirited, impressionable and naturally happy. As a young New Yorker, he shrewdly observed the ways of the town, for he was in temperament urban and always remained so. Before Irving was twenty-three, he had spent two years in Europe. His brothers were troubled about his health, for he seemed to be consumptive, and they thought a leisurely tour would be excellent for this.

Back in New York, with health restored, a young man of fashion, Irving rejoiced in the growth of the town, where magazines, books and plays were multiplying and everyone was reading Scott, Thomas Moore and Thomas Campbell.

As for Irving's work as a lawyer, he did not take this seriously, — he was said to have had but one client, whom he left in the lurch; but his brothers were glad to keep him going and even made him a nominal partner, so that he might have leisure to follow his tastes.

❧

On Saturdays and Sundays, with his brother William, James K. Paulding and Gouverneur Kemble, Irving and his friends drove to "Cockloft Hall" on the outskirts of Newark. They played leap-frog on the lawn and talked over their plans.

*Irving joined in convivial gatherings in New York taverns and clubs.*

RADISHES!

" *Radishes! Any Radishes!*
" *Here's your fine Radishes!*"
Radishes! Radishes!
I hold them to view,
Turnip or carrot form,
As fine as e'er grew.

CLAMS! CLAMS!

" *Here's your fine Rockaway Clams! Here they G-O!*"

Fine Rockaway Clams,
Just out of the boat,
Buy a few hundred,
They're an excellent lot.

*Through the open windows one heard the street criers announcing their wares.*

One Salmagundi essay suggested "Baby culture by improved methods."

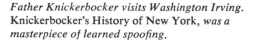

A Dutch courtship.

Father Knickerbocker visits Washington Irving. Knickerbocker's History of New York, *was a masterpiece of learned spoofing.*

They made this old house famous in *Salmagundi,* in which Paulding, William Irving and Washington Irving appeared as a club of eccentrics, Anthony Evergreen, Langstaff and William Wizard. Published in a yellow cover, this occasional magazine was modelled on *The Spectator* and *The Citizen of the World,* which still seemed new and exciting in little New York. The paper proved a profitable venture. Eight hundred copies were sold in a single day. *Salmagundi* had a great vogue as a mildly satirical series of comments on life in the town which the authors first called "Gotham."

The Knickerbocker *History of New York* grew out of *Salmagundi.* Irving had been surprised to find how few of his fellow-citizens were aware that the town had a history extending back into the regions of doubt and fable. He wished to provide the town with local tales and pleasantries that might season its civic festivities as rallying-points of home-feeling. How few American scenes and places possessed the familiar associations that lived like spells about the old-world cities, binding to their homes the hearts of the natives. So it was that he conceived the history of Dietrich Knickerbocker, the doting antiquarian of old New York. He had the air of a country schoolmaster, and his history was the whole business of a dedicated life. In this figure Irving burlesqued the vainglorious pedantry of previous historians.

This masterpiece of learned spoofing offended some of the older New Yorkers. But who could quarrel seriously with such a ripe expression of a mind that was so well-furnished and so good-natured? It was in this book that Irving's talent declared itself, the first high literary talent the country had known.

*Malvolio Dubster, New York Dandy: "I have went to great expense but can scarcely get a partner to a tea dance". From* Salmagundi *a mildly satirical series of comments on life in "Gotham"*

# Irving and Scott

*both writers rambled over the Scottish hills,*

*reciting border ballads, exchanging ideas.*

*Abbotsford — a striking symbol of
the new cult of the Middle Ages.*

*In 1815, Washington Irving,* at loose ends in New York, six years after publishing *Knickerbocker,* drifted over to England with no particular plans in mind.

Irving was not a stranger in England, with which his ancestral ties were deep. There he had many well-wishers. Henry Brevoort had passed through England, scattering copies of *Knickerbocker.* Coleridge had picked up the book on the table of an inn. He could not put it down, and he was still reading it in the morning, with the lights burning at ten o'clock. Byron delighted in *Knickerbocker,* and Scott had written a letter to Irving, while he was still in New York, acclaiming the

*Irving was always drawn to painters, and he had some talent for drawing himself. His writing was pictorial and sympathetic to men of the brush. He had chosen his pen-*

*name "Geoffrey Crayon" with reason. The sketch below is from his diary recording his impressions of the American West after his return from England.*

youthful writer as already a master.

Irving was to live for seventeen years in Europe, but he had no notion of this when he left New York.

A high point of Irving's first English travels was the four days he spent with Scott at Abbotsford. Scott, with his American visitor, talked and walked from breakfast till bedtime, — with his dogs and his children, reciting border ballads in a growling voice, limping along with his big stick, happy to find that this pleasant young man had known the Scottish lore from his earliest childhood.

The novelist's own house Abbotsford was a striking symbol of the new spirit with its cult of the Middle Ages and the picturesque. Almost everything that was old enchanted Europeans now, as it enchanted Americans who returned to the scenes of their forbears.

Abbotsford was full of all the new German romantic writers, whom Irving had himself begun to study. It was in these romances that he found the kernel of his own *Rip van Winkle*. He wrote shortly afterward this tale of the Catskill ne'er-do-well, the hen-pecked friend of all the village boys, who wandered off with his dog and his fowling-piece and fell in with gnomes at their nine-pins in a hollow of the mountains. At about the same time he wrote the *Legend of Sleepy Hollow*, remembering the haunted region he had known in his boyhood, the valley by the Hudson where the old Dutch farms had breathed for him an atmosphere of dreams and fancies. He longed to give his own country a colour of romance and tradition, and the great-hearted Scott, who freely prophesied his fame, confirmed his ambitions and interests.

It was Irving's musical, rhythmical style, his quiet humour and dreamy charm that accounted for the triumph of these stories and the other essays embodied in the *Sketch Book* (1820). While it was published first in America, English readers were also drawn by the modesty, sweetness and candour of this American author. His style, so elegant and so simple, was to mark all of Irving's work, the sign of his cheerful good nature and transparent good taste; and meanwhile, at home, the book absorbed the whole attention of the small reading public that was at once informed and alert. That an American author should have produced this model of prose was a matter of national self-congratulation, and his countrymen were prepared to share his feeling about England, while they rejoiced in his American sentiments and legends.

*Ichabod Crane and Rip Van Winkle became the possession of every American mind.*

*Rip and his scolding wife.*

*Rip snubbed by his dog.*

*The return of Rip Van Winkle.*

*Americans were all the more disposed to feel* their attachment to English traditions when the ties of the mother-country were broken, when the relics of England vanished at home and their own civilization rose about them. Whatever spoke of an older England became doubly dear to them, as the home of their memories and their culture; and, while they made no effort to preserve their own historical monuments, they worshipped at the old-world shrines of Europe.

Such was the mood of Irving's stories dealing with Old England contained in the *Sketch Book* and the somewhat later *Bracebridge Hall.* This was the story of an ancient manor-house where customs, forgotten in the towns, survived in the country. Irving had stayed in one of these houses during the holiday season, when the old Christmas ceremonies were still kept up, the Yule log, the wassail bowl, the boar's head crowned with rosemary, the waits, the morris dances, the carols and the mummers, and the sword-dance handed down from the time of the Romans. The harper, the Christmas candles, the spiced wines, the mistletoe possessed for him a magic of the glamorous past; and so it was with everything else that he observed about him and that only an American perhaps could feel so fully.

It was in 1826, after a stay in Paris, that Washington Irving set out for his visit to Spain. This journey was a sort of second birth for him. He fell completely under the spell of the Spanish literature of old, the luxuriance and vigour of its chronicles, romances and plays, abounding in generous sentiments and oriental flavour.

Betweenwhiles he visited many parts of Spain, travelling sometimes alone, sometimes with friends. In 1829 Irving passed an enchanted summer in the Alhambra. A ragged brood of peasants and invalid soldiers inhabited its corridors and courts. There old women, vagrants and curious do-nothing folk sat on the stone benches and dawdled and gossiped, while loitering housewives listened to the endless tattle. Irving passed the greater part of his days assembling the tales that later appeared in his book, *The Alhambra.* He mingled history and fiction together, gathering the scattered members of popular traditions and skilfully working them into shape and form.

*Christmas magic of the glamorous past, recreated in Irving's Sketch Book. Whatever spoke of an older England became dear to Americans, for it was the homeland of their culture.*

In 1832, after living for seventeen years in Europe, Washington Irving returned to his native New York. Now, in his fiftieth year, he found himself a national figure, as famous all over the country as Calhoun and Clay.

Washington Irving passed most of his later years at Sunnyside, with long visits in Spain, when he was American minister from 1842-1846. He had bought in 1835 a small stone Dutch cottage overlooking the Hudson, and there he was living in the early forties, on a cove at the end of a quiet lane, within strolling distance of the church at Sleepy Hollow. Sunnyside, as he presently called it, bristled with crow-stepped gables and chimneys and porches, hung with trumpet-creepers and honeysuckles alive with bees and ivy from Abbotsford.

The house soon became a resort of literary pilgrims, some of whom attempted to borrow the master's form and style while others were content with scraps of his blotting-paper. They agreed with Poe that Irving was "the most deservedly eminent among all the pioneers of American literature," partly because he was first in the field, partly because of his tone and manner and partly because of his influence on other writers. In the absence of bolder talents that could rival his in charm and skill, this was indeed the age of Washington Irving, the man of letters who had established a name for his country in literature.

*The master of Sunnyside, where in later years Irving was host to many writers.*

*Irving with his nieces on the lawn of Sunnyside. All his life an incorrigible bachelor, he outlived many authors of higher power because of his geniality and grace.*

Cooper had the air of a sailor, at times brusque, always sure of his opinions.

# James Fenimore Cooper

*knew well the pleasures of the pathless woods, the rapture on the lonely shore.*

*While Irving was exploring England,* another New Yorker, six years younger, who had served for a while in the navy after going to Yale, had married and settled in Westchester County, where he lived as a country gentleman without so much as a thought of writing a book.

Cooper had inherited from the founder of Cooperstown, his father, a sufficiently ample fortune and twenty-three farms, and his wife was one of the De Lanceys, the old New York Huguenot family, who had connections in New Rochelle, near by. He had spent some years at sea in his adventurous youth.

He had the air of a sailor or a man of affairs. With his wind-blown look and bright grey eyes, he was an out-of-doors man, sometimes boisterous, often brusque and always sure of his opinions.

From Cooper's farm at Scarsdale, it was an easy drive to Bedford, over the winding roads of the Westchester hills. There lived John Jay, the former Chief Justice, to Cooper almost an uncle. Cooper delightedly listened while Jay related stories of the Revolution. At one time Jay had been chairman of a committee that was appointed by Congress to gather news about the British plans. He had employed a secret agent whom he described to Cooper and who reappeared soon afterward in the fictional character of Harvey Birch. For it was then that Cooper wrote *The Spy,* influenced no doubt by Scott, to retrieve the heroic past and the beauty of his country.

For Cooper, a patriot first, last and all the time, was ardently and eagerly interested in the history of the country and especially of his own beloved state of New York. He knew much of the state of New York by heart, for he had lived all over it,

*Scene from Cooper's* The Spy *painted by William Dunlap. (New York State Hist. Soc.)*

16

The Pilot *was the first long story dealing with the life of sailors. As Joseph Conrad said, Cooper really invented the sea-story.*

at Cooperstown, in Albany and now in this Westchester village with a view of the Sound. He knew the lovely New York lakes, Champlain, Cayuga, Seneca, Oneida.

He knew the ocean, meanwhile, as well as the woods. For Cooper had spent three years in the navy and had previously served in the merchant marine, the usual way of acquiring training. It left more traces than any other in his novels later, — memories of the Spanish coast, Gibraltar and the Mediterranean as well as Falmouth, London and the Isle of Wight.

During these years of active naval service, Cooper amassed a prodigious knowledge of ships and the "sea dialect" and sailors. He really invented the sea-novel, for *The Pilot* was the first long story that pictured in detail the movement and handling of vessels, and he wrote at one time or another a dozen sea-tales, some of which were certainly among his best. Cooper himself, besides, had many of the traits of a sailor, a seadog of the old-fashioned kind for whom everything was black or white and who defended flogging at sea and whipping-posts at home.

In Cooper's novels, from first to last, the sea was to rival the forest, and one might have said that Cooper's solution for all the problems of fiction was to take his readers on a voyage. At least, he did so frequently when he found himself in a tight place, just as he usually provided a beautiful girl and placed her in a position to be rescued. He

*Cooper's History of the Navy bristled with exploits that delighted the hearts of Americans.*

had spent at sea the most susceptible years of his youth. Many of his young heroes followed the sea, — Mark Woolston and Miles Wallingford, for instance, — and he was almost always ready to oblige when his friends called for "more ship." He knew the terrors of the sea, yet it gladdened his heart, and the sailors' toast "sweethearts and wives" resounded in the novels in which he recorded his joy in everything that floated.

*But Cooper loved the wilderness* even more than the sea, that other world where men "breathed freely", for he was, after all, a child of the forest and the frontier and the earliest of his impressions were his deepest and dearest. Before he established himself at Scarsdale, he had taken his wife to Cooperstown, driving in a gig through the forest on the corduroy roads, and there for three years the family lived in a house that he built near Otsego Hall beside the sylvan lake that glittered in the sun. In its repose and solitude, the lake, as it placidly mirrored the sky, with its dark setting of woods and the trees overhanging, was a haunting symbol for Cooper of the grandeur of the forest, sublime in the light of the moon, lovely by day.

The region of the Leather-Stocking Tales was the southwestward-facing angle that was formed by the junction of the Mohawk River and the Hudson, stretching as far as Lake Ontario, together with Lake George to the north. Lake Otsego evoked the still earlier day when the dark and interminable forest had scarcely as yet been disturbed by the struggles of men. Then the youthful Natty Bumppo had first beheld the Glimmerglass and met his friend Chingachgook at the rock. Cooper was possessed by the image of the tall, gaunt hunter Natty Bumppo. A whole cycle of stories rose in his mind of which Natty was always the central figure, as the lake-strewn forest was the scene of the Deerslayer's exploits. The Deerslayer, the Pathfinder and Leather-Stocking were one and the same, and sometimes Natty also appeared as Hawkeye, the poet of the wilderness who loved to speak in favour of a friend and who never clung too eagerly and fondly to life.

Cooper, in the course of thirty years, was to write thirty-three novels, as well as many books of other kinds. These novels were of all types, simple romances, tales of adventure, historical stories, satires, pictures of manners, and they varied in their degrees of merit as in the range of their characters and settings, which in the end proved to be very wide. Disregarding his tales of Europe, Cooper's scope was national, — he was by no means a regional or sectional writer, — and he was successful, on the whole, in his portrayal of local types and the characteristic scenes of many regions. Cooper's all-American imagination ranged widely. He delighted in the chivalrous rivalry of the captains in *The Sea Lions,* in the high courtesy and

*Otsego Lake with Otsego Hall, seat of the Cooper family. The lake and its surrounding woods, compact with magical memories for Cooper, became the setting for his Leather-Stocking Tales.*

*Cooper moved to Otsego Hall in 1834. Morse had remodelled the house and built castellated cornices around the roof. Cooper returned to farming, the life he had loved in earlier years.*

*The study in Otsego Hall where Cooper wrote most of his later books.*

*Deerslayer, Pathfinder and Leather-Stocking were the same — one symbol of the frontier's bravery, gallantry and courage.*

fortitude of his Indian braves, in the true freedom of the American borderer, honourable and fearless, in the valour of ingenious men contending with the sea. A noble nature shone through Cooper's novels, and, roughly written as most of them were, full of improbabilities, as rudely built as cabins of the pioneers, they lived very largely by virtue of this and the wonderful eye for the forest and the sea that made Cooper, as Balzac said, the master of literary landscape-painters. Both the sea-tales and frontier romances struck some deep ancestral chord in the hearts of men. Cooper deeply understood the passion for a solitary life that went with a feeling for the vastness and freshness of the forest and that sometimes bred elevated characters, steady as the pines, with head erect, at once humble and grand.

Many of these American stories were written abroad. Cooper and his wife and daughters spent seven years largely in Paris, though they wintered in Florence, Rome and Dresden. He had castles placed at his disposal, while his books were not only praised by the greatest novelists and critics in Europe but had begun to influence generations of writers.

After his return home, Cooper soon retired to Cooperstown, and, save for occasional winters in New York and Philadelphia, there he continued to live for the rest of his days. He bought back Otsego Hall, which had been sold when his mother died, and his friend Morse remodelled it, gothicized the windows and built a castellated cornice around the roof. The grounds were elaborately laid out, and Cooper returned to gardening and farming, the life he had loved at Scarsdale in earlier years. He often composed on walks through the woods, following mountain paths or strolling along the lake-shore to his farm, the Châlet. Immensely productive as always, he wrote the long series of books of travel that recorded his memories and his pleasure in the scenery of Europe. Cooper's power of invention was inexhaustible.

Which were his vividest characters? They were all men of the humbler sort who were essentially noble in their low disguises, Harvey Birch, Long Tom, Natty Bumppo, natural gentlemen, Indians and sailors to whom Cooper's heart went out, in his revulsion against the unworthy present. One and all were of the type that Melville called the "kingly commons." These were the men that Cooper's genius loved.

# Later Knickerbockers

*Halleck had the jaunty air supposed to be typical of a New Yorker.*

*Halleck's poem* Fanny, *a satire of New York society, pleased the town.*

*Paulding loved the Knickerbocker past that Irving had laughed at and had made merry with.*

*Paulding's* John Bull *ridiculed those who thought America a barbarous land.*

The two important New York writers, Washington Irving and Fenimore Cooper, preferred country life to life in the town. A lover of the old agrarian world, Cooper despised the commercial metropolis and returned in 1834 to the home of his childhood in Cooperstown. Irving, a merchant's son, was more at home with business men, but he too liked haunts of ancient peace. In 1836 he settled at Sunnyside, his remodelled old Dutch house near Tarrytown.

Meanwhile, New York was more and more becoming a focus for things of the mind, replacing Philadelphia as the literary centre. The town was a curious mixture of the countrified and the cosmopolitan. Many of the merchants had come to town from farms and so had many of the poets, writers and journalists.

Halleck had come from Guilford, Connecticut, where his father kept a country store. He himself had opened there an evening school for bookkeeping, for he was a methodical man with the habits of a clerk. Arriving in New York, as early as 1811, he became the private secretary of John Jacob Astor, meanwhile developing a graceful talent as a writer of light verse who was known as a sort of local Horace. He had the sprightly step and the jaunty air that were supposed to characterize New Yorkers; and his *Fanny* pleased the town with its touch-and-go allusions to Weehawken, Saratoga and the Falls of Cohoes.

Meanwhile, in Washington Irving's absence James Kirke Paulding had become a leading New York writer, casual and hasty as he was, — and lighthearted about it, — a shadow and understudy of Irving. He shared the antiquarian feeling that was strong in his old comrade.

He loved the Knickerbocker past. This feeling gave birth to the best of his novels, *The Dutchman's Fireside,* a charming tale of the northern country in the days of the French and Indian war. The Dutch tradition was rapidly fading, but Paulding blew on its dying embers.

A gradual, general change in the literary climate was taking place. In this age of sensibility, the female mind spread through the press and filled the annuals and the magazines, the "Souvenirs" and "Tokens."

This tendency of the new generation, the Bul-

werism and "elegant polish," the feminine sensibility and the hankering for Europe were all expressed in a writer of the thirties. Another transplanted New Englander, like Bryant and Halleck, and, like Cooper, an offspring of Yale, Nathaniel Parker Willis described himself as a "here-and-there-ian" and a "constant servant of the ladies." There was something infectious in his appetite for novelty and adventure, and he gave so much pleasure because he was so ready to be pleased.

The steep and thorny ways were not for Willis. He preferred the dalliance and the perfumes of the primrose path. Long before he left Yale he knew the fashionable watering-places where the belles and the beaux philandered in the big hotels, and he was planning stories already about young men at these resorts, wandering from one to another, dancing and flirting. Willis stood for a hundred poets of the day. His specialties were moonlight on the lake and twilight in the vale and the love that did *not* wish to live in a cottage.

Like later American writers he was drawn to the world of gilded youth, and he was much more concerned with the women than he was with the men, — the belles of New York and the Southern beauties from the "latitudes of lovely languor." The spas and springs and watering-places were Willis's happy hunting grounds. There were moments in Willis's stories that suggested the younger Henry James, alike in their characters and settings and lightness of touch, while Willis conveyed, as no one else, the glamour of youth in this earlier time. He might have been described three generations later as the Scott Fitzgerald of the belles of Saratoga.

*Willis described the world of gilded youth at Saratoga and other spas.*

*His stories centred around the belles "from the latitudes of lovely languor."*

# The West

*the region brimmed over with heroes for poets to come:*

*folklore of the Indians passed into tales and poems.*

*The new states of the Middle West* swarmed with pioneers. The early settlers had clung to the rivers, while now they were moving out on the prairie, hoping for a "chance." Almost every square mile was marked out by blazed trees, and homesteaders searched the woods with maps and pocket-compasses looking for their sections and quarter-stakes. Before long big barns, with sheds and stables,

*Davy Crockett, gargantuan symbol of a world that knew no metes and bounds.*

poultry-yards and well-built houses rose overnight amid well-fenced fields of grain.

There were no American poets as yet to celebrate the "all-conquering ploughshare" and the "unsubduable fire" of the Western settlers, but there were heroes of poets to come in many a keelboat and cabin; and the frontier life brimmed over with comic stories, ballads and songs, the wild native seeds of a literature of the future.

Abraham Lincoln was growing up in Illinois. Twice, on a flatboat, he had floated down the Mississippi, with flour, meal, pork and potatoes for the New Orleans market. Mike Fink had already become a legend, the river man who had clung to his broadhorn after the steamboats came. Another of these men was Jim Bridger, who had discovered the Great Salt Lake, a hero of the dime novels of after years.

Among these men who were living legends, half hidden by their forest life, Davy Crockett perhaps was the most renowned, the successor of Boone in the popular fancy as a master of woodcraft, a mighty hunter and a story-teller beyond compare in his "great garden" of Tennessee. In the savage "shakes" there, a region despised in Knoxville and Nashville, Davy was famous at shooting-matches, flax-pullings and tavern-frolics, and everyone had heard of his exploits, how he had outshot Mike Fink and killed a hundred bears.

He even wrote the story of his life, in which a friend helped him to "classify the matter." He liked the kind of real life that made a book "jump out of the press like a new dollar from a mint-hopper," he said; and this *Narrative,* with its fresh images and homespun style, at once became and remained a frontier classic.

*Mike Fink, a teller of river tales as fabulous as Paul Bunyan's*

*Jim Bridger, Great Salt Lake scout, became a hero of the dime novels.*

*Abraham Lincoln, rangy, strong, floated down the river on a raft.*

The tall tales that flourished in the West were the natural growths of a world that had burst its bonds, a young mind that had cast the skin of ancestral conventions and social forms and exulted in a freedom that knew no limit. In this sense the frontier had something in common with Rabelais, who spoke for a lusty France that was trying its strength after the long constriction of the Middle Ages.

Here and there an Eastern mind was becoming aware of the Western lore and its meaning for the America of the future. "Our eyes will be turned westward," Emerson said in the *Dial,* 1843, "and a new and stronger tone in literature will be the result."

If not a poet-writer, the frontier produced a poet-painter. Audubon surveyed and reported the primal American world, observing, while he drew the birds, the human *dramatis personae* of a rising civilization in its elemental phases. He saw, with an eye as genial as Whitman's, with a simple heart and a spacious mind, the frontiersman, the hunter, the trapper, the whaler and the sailor, the farmer and the fisherman, the lumberer and the pioneer who were building a world for Americans to find a home in. Through the opening years of the nineteenth century, and even as late as the forties, while literature in America dawned and spread, Audubon haunted the frontiers, north, south and west, that encircled the centres of culture and their

men of thought. His *Episodes* were a cyclorama of the primitive scenes of these frontiers, and he spoke words of good cheer for the future of the race.

*Audubon's journals were written with the freshness of morning in the woods.*

23

*The Indians were still in their heyday. Catlin drew them in all their splendour of gait and costume. Thousands of later stories were based on his sketches.*

*There were many other wanderers* who could scarcely bear to leave the plains. George Catlin, born in 1796, went west in 1832 and lived for eight years among the Indians painting their warriors, medicine men and chiefs. The Indians were still in their heyday in all their splendor of gait and costume. Catlin made up his mind to visit all the continental tribes and make a pictorial record of their vanishing life.

Catlin, the showman, was a sincere enthusiast who believed in the honour of the Indians. He had seen them in full bloom. Thousands of later stories were based on his descriptions and countless illustrations were redrawn from his pictures.

Catlin depicted the outward and visible life of the Indians. At the same time Henry Rowe Schoolcraft explored and described their inner and spiritual existence. Not how they lived, dressed and amused themselves, but how they thought and felt was Schoolcraft's preoccupation, and he was astonished by their parables and allegories, which he published in his *Algic Researches* and his voluminous *History of the Indian Tribes*. Schoolcraft had set out to search the dark cave of the Indian mind, and here, among these Indian tales of the charmed arrow, the summer-maker, the red swan and the origin of Indian corn, first appeared the story of Hiawatha.

It was in Schoolcraft that Longfellow found this foremost of the Indian myths, which hallowed the lakes and streams of the northern frontier. Schoolcraft's writings were the gate through which all of the lore of the Indian passed gradually into American literature.

❋

*The frontier was tumultuous,* and the freedom of this ungoverned country demoralized many an exile from the stable East. The lonely and perilous frontier life was favourable to emotional religion. The Presbyterian church was the cult of the well-

# to National Literature

*fervour reverberates in later writing.*

to-do, but the Methodists, following the Baptists, appealed to the people, for they preached free will and universal grace. A team of preachers came together, as many as twenty or thirty, and preached for four or five days, by day and by night. These camp meetings provided a natural outlet for penned-up frontier emotionalism. The red glare of the campfires was reflected from the tents, surrounded by the blackness of the forest. A hundred victims would fall like dead men under one powerful sermon, while the groans of the spiritually wounded echoed through the woods.

Some of these ministers, called "sons of thunder," were mighty men. They were even remarkable writers, too, and a handful of their journals were perhaps the most interesting books that arose from the turbulent Western life of the time. Aside from the dignified Francis Asbury, who disliked all eccentricity, the noble Peter Cartwright was the greatest of them, and they all roamed from region to region, with or without road or path, with stools for chairs and dirt floors for carpets, sleeping on bear and buffalo skins. Lorenzo Dow would emerge from the woods, melancholy, tall and cadaverous, with his long black cloak and reddish beard and the wild hair streaming over his shoulder. Peter Cartwright remained for half a century the most famous and the grandest of the backwoods preachers, living on forty dollars a year, with whatever food and clothing his followers gave him.

This double-barrelled "old religion," as people called it in later years, was to leave profound impressions on the character of the West. Evoked by the life of the pioneers, it expressed the race, the place, the moment; and its narrowness and grimness, together with its joys and terrors, very largely shaped the Western mind, which remained by turns repressive and explosive. Even five generations later the literature of the Middle West was coloured and scarred by the traces of this old religion.

*One heard the sobs and shrieks of the downcast mingling with the shouts of praise of those who had crossed the threshold of the land of Beulah.*

*Peter Cartwright:
The New Englanders disliked
the loudness of this
Kentuckian, one of the
"sons of thunder."*

# The South

*with its fine social culture, it lived at the expense of the present in a world of tradition.*

*If the West was tumultuous* and showed signs of intellectual awakening, the South remained static. On the whole its leaders were indifferent if not hostile to literary interests.

In this plantation world of leisure, there was time for sports and horsemanship. It was a life of out-of-door activity, easygoing, generous, hearty and free, where nothing seemed remoter than the kind of introspection that flourished in the Northern regions, especially New England.

On the other hand, the great class of the Southern planters, small in number but large in mind, had been singularly prolific of eminent statesmen. The Southerners were congenital politicians; for the plantation was a school of statesmanship, and the management of a great estate trained one to manage a larger world.

More than by anyone else indeed the political creed of Americanism was first conceived by Virginians of a certain type, planters such as Jefferson, Patrick Henry and John Marshall, who, whatever else they were, had roots in the hinterland, which they called "the forest." So this Virginia school of democracy was the great school of American statecraft, and Jefferson, who looked to the people, was trusted by the people in turn. Thus, one found in Jefferson's writings the earliest crystallization of what might be called the American prophetic tradition, of Whitman's *Pioneers,* the "Trust thyself" of Emerson, and Lincoln's mystical faith in the wisdom of the people. He expressed an American way of thinking that had never been put into words before.

With the passing of Jefferson and other Virginia minds in the early decades of the nineteenth century, new statesmen had emerged who were by no means men of such wide horizons. The contrast between the old and the new was especially striking below the Potomac, for the South had withdrawn more than any other region from the movement of the world. Closing door after door through which the thought of mankind had passed, it was to become by its own desire a forbidden region.

This was an atmosphere in which literature was

not apt to flourish. The older Virginians were realistic and had had small use for "mere romances" that pictured men as they should be, not as they were. But the realistic mind had vanished for a while in the South. The new generation preferred to cherish illusions, and one of these illusions was that the age of chivalry was not gone and that they could perpetuate feudalism in the teeth of the world. Quite naturally tales of contemporary life were rare in this region, while the love of historical romance was wide-spread. The passion for Sir Walter Scott was foreordained throughout the South, for his note was loyalty to the soil, to the family, to the clan. Scott pictured brave men and heroic deeds, and he spoke for all the primary virtues of an unchanging order. A northern bookseller remarked that he sent Scott's novels below the Potomac by the train-load.

At the moment John Randolph symbolized the

*John Randolph typified the Southern literary man. He once fought a duel over a question of pronunciation.*

*"Our Domestic Institution" was tenaciously upheld by Southerners.*

*Scott's novels glorifying feudalism appealed to the Southern mind.*

life of the Southern man of letters, for Randolph was distinctly of the literary order. His speeches were improvisations, but what invariably distinguished them was his literary feeling, his reading and his gift of the phrase, and as he poured out his beautiful sentences, lolling in the House, one realized that Randolph was an artist. His voice was as sweet as a flute, Lord Melbourne said. But Randolph published nothing and seldom wrote.

In spite of these retrogressive conditions, the South was to produce some writers of note. Simms, J. P. Kennedy, Longstreet and others, not to mention Poe, were proofs of the tenacity of its literary instinct.

*"Woodlands," near Charleston, where William Gilmore Simms lived. He boasted of fifteen children and a library of ten thousand books.*

## THE SOUTH—Continued

*There was more intellectual life* in Charleston during these years and for decades to come than in any other city of the South, and the founding of the *Southern Review* in 1827 gave it a forum and a focus. Charleston was a centre for numbers of writers and men of science who lived there or gathered there from other towns or their own plantations. The Charleston intellect was awake and alert, and the people retained the high spirits and the joy of living that nourish and often quicken the life of the mind.

In this circle William Gilmore Simms was the greatest man, immensely productive, impulsive, vigorous and sanguine, a poet as well as a novelist. Strong of will and large of heart, strikingly handsome, prodigally generous, he was the living emblem in letters of all that made the South attractive.

He was especially devoted to the New York writers Cooper and Bryant. He was grateful to Cooper for awakening Americans to a sense of their historical and mental resources. Cooper had preceded him in picturing the American border, the life of the pioneers and the mysteries of the woods. These were the themes of his own work, although his particular field was the Southern border.

Simms was a lover of South Carolina; there was scarcely a spot on a muddy road in all the state that was not invested with glory or charm for Simms. Every crossroads, gate or wall had its befitting moral for him and teemed with associations of persons and events.

Simms knew the border Indians too, the Chero-

kees and Choctaws, whose legends he related in several of his poems, and later, in *The Yemassee,* he presented extraordinary scenes of Indian life, especially in the older days.

These were only a few of Simms' themes. His work ranged far and wide in genre and in setting. Once, James Harper, the publisher, said Simms wrote in half an hour more copy than the printers could set up in a week.

Yet Simms took pains with his documentation, and he had a realistic eye. In fact it was his realism that kept his work alive when readers lost their taste for other romancers.

*A writer of imposing talent, William Gilmore Simms was a living emblem of all that made the South attractive.*

*Simms wrote many fine novels on border warfare in revolutionary South Carolina.*

Meanwhile, the new Southwestern settlers began to appear in comic tales that were fresh in form and feeling and intensely local and that followed more or less the pattern set by Longstreet's *Georgia Scenes,* which was published in 1835.

In their perfect naturalness, Longstreet's sketches, shapely, racy and crisp in style, reflecting this rough and virile pioneer life, were destined, thanks to the acid and salt that preserved them, to survive whole shelves of contemporary romances and novels.

*Augustus Longstreet, writer, lawyer, college president and Methodist divine.*

*Georgia Scenes (1835) described hearty customs during the region's pioneer days.*

❧

Turning further north one found Baltimore, a half-Southern city, active intellectually. This city showed how the Southern mind responded to the spur of an urban existence.

Perhaps the most important among the Marylanders was the half-Virginian John P. Kennedy, a sort of Southern Washington Irving and an intimate friend of Irving himself. The graceful, cheerful, fox-hunting Kennedy had often visited as a child on several Virginia plantations. With a singular gift for happy titles, he wrote *Swallow Barn,* a Virginian variation of *Bracebridge Hall,* describing the household ways and pastimes of an old brick plantation-house on the banks of the river James about 1800.

This engaging book established a pattern that was followed by three generations of authors in the literary treatment of the Southern plantation. Later, Kennedy turned away from the living Virginian scene and wrote *Horse Shoe Robinson.* This woodman, a South Carolina Natty Bumppo, told Kennedy his story, and he presently reappeared as the giant Horse Shoe Robinson in the stirring though prolix romance that bore this name.

*John P. Kennedy, Baltimore author and a friend of Poe, described in* Swallow Barn *the sunny days of Virginia plantation life.*

# Edgar Allan Poe

*a literary genius without a*

*parallel on the American scene.*

*It was on Sullivan's Island* near Charleston that the South's great literary genius found his inspiration.... Edgar Allan Poe, artillery man, alias Edgar Perry, was stationed at Fort Moultrie in 1827. Here he had listened to the "sounding sea" that one heard in his poems and stories later.

Edgar Allan Poe, who had spent five years of his childhood at school in England, had grown up in Richmond as a ward of John Allan, the merchant, whose wife was the daughter of one of the Virginia planters. Edgar, petted and rather spoiled, with his air of a Little Lord Fauntleroy, graceful, exceptionally handsome, winning in manner, had become an imperious older boy, a capital horseman, fencer and shot and a leader of the other boys at his school in Richmond.

By 1826, when Poe was sent to the University of Virginia, he was erect, pale, slender and seventeen, with large, grey, luminous, liquid eyes. Surrounded with tutors, servants, horses and dogs, with clothes of the best that the tailors of Richmond afforded, he was regarded in fact as the heir of one of the richest men in the state, for Allan, who had no legitimate children, had recently inherited a fortune of something round three quarters of a million dollars.

Meanwhile, Poe acquired at the University of Virginia in Charlottesville a good part of the store of learning that marked his tales and his criticism in after years. In those days, and later, Poe was accused of all manner of dodges in the way of pretending to a learning he did not possess, but were they not occasionally admirable for just this rea-

*There was no doubt of the presence of incipient madness
in the marvellous imagination that conceived these tales ...*

*Throughout his life Poe thought of Richmond as his home because of the happiness he had known there as a child . . .*

son? Much of the wondrous atmosphere of tales like *The Fall of the House of Usher* was a result of these allusions to strange and exotic books and authors.

He was a constant reader of the current magazines, and he had formed the habit of reading the foreign periodicals as a boy in the book loft of Allan's warehouse. He had, in a rudimentary form, a universal mind, together with astonishing powers of concentration.

But while outwardly the attractive Poe was a clever young man of the ruling class, his life was built on quicksand. John Allan had never adopted him and may have turned against him because Poe happened to know too much about his private life. He refused to pay Poe's expenses at college, as afterwards at West Point.

An outsider among the young Virginians, and constantly reminded of it, with a natural and life-long craving for the sympathy of women, he was desolated as a boy by the death of the mother of one of his friends, the beautiful Mrs. Stanard of the poem *To Helen*. Then Mrs. Allan also died, — the radiant foster mother who had stood between Poe and the feelingless caprices of her husband. A young man who was an orphan too might well have felt that the "conqueror worm" was the hero of his tragedy already.

Long before Poe came of age he knew the sorrowful juxtapositions of luxury and squalor that were to make him a pre-eminent type of the romantic. He began to be haunted by nightmares at about the age of fifteen; and he broke down a few years later and showed many of the signs of insanity.

*Elizabeth, Poe's poor little mother, who dragged him as a child from theatre to theatre.*

*Mrs. Allan, Poe's foster mother, who stood between Poe and the caprices of her husband.*

*John Allan, Poe's foster father, a Virginia millionaire, quarrelled with young Poe and withdrew his support.*

31

Poe in later years. Photograph taken by S. W. Hartshorne, Providence, R. I.

*Poe had received an appointment* to West Point in 1831. However, he was court martialled and dismissed from this school in the same year. Having lost favour with the Allans, he had gone to Baltimore to join his father's family. The Poes there had fallen on evil days. Mrs. Clemm, Poe's aunt, the sister of his father, supported the struggling little group as a Baltimore seamstress. Poe shared the garret of her wretched house with his drunken dying brother, and there he wrote some of his tales. *The Manuscript Found in a Bottle* was one of the first.

In Baltimore he fell in with the writers John P. Kennedy, William Wirt and Holley Chivers, all of whom were ready to help him. In spite of the legend that later arose, Poe found the world in general well-disposed. He was never by choice a bohemian, he was far from irresponsible, and he never blamed others for the "unmerciful disaster" that followed him "faster and faster."

He began to break down physically about 1832. There was more of the tragic in the life of Poe than any sensitive man could bear, and he took opiates occasionally and drank too much. Was he not, besides, a victim of the "Imp of the Perverse," like the hero of the tale that bore this name?

After four years of Baltimore, Edgar Allan Poe returned in 1835 for a stay in Richmond, and there he edited a magazine, the *Southern Literary Messenger,* and married his little cousin, Virginia Clemm. He had been a success as an editor, and later, in New York, *Graham's* became, under his editorship, the foremost monthly journal in the country.

His association with magazines affected Poe's life and work in many ways. It developed his critical faculty, for instance, for he was a regular book-reviewer who first undertook this kind of writing as an editor in Richmond. He made the *Southern Literary Messenger* famous all over the nation for the clear and fearless authority of its reviews. Poe professed "*that* nationality which defends our own literature, sustains our own men of letters, upholds our own dignity and depends upon our own resources"; and he believed that American literature had at last reached a condition where it was ready, as he said, for criticism. This was a time

*The house in Richmond where Poe edited "The Southern Literary Messenger". Receiving a very low salary he made this magazine a leader in American criticism.*

for critical standards, a rigorous plain speaking and a serious effort to uphold the dignity of genius. The magazine-habit brought Poe, moreover, in ever closer touch with current events and tendencies in the world of thought. He shared the typical American interest in practical science, for instance, an interest that also included the subliminal mind, and his tales ranged in their subject-matter from notorious murders to electro-magnetics, phrenology, animal magnetism, the telegraph and ballooning.

His editorial work, besides, brought Poe into contact with many of the other contemporary American authors. He had met or corresponded in Baltimore with the best writers of the South, and in Philadelphia he encountered the baleful Rufus Griswold, who traduced him later. Griswold created the popular myth of the life of Poe that prevailed for at least three generations. This rather low vindictive creature went so far as to say that Poe had had criminal relations with his aunt, Virginia's mother. He accused Poe of every kind of baseness.

Poe was not a great critic, but just because he dwelt so much on the art of composition he was a valuable critic for the moment, for the place. He wrote about literature as an art when this was the one thing necessary, at an hour of triumphant democracy when a multitude had begun to write who had never known the discipline of the cultivated few.

Poe had accepted in his last year a post on the Richmond *Examiner,* — his life in a sense had come full circle. One seemed to discern this tendency at least in the chaos of his neurotic and erratic movements. At the end, however, every city was a City of Dreadful Night for Poe, for he had developed many of the symptoms of madness. His nervous instability increased with every year and he made enemies everywhere and quarrelled with his friends. He was to publish *The Raven* in 1845, while some of the finest of his poems, *Ulalume* and *Annabel Lee,* were fruits of his tragic life in the cottage at Fordham, where, wrapped in his old black military cloak, Virginia died on her mattress of straw, hugging the tortoise-shell cat to keep her warm. Meanwhile, he had written the *House of Usher, Ligeia* and the *Murders in the Rue Morgue* before he left Philadelphia in 1844 and moved to New York for those last five years that witnessed the climax of his misery and the height of his fame.

All the years of Poe's life were passed on the great Atlantic highway that ran from Boston and Providence to Richmond and Charleston,—Boston, his birthplace, Providence, where Mrs. Whitman lived, — the Rhode Island poet who became engaged to Poe in 1848, — Richmond, which he regarded as his home, and Charleston, the centre of his life as a soldier. Along this route, from city to city, his mother had wandered before him, living, like himself, in humble quarters, and dying as it were on the road, as Poe was to die in Baltimore in 1849, at a time when his thoughts and his hopes had returned to the Southland.

*Sarah Helen Whitman, Rhode Island poet, broke up her engagement to Poe. She had inspired his poem "To Helen".*

*Virginia Clemm, Poe's cousin whom he married when she was thirteen years old.*

*In Fordham cottage, New York, Poe spent his days of greatest misery and highest fame.*

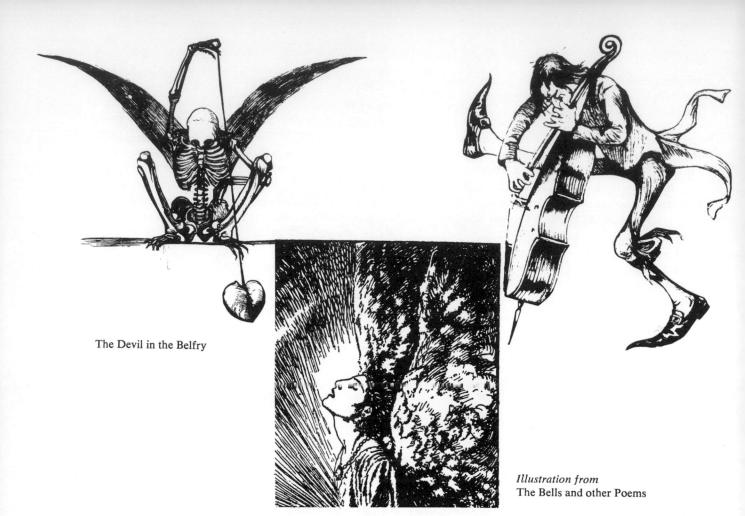

The Devil in the Belfry

Illustration from
The Bells and other Poems

*Poe's complex insecurity,* — physical, social, financial alike, — explained in large measure his character, as it also accounted for the nature of much of his writing. To bolster his self-esteem in the sad and ambiguous position in which he found himself throughout his life, he liked to assume the role of the man of the world whom no one could dislodge or baffle.

He liked to play for a similar reason the part of a solver of cryptograms, a reader of riddles, a peerless detector of crimes for whom the official police were mere idiots and infants. He felt a need of being a romantic hero. There was much of the actor in him, which made him a capital public reader. He had sometimes the air of a stage Virginian, who exaggerated the part a little, because it was not really his by right, and his tales and his poems were full of the imagery of the theatre, mimes and mummers and masquerades, shifting scenery, phantom forms and the "gala night," for example, of *The Conqueror Worm.*

Meanwhile, he possessed a literary genius that had had no parallel as yet on the American scene.

This genius, moreover, was supremely artistic. Poe was a craftsman of exquisite skill in prose and verse alike. He was an innovator in verse, a creator of "novel forms of beauty," who influenced poets elsewhere for an age to come. He sought "the unknown — the vague — the uncomprehended." His images, instead of creating specific pictures in the mind, evoked a world of sorrowful associations, remote, dim, sinister, melancholy, majestic, his refrains suggested echoes from bottomless gulfs, and when he repeated a word in a rhyme the sound seemed magically altered by the new collocation.

Already by 1831, when the third of his little collections was published, Poe had written *To Helen, The City in the Sea, Israfel, The Lake* and others of more than a dozen poems in which he emerged as a new voice in the language. In the end he wrote two score and ten, and perhaps fifteen of these bore the stamp of Poe's true genius.

The tales that Poe was writing had much in common with his poems, — they were sometimes even as musical in the beauty of their prose, — and there one also found dim tarns, wild and dreary

34

landscapes and phantom figures flitting to and fro. Evil things in robes of sorrow presided over some of these tales, with their strange effects of horror, the macabre and the grotesque, a world of the phantasmagoric, suggesting the dreams of an opium-eater. A lover of melancholy, mystery, the horrible and the dire, Poe was bathed in the air of his time, and he was a man of a time when people were living "Gothically" all about him, when they were building Gothic houses that recalled the school of his childhood in England, with its gates and its pointed windows and ceilings of oak.

There was no doubt of the presence of incipient madness in the marvellous imagination that conceived these tales, an imagination all compact of gloom, despair, sepulchral thoughts, grim fantasies and the fear of impending mental decay. The typical heroes of these tales were victims of neuroses. They were ridden, for example, by a conviction that they were destined to be buried alive, while they doubted the fidelity of their closest friends. Their sanguinary heads rolled from the tops of steeples into the gutter. They went home in high glee with dislocated necks or they placed corpses in boxes that were supposed to contain champagne with springs to make the corpse rise when the box was opened.

The tales of Poe were impressive precisely because they were *not* fabrications but involuntary ebullitions of his own sick mind. "Wild visions, opium-engendered, flitted, shadow-like" before his eyes, as before the eyes of the narrator of *Ligeia,* with the tottering figures of pallid tenants of tombs.

"To dream," said the lover in *The Assignation,* "has been the business of my life." So it was with Poe, who wrote the story, and in some of his dreams he carried out the dearest wishes of his heart: he had moments of happiness there that life denied him.

Poe longed for material luxuries but he was a lover of spiritual beauty, and occasionally, in his prose and verse, his love and genius crystallized and formed a gem of purest ray serene. Moreover, one absolutely believed the impossible when the art of Poe presented it, so great was the force of his imagination and the skill with which he introduced the trivial and precise details that imparted to the whole effect an air of truth. It was this power of the factual detail that carried one, helpless with terror, to the bottom of the hideous gulf in the *Descent into the Maelstrom* and roped one down with the rats in the Spanish pit. One shared Poe's nightmares more vividly than one felt one's own.

The Pit and the Pendulum

The Murders in the Rue Morgue

35

# William Cullen Bryant

## *"the father of American Song."*

*Illustration to Bryant's poem* The Fountain.

*Bryant, grave, austere and sensitive, sincerely
expressed a whole-souled joy in the American
spirit and the American scene.*

*Poe, living in New York, was* hardly a part of the
literary scene. The centre of the writing community,
as of journalism and politics, — a great citizen and
lover of his country, — was William Cullen Bryant.

A Massachusetts man, a lawyer at Great Barring-
ton, Bryant was thirty-one when he settled in New
York, and he had already written some of his best
poems. He seemed to be predestined to become the
"Father of American Song."

When Bryant was only eight years old, his far-
mer-grandfather had set him the task of turning
into rhymes the Book of Job and gave him a nine-
penny coin when he had achieved it. What was
quite as important for him, his father ridiculed the
rhymes and would not "allow this doggerel to
stand," as he said. Later he showed in all his work
a feeling for perfection that was without precedent
in the American verse of the time, and for this no
doubt he was largely indebted to his father.

Bryant was only seventeen when he composed

*For Bryant the woods abounded in Indian legends.
These he wove into his poems.*

*Thanatopsis,* the lines that opened an epoch in American verse. The autumnal decay of nature suggested this "view of death," so youthful in its melancholy, so noble in its feeling, so typically an expression of the moment and the place. Bryant had also really discovered his country and freed it from the faded fancies of an older world.

Bryant, keenly interested in botany, had studied Linnæus as closely as the Bible, and the delicate descriptive touches in his flower pieces were drawn from exact observation and definite knowledge. All the earlier poets had clung to conventional imagery. His images were fresh and clear and one heard in his poems the sounds of the woods, the hum of the bee and the chirp of the wren, as one scented the stream of odours flowing by.

Then for Bryant on his lonely walks the woods abounded in Indian legends, and he liked to weave these into his poems as well. With all his diffuseness and lack of intensity there was something noble in his air that lifted him over the heads of common poets. In the minds of remote generations and by virtue of some of his poems, Bryant remained the bard of the early republic.

There was a touch of the seer in him and something heroic and hardy that sang in the "Forest Hymn," "The Sower" and especially "To a Waterfowl," the most intense of all his poems, in which for a moment he entered the realm of magic.

Bryant had found himself as a poet before he arrived in New York, and his note never changed in later years. Moreover, his work was accepted at once, like the novels of Cooper and *Rip Van Winkle,* that earlier forest tale. Its freshness, its veracity, its rendering of a world of nature that had never before appeared in moving verse, all this gave Bryant an immediate place that others had to struggle for and raised him for a decade or two above all rivals.

*Every summer afternoon Bryant escaped from the city seeking refuge among the groves that lined the quiet Hudson. Or he took a ferry to Brooklyn. Years later, for walks he joined Walt Whitman there, when this young man was editing the* Brooklyn Eagle.

*Asher B. Durand: Kindred Spirits. William Cullen Bryant during an outing in the Catskills.*

# Painters and Writers

*they waken the nation to a sense of its own mental and imaginative resources.*

*While hopeful signs of a* flowering of literature in the West and the South were appearing, it was the valley of the Hudson that during these years became the literary focus of the country. Cooper and Bryant were constantly there and numbers of other well-known writers lived, like Irving himself, on the banks of the river. Willis was to settle soon at Idlewild, near Cornwall. Paulding moved to his farm "Placentia" in 1844, just above Poughkeepsie, while Audubon had built a house at Minnie's Land near the village of Harlem, not far from the Fordham cottage of Edgar Poe.

Bryant's farm was at Roslyn, Long Island. He often ascended the wild Housatonic, with its islands of rocks and hanging trees, but he always returned to the valley of the Hudson which, largely thanks to him, had also become a focus of the painters of the country.

For the so-called Hudson River School expressed a feeling for American scenery that Irving, Cooper and Bryant had already awakened, and it was Bryant who kindled Inman and Thomas Cole when he told them to "Go forth . . . and list to Nature's teachings." Bryant, the inseparable friend of Cole, excited in Durand and others a passion for the wild scenes along the river. Leaving the "maze of dusty streets" in which he never felt at home, he went on walking tours with Durand and Cole, delighting in the rocky glens, the forest knolls and the plunging streams that appeared in his poems and their pictures. Together they scaled the Catskill crests and unfrequented precipices, shaggy with rocks and pines and hidden cascades.

These artists glorified a river which the rising generation regarded more and more with pleasure and pride. The Hudson River School expressed the mood of the decade. America had passed beyond the stress of pioneering. A moment of self-realization had arrived. Americans had settled a homeland which they loved and more and more delighted in.

Its most notable aspect perhaps was this national mood of self-awareness for which the American writers had prepared the way. For it was largely thanks to these writers that Americans had become conscious of their country, its woods and fields, its rivers and mountains and its intellect and history too. Young as it was, American literature already had much to be proud of, though the most intelligent foreign visitors were scarcely aware that it even existed.

Perhaps it was true, as Poe said, that New York was the focus of this renascence of American letters, as Philadelphia had been years before; but Boston had reasons at the moment for disputing the claim. In Massachusetts, which Audubon called the "reading state," — especially in the capital Boston, in Cambridge and in Concord, — a literary movement was under way that spread its influence far and wide and even swayed minds in every part of the country. Boston was unique indeed as a centre of powerful minds in the following generation that witnessed the flowering of New England.

*Bryant writing in his study in Roslyn, L. I.*

*Durand painting a Hudson River landscape.*

*Book Two*

# The
# Flowering of New England

*The age of Washington Irving* brought forth a number of writers who gave the country a sense of self-realization. Thanks largely to Cooper, Irving and Bryant, the Americans were able to feel that they were no longer colonials but men of a race with a mind, a history, a literature and a nation of their own, a nation that was passing "from the gristle into the bone," as Cooper, the novelist, said in the eighteen-forties. As Audubon "discovered" the American birds and Catlin discovered the Indians, these writers discovered, for Americans, their woods and fields, their scenery, their flowers, their rivers and prairies and mountains. So William Dunlap discovered American art.

This literary phase fulfilled a rule in the evolution of peoples and nations, the rule that writers appear at the stage of progress following great struggles for the freedom and shaping of the state; and the atmosphere these writers breathed was leisurely and spacious. They had some of the breadth and sweep of patriarchal times, they were emotionally uncomplicated and seemed, in general, happy in comparison with many writers of later epochs. Their minds were, on the whole, focussed on the outer world, and they were at home with men of enterprise and action.

But the second literary phase that opened with the New England renascence was marked by a greater variety, unity and depth. Its writers expressed a collective impulse and passed through a true Spenglerian "culture cycle."

Here was a homogeneous people, living close to the soil, intensely religious, unself-conscious, unexpressed in art and letters, with a strong sense of home and fatherland. One of its towns became a "culture-city," for Boston, with Cambridge and Concord considered as suburbs, answered to this name, which Spengler accords to Florence, Bruges and Weimar, as no other town has ever answered in either of the Americas. There was a springtime feeling in the air, a joyous sense of awakening, a free creativeness, an unconscious pride, expressed in the founding of institutions, intellectual, humanitarian, artistic; and, — at first a little timid, cold and shy, — the mind began to shape into myths and stories the dreams of the preurban countryside.

"Men are free," said D. H. Lawrence, "when they are in a living homeland, a living organic, believing community, active in fulfilling some unfulfilled, perhaps unrealized purpose." This was the case with the New England authors, in the epoch of the building of the nation. Perhaps it was never more truly the case with any group of authors, all question of intensity aside. They were as completely of their people as any authors of the oldest nations; and they saw, if not themselves, — for they were not self-conscious, — at least their profession as having a Promethean role to play. They were teachers, educators and bringers of light, with a deep and affectionate feeling of obligation towards the young republic their fathers had brought into being.

The breadth of their conscious horizon, the healthy objectivity of their minds, their absorption in large preoccupations, historical, political, religious, joined with their literary feeling, — a blend of the traditional and the local, — gave the local wider currency while it brought the traditional home to men's business and bosoms. They filled the New England scene with associations and set it, as it were, in three dimensions, creating the visible foreground it had never possessed. They helped to make their countrypeople conscious of the great world-movements of thought and feeling in which they played parts side by side with the intellectual leaders of the older countries.

*<br>*   *

All over New England, not only in the "Literary Emporium," as Boston was called far and wide, there was a passionate interest in self-culture. Children of the poorer families, who could not afford to buy paper and ink, made their own, or used chalk or charcoal, and learned to write on the kitchen floor. This interest in reading and study, in books and authors, laid trains of feeling in the general mind that were about to burst into expression. Throughout the region, as throughout the nation, there was a widely spread presentiment that a great native American literature was about to make its appearance. Everyone read English books, histories, poems, essays, in which people found the moulds of their minds and manners; but they already felt that these English authors described a world that had ceased to be their own.

They were ready to welcome tales and poems without the English kings, menials and beggars, — with fresh American flowers instead of the far-away verdure of the British poets. They were ready for historians and poets who might prove to be as independent as their statesmen had already been. The New England air was filled with a sense of expectation.

*Tremont Street, Boston, ca. 1840. Painting by Philip Harry. Karolik Collection, Museum of Fine Arts, Boston. On the left appears the Tremont House. Built in 1829, this was the first truly modern Hotel in America, famous for its comfort and service. On the opposite side of the street, the Tremont Theater, which is still standing.*

42

# Boston and Cambridge

*Since the eighteen-twenties, Boston had* tingled with a new ambition. In its spirit of emulation the town suggested Florence. Everyone with talent was impelled to struggle. Everyone laboured to be foremost. Learning was endemic in the Boston mind as befitted a town whose first inhabitant, the Cambridge scholar Blaxton, had brought his library with him. There had been books on the slope of Beacon Hill when the wolves still howled on the summit. And now that the nation seemed to be on a solid footing, the intellectual life grew apace.

Various institutions of learning marked the coming of age of the Boston mind. The Boston Athenæum was largely the work of Buckminster, who had spent most of his little fortune buying books in Paris. He had sent three thousand volumes home, sets of the British essayists and poets, works on Greece and Rome that brought the classical world before one's eyes. The first wistaria vine, the first mimosa was scarcely more of a novelty in Boston than some of these intellectual plants and vines that were to scatter their seeds across New England.

The culture of the immediate past and present found expression through another organ. The Anthology Society, devoted to literary interests, numbered among its members Buckminster, Channing, President Kirkland of Harvard, John Lowell and other well-known men. The members met one evening every week to discuss the manuscripts for their magazine, the *Monthly Anthology,* over a modest supper of widgeons and teal, brants or a mongrel goose, with some good claret. There was too little intercourse, they felt, among Americans who cared for letters. They even hoped that their review, the first of its kind in the country, which had succeeded many feebler efforts, might foster the growth of a national literature.

The magazine, though somewhat staid in manner, decidedly starched and impersonal, was yet an enterprise that promised much. It deplored the backward state of American letters, the servile imitation of England, the fruits of a superficial education. Whatever the future might produce, the writers of the review showed that Boston had roused itself out of its ancient slumbers.

*The magazine published by members of the Anthology Society was well informed. It reviewed exhibits, theatre, books.*

*Buckminster helped to establish the Athenaeum. He spent considerable sums buying books for its library in Europe.*

*Most of the men of the* mind in and around Boston had come to nurse in Cambridge. Learning was immemorial in Cambridge, omnipresent at Harvard. The shopkeepers around the square added tags of Latin to their signs. The janitor of the newly-established Law School was a notable spouter of Virgil.

Harvard College was the heart of Cambridge, and the patrician families of Boston regarded it as more than a family affair, — it was a family responsibility.

The object of study at Harvard was to form the mind, a clear, distinct mentality, a strong distaste for nonsense, steady composure, a calm and gentle demeanour, stability, good principles, intelligence, a habit of understatement. The surface, at least, seemed somewhat tame, suited for the merchant and the lawyer, and the man of God after the Boston fashion.

The mainspring was useful common sense. In a word, the students learned to think. Moreover, they learned to write. Their style was almost sure to be marked by grace and, as often as not, by force. Their scholarship was sure to be exacting, especially when Edward Tyrrel Channing, the younger brother of Dr. Channing, became professor of rhetoric, — two years after the birth of a Concord boy, Henry Thoreau by name, who was to acknowledge, in later years, that he had learned to write as Channing's pupil. In fact, the whole New England "renascence" was to spring so largely from Channing's pupils, Emerson, Holmes, Dana, Motley, Parkman, to name only a few, that the question might have been asked, Did Channing cause it?

> Channing, with his bland, superior look,
> Cold as a moonbeam on a frozen brook,
> While the pale student, shivering in his shoes,
> Sees from his theme the turgid rhetoric ooze.
>
> *Holmes*

He had a remorseless eye for the high-falutin, the swelling period, the emphatic word, morbid tissue to this ruthless surgeon. Channing sowed more of the seeds that make a man of letters than all other teachers that have taught a much taught country.

*Summer costume of the Cambridge students; a pencil sketch found among the papers of Edward Everett Hale, probably drawn by Samuel Longfellow, 1838.*

*Professor Edward T. Channing taught his students to write with grace and force. Thoreau and many other writers studied with him.*

*Genial President Kirkland, naturally frank and cordial, finished off examinations by offering the candidates a dish of pears.*

45

*Not in Boston alone but in every* corner of New England a fresh and more vigorous spirit was plainly astir. On the granite ledges of New Hampshire, along the Merrimac River, in Essex and Middlesex Counties where the spindles whirred, or westward on the lovely Housatonic, life was filled with a kind of electric excitement.

For two hundred years the New England people had been actively working their minds. They had been striving to educate themselves, thinking, brooding, keeping their journals, reading their Bibles, their classics, their books of sermons; and all this life was preparing to bear its fruit.

At Newport, Salem, Portsmouth there were notable scholars in charge of the young, Harvard men or Englishmen, French tutors, Italian dancing masters, the dim dawn of a cosmopolitan culture. There were public reading-rooms in Newport and Portsmouth. Salem, like Boston, had its Athenæum and a large library.

All these towns abounded in interesting persons, sometimes droll and quaint, often witty, almost always learned. At Salem, the most imposing of the seaports, dwelt a circle of distinguished men who were to leave their mark in American history.

## NATHANIEL BOWDITCH

The most illustrious of the Salem worthies was the great mathematician, Nathaniel Bowditch, the author of *The Practical Navigator*. This second Benjamin Franklin had learned his Latin as a boy in order to read Newton's *Principia,* — in which he found an error. The book he had written, the *Practical Navigator,* had saved countless lives and made the American ships the swiftest that had ever sailed. Here was an American book that every British seaman had to read if he hoped to get ahead of the Yankee skippers. If the Yankee mind could produce a work like this, what could not the Yankee mind produce when it turned its faculties in other directions?

## NOAH WEBSTER

The Connecticut mind, as travelers often noted, was keen, strong and witty, but usually narrow, educated rather than cultivated. The only important Connecticut man of letters, a symbol of his world in many ways, was the famous lexicographer, Noah Webster, who was more concerned with "education" than he was ever concerned with "cultivation," but who was doing more with his education than all the American pedagogues put together. He was at work, at New Haven, writing his Dic-

tionary, a new Declaration of Independence. His object was to establish a national language as a bond of "national union." A spirit of the blindest imitation stifled all American enquiry, benumbed the intellectual faculties. He had worked up his own vernacular word-book, based on the common usage of New England. The store-keepers, up and down the country, laid in supplies of Webster's Speller, along with their hogsheads of rum and their kegs of molasses. The pedlars carried it from door to door, until, as the decades passed, fifty million copies had been sold. It had given the population a uniform spelling.

He did his task so well, within his limits, that "Webster," with its countless modifications, was destined to remain a standard work for the English-speaking peoples of the world.

*Noah Webster's object was to establish a national language as a bond of national union.*

*Channing proclaimed his inextinguishable faith in the natural possibilities of man. By raising the estimate of human nature he gave the creative life a prodigious impulse.*

## WILLIAM ELLERY CHANNING

*Newport was already reaping its* harvest, for there the Channing family lived. William Ellery Channing, the Boston preacher, had spent half the hours of his childhood wandering about the beach and the towering rocks, listening to the music of the waves, with the wide ocean before him, filled with a sense of awe and rapture.

Newport, the "American Eden," so like the Isle of Wight, had fostered in Channing a feeling for Wordsworth and Byron, those two romantic poets who had shared his moods. The slender, pallid, nervous little man, grave, reflective, fond of lonely rambles, teemed with the new ideas that were slowly coming to birth along the seacoast.

Channing was a poet and a saint; and he shared and led, as no one else could lead them, the deeply devout religious conversations that occupied so many Boston minds. He did not care to discuss the minutiae of theology, for the Unitarian leaven that worked in Channing was of a much more fundamental kind. He pondered in his heart the question of convincing human beings that they were parts of a great whole, bound to work for the welfare of this whole. In after years, as a preacher in Boston, he mounted his pulpit every Sunday and poured into the ears of his congregation, willing or unwilling, large draughts of intellectual day.

He had a large opinion of human nature. The adoration of goodness was his religion. He hungered and thirsted for it; and the great, wide, ingenuous eyes that beamed under his broad-brimmed hat and lighted up the little figure, wasted by so many sufferings, proclaimed his inextinguishable faith in the natural possibilities of men. He detested the jealous caution of New England, the insane love of money that pervaded the trading world, the coldness of the calculating mind, the dullness and timidity of provincial manners.

Everyone could see, in after times, that Channing had been the great awakener. He harrowed the ground for literature, first by his harrowing of the ground for life, and also by his intuitive understanding of the function of art and letters.

## DANIEL WEBSTER

*If Channing was New England's* spiritual awakener, Daniel Webster symbolized New England in its political convictions. He was a demon of a man, a full-blooded, exuberant Philistine, with a demiurgic brain and a bull's body, with an all-subduing personal force, an eye as black as death and a look like a lion's. As a lawyer, he was unapproachable. He could invest a common murder-case with the atmosphere of an Aeschylean drama.

All his traits, his references, his habits bore witness to the national character and buttressed it with the kind of authority that could not be gainsaid. When he spoke of the Bay State and Bunker Hill, of Plymouth Rock, Lexington and Concord, one felt that to belong to Massachusetts was the noblest privilege of history.

*Daniel Webster: a New England statesman who spoke for the nation.*

# Widening Horizons

*George Ticknor awakened interest in native*

*legendary lore through foreign balladry.*

*While there was much home-grown* talent in New England, some of the younger scholars were eager to widen their horizon, and the news had reached Boston of the German universities that were still little known even in England. They read accounts of the great library at Göttingen and they set to work to learn the German language, which only a few could read in the English-speaking countries. They were anxious to expose themselves to the culture of the old world and all its intellectual, poetic and linguistic riches; and they exercised, returning to Boston after their studies abroad, a catalytic power, inspiring, in certain cases, the native genius.

It was this aspiration that prompted two young Boston men in the spring of 1815 to embark on a journey of discovery. Not content with the state of affairs at Harvard, they had made up their minds to go to Germany and investigate the reports that had come to Boston about the prodigious progress of German scholarship. George Ticknor, a lawyer, and Edward Everett, a brilliant young minister of twenty, had sailed for Liverpool, the first stage for Germany, along with a party of other Boston friends. George Ticknor was positive, self-assured in the Boston way, not by any means a man of genius, or he would not have been so self-assured, but certainly a man of remarkable talents. Everett was considered the brightest student who had ever passed through Harvard. John Adams called him "our most celebrated youth."

*George Ticknor: Never before in America had anyone invested with such glamour the life of the poet.*

Going to Germany was not a lark for a man like Ticknor. His country, he felt, was in urgent need of scholars, not the musty theologues of old but well-trained teachers and men of letters. In this capacity he could be useful, especially if he had seen the world.

Before leaving, both Ticknor and Everett had gone on an American tour. Ticknor had visited Jefferson at Monticello, who gave his young friend letters to many European scholars and men of af-

*American scholars went to school again in Göttingen. Its professors were as formidable in the field of studies as Frederick the Great had been in the field of arms.*

*Ticknor's handsome Georgian mansion at the head of Park Street. When later in life Ticknor became a chilly old scholar, his house was to be known as "Ticknor's Iceberg."*

fairs; and Everett, who had seen Madison, was also equipped with letters that opened every European door.

The heads of these two young men might well have been turned. For what young men of any other country could have had quite their opportunities, as the first young scholars, with attractive manners, or, rather, the first after Washington Irving, who represented the new American nation upon which so many hopes of humanity rested? What were they to say and feel when Madame de Staël remarked to them, "You are the advance-guard of the human race," when Lafayette, Chateaubriand, Benjamin Constant greeted them in the same soul-stirring fashion?

In Germany they were soon to meet scholars who had put the English philologists to the blush. In fact, these German professors were something new under the sun, as formidable in the field of studies as Frederick the Great had been in the field of arms.

Here was little Dissen of Göttingen who had spent no less than eighteen years, at sixteen hours a day, on Greek and nothing but Greek, and who said that even now he could not read Aeschylus without a dictionary. It all depended on what one meant by "knowing." No one who had ever seen a German could ever again call a man a scholar

unless he was willing to follow Eichhorn's programme: 5 a.m. to 9 p.m., with half-hour intervals for meals. As for the poor little Harvard library, it was a good half-century behind the times.

Ticknor and Everett were glad to go to school again, with their big portfolios under their arms, just like two boys who fear the birch.

Ticknor had been appointed, in his absence, the Smith Professor of Belles-Lettres at Harvard. He was expected to teach Popular Latin, Old French, Provençal, Spanish and Portuguese. All this was to have its effect on the rising generation of American poets, so many of whom were to study under him. For Ticknor was not only to sow at Harvard, in a ground already prepared, the seeds of the modern literatures of Europe; he was to stimulate, in some of his pupils, — by opening up these veins of popular legend, the balladry of Spain, Provence and Scotland, — a feeling that was already half-awake for the legendary lore of their own country. Every river-valley in New England teemed with similar legends, waiting for other Irvings, in prose or verse.

In fact, as one followed Ticknor on his travels, one could imagine already how he was destined to stir his Harvard class-room. Although his main concerns were prosaic enough, — philological data, sober facts of literary history, — still, the lives that he was to talk about, Cervantes, Lope de Vega, Dante, Petrarch, Froissart, Calderon, the old explorers and soldier and sailor poets, were quite enough to excite a roomful of boys who were able to do their own embroidering. He opened up vistas of adventure, unheard-of prospects for a poet's life. And if, without wishing to spread the peacock's feathers, he dropped, in those years to come, into reminiscence, he could unfold a world-panorama such as few in Cambridge had ever dreamed of.

Never before, in America, had anyone invested with such glamour the life of the poet and the man of letters.

*Dante Calderon Cervantes*

49

# New England Historians Fulfill Vital Function

*Ticknor and his friends had stirred* the country's poetic imagination by bringing to the fore the balladry of other lands. At the same time the historical mind was extraordinarily busy. Young men with literary tastes were drawn into historical research largely for want of other choices, because there was little else for them to read. Everything had prepared the Boston mind to centre its thoughts on history, as it had chosen theology in the past; and the general interest that filled the libraries with an ample apparatus of research animated the young historians and gave them a sympathetic welcome.

With all these new facilities, the studies of the historians made rapid progress. George Bancroft, Jared Sparks, and William Hickling Prescott were preparing a series of monumental works. Sparks, the "American Plutarch," was working on his "lives," the *Library of American Biography*. His writings, however useful, were hardly exciting, at least to later readers.

Still, the fame of his work showed what an audi-ence awaited the coming historians, and what a social function they fulfilled, a function as vital as that of the orators, the ministers, the scholars and the portrait-painters. For the twelve volumes of the *Washington,* of Jared Sparks, orders came from the remotest hamlets. The *Franklin* was translated presently into one of the dialects of Hindustani.

But Sparks' vogue was slight beside that of Bancroft, whose *History of the United States* began to appear in 1843. Never before had anyone attempted to tell the whole story of the nation, and the poor little dry chronicles and annals that stood for American history were swept from the shelves by Bancroft's enterprise. There were reasons for Bancroft's renown. He was learned enough to place American history in the main stream of historical events. It was true that, in the first editions, before Bancroft "slaughtered the adjectives," the book was like a Fourth of July oration, like one of Everett's speeches long drawn out, with the Stars and Stripes streaming from the author's hands. For Bancroft, God was visible in history and history culminated in the United States.

One still recaptured later, turning its pages, the pride that thrilled the bosoms of the forbears for whom the glowing historian first unrolled the panorama of the national epos. The forbears themselves

*George Bancroft was the first to unroll a glowing panorama of the nation's history.*

*George Bancroft lecturing at the New York Historical Society in 1852.*

*The house of William Hickling Prescott in Beacon Street in Boston, facing the Frog Pond.*

shared Bancroft's fervour. The young republic shared it; and the republic saw itself reflected in Bancroft's flattering mirror.

Suddenly, in 1837, out of this throng of historical studies, honest and laborious, some of them fervent, none of them august, a great work appeared, like a wonder of nature, as it seemed to American readers, — *The Reign of Ferdinand and Isabella.* It was a brilliant performance, as any child could see and no scholar was ever to deny. As a work of art, a great historical narrative, grounded at every point in historical fact, and with all the glow and colour of Livy and Froissart, it was a magnificent success.

It was the work of William Hickling Prescott. Prescott? — who could believe it? He was partly blind, and he had an extravagant love of jolly parties. He talked with a joyous abandon, running over with animal spirits, laughing at his own inconsequences, with always some new joke or witty sally.

His book had been born a classic. It was a conquest of personality. Prescott was a first-rate human being, exuberant, gallant, wilful, devoted, and his temperament fitted him to understand an age of courageous exploits.

But how could a half-blind man write a history, based on unpublished documents in several foreign languages? With the aid of a friend and a sister and later of a competent secretary, he made his ears do the work of his eyes. He taught himself to use a noctograph, by means of which, with the aid of an ivory stylus, pressing on a sheet of carbon-paper, he took his notes and wrote his manuscripts.

Meanwhile, he had learned to memorize, composing in his memory to such an extent that he could often carry in his mind as many as three chapters of one of his books, seventy-two pages of printed text.

Few could have dreamed that a work on such a subject could have been received with such hosannas. Prescott never guessed how hungry his countrymen were for the brilliant glow and colour that he gave them, the pageantry of kings and queens and battles.

After his first great effort new plans rose in Prescott's mind, shoots from his Spanish studies. Why should not he, like the Spaniards, gather gold in Mexico and the Andes? The drama of *The Conquest of Mexico* shaped itself. He set the stage with a panorama of Montezuma's empire. From the moment when Cortez, burning his boats and landing at Vera Cruz, began his march to the capital, the story moved on to its final result with the frightful inevitability of some drama of nature. The Aztecs, like the Incas, in *The Conquest of Peru,* the work that rapidly followed, were painted as the chroniclers had seen them. Generations passed before anyone challenged the truth of the picture that Prescott drew of the conquest, grandly in the Mexico book, only less grandly in the tale of Peru. Everything that Prescott wrote had the same solidity, and he told these two great stories with an air of effortless ease. Massive but alive in all their parts, they were full of colour and vigorous movement. They were partly composed on horseback. Prescott mentally wrote the final chapter in a gallop through the woods at Pepperell.

*John Lothrop Motley, by celebrating the rise of the Dutch Republic, celebrated the American type in its first historical appearance.*

*Motley's family home, Jamaica Plain, Boston. Here every Saturday afternoon young Motley with his friends wearing cloaks had acted out historical melodramas.*

*Boston, which had produced a Prescott,* brought forth another writer in the eighteen-fifties whom readers were to enjoy for generations. John Lothrop Motley, the son of a merchant, had much in common with his predecessor. Born in similar surroundings, a few years later, in one of those households where Scott was the staple of reading and Irving and Channing were read as American classics, Motley was a high-spirited boy of whom the last thing to be expected was the drudgery of a scholar's life.

His gift for historical writing first revealed itself in an essay on Peter the Great, suggested perhaps by Motley's one-year stay in Russia. The story of Peter the Great led naturally to Holland where the Emperor, a Russian Yankee, had worked as a shipbuilder. One day, a friend found Motley at work with a huge Dutch folio and a dictionary. He had turned to another use than novel-writing his art of painting scenes and characters, though few could have seen the connection between the histories of Holland and the American republic. But for Motley the United Provinces, in their struggle to liberate themselves from Spain, suggested the struggle of the United States. William the Silent, for him, was a prototype of Washington. This was the larger meaning of Motley's work, the motive, scarcely expressed, that gave him his vast popularity.

In later life, as minister to Austria and England, Motley was immersed in politics. *The History of the United Netherlands* and *The Life and Death of John of Barneveld* reflected his interests. These works were almost exclusively concerned with statesmanship. But Motley was a preëminent story-teller, and some of his writings were to live with the best of Prescott and Parkman.

*A greater writer perhaps than Prescott,* who had shared his physical disabilities, and certainly greater than Motley, Parkman was the climax of the Boston historical school. The last romantic historian, deriving his impulse from Scott, as he drew his design from Gibbon, Parkman was a lonely man who stood outside his epoch, an aristocrat, a stoic and an artist.

In 1846, at 23, he had made a trip west to regain his health, impaired already by overwork. He had crossed the plains on the Oregon trail, an undertaking as dangerous as that of Columbus when he crossed the sea. The tale of his adventures, *The Oregon Trail,* which appeared in 1849, had opened a new world for story-tellers. The book was boyishly vigorous, fresh and frank, and he wrote as if he rather wished his pen had been a sword.

From his earliest childhood, Parkman's tastes and interests had converged to form his will. For, while he was a man of the world, he was a woodsman born. His element was the Border, and the life of the Border, where the primitive and the civilized were in conflict. The life of the pioneers had for him a resistless charm.

These interests prompted him to form an ambitious plan: to write what he called the history of the American forest, — the history of the "old French War," — the contest of the French and the English for the control of the continent.

Only after incredible odds was he able to complete this vast historical canvas, the seven separate works describing the conflict for the domination of the New World.

Parkman's life at best was a purgatory. As a delicate, sensitive boy, with a passion for adventure, he had lived in a state of constant tension. While his energy was super-normal, his constitution could not bear the strain. He had broken down. His eyes had given way from excessive reading. At any attempt to write, he felt an iron band about his head that seemed to contract with force. He could not read continuously for more than five minutes, and he usually read a minute at a time.

With all this he had to restrain his passion for action. All he could do was to ride his wheel-chair as if it were a saddle. He had to sublimate his love of danger, he had to repress his energy to save his nerves. His mind was like a bow, too tightly strung; and this tension appeared in his work, in its frequent speed and picturesqueness. One felt the virile force of the writer, his pleasure in the savage and the vast.

His contempt for physical weakness grew with his own infirmities and suggested the "hard-boiled" mind of a later epoch. What he really hated was the weakness in himself, and in this he resembled all the "hard-boiled" writers.

In the face of incredible odds his work advanced, volume by volume, till the series came to an end, proving beyond a doubt that he was a great historian, the greatest perhaps who had ever appeared in the country. Parkman had made Pontiac, Champlain, LaSalle and Wolfe historic figures like Charlemagne and Peter the Great. Until he wrote, students who thought the Tudors all-important saw nothing in the conflict in the forest that had made the American nation what it was; and Parkman, who had discovered his theme, created a form that matched his theme in grandeur.

*Francis Parkman: His element was the life of the border, where the primitive and the civilized were in conflict.*

*Father Jogues, French Jesuit missionary addressing the Mohawks.*

*Francis Parkman, photographed by Mrs. Henry Adams during a visit to the Adams summer home, at Beverly.*

# The Hour Had Struck for Poets

*Henry Wadsworth Longfellow, a born poet whose*

*every fancy clothed itself in images and rhymes.*

*The spreading chestunt tree — one
of Longfellow's own drawings.*

*The Craigie House in Cambridge had* grown accustomed to distinguished lodgers, such as Jared Sparks, the historian, Edward Everett and Dr. Joseph Worcester, the lexicographer. Then in the summer of 1837, a young man of thirty, Henry Wadsworth Longfellow, the new professor of modern languages at Harvard, applied at Mrs. Craigie's door for chambers. He got his own tea and toast for breakfast and quietly went about his college duties.

He was a romantic soul. He was a born poet whose every fancy clothed itself in images and rhymes. He was also a scholar, the man in all America best fitted to fill Professor Ticknor's vacant chair. Longfellow had spent four years wandering over all Europe in preparation for his new position. He had learned not only the usual languages, all that Ticknor knew, but also Finnish and Swedish, and he had published several text-books, French and Italian grammars, and a Spanish reader. But he was a poet all the time. Everywhere the Europe that he witnessed had gone back to its national origins. The poet had become again the singer and the moulder of the national life. Longfellow had felt this world-impulse and so had become conscious of his own mission.

In his Cambridge classes he found willing ears. He taught with a feeling for the romance of letters more intimate than Ticknor's. His mind was like a music-box, charged with all the poetry of the world. Ballads that rippled with the River Neckar.

Spanish, Swedish, Danish ballads. Epics and fragments of epics, like *Frithiof's Saga*. Sagas of ships and sea-craft and laughing Saxons, dashing their beards with wine. The music-box unrolled its coloured stream; the lecturer spoke with a mildly apostolic fervour. Henceforth, let it be understood that he who, in the solitude of his chamber, quickened the inner life of his countrymen, lived not for himself or lived in vain. The hour had struck for poets. A national literature ought to be built, as the robin builds its nest, out of the twigs and straws of one's native meadows.

Cambridge, like all New England, like New York, was ready for its poets and its tellers of tales.

Cambridge had ripened, in these few short years,

*Longfellow during his stay at Göttingen,
where he studied modern languages.*

as a well-tended garden ripens in June. All in a mist of birds and honeysuckle, the literary mind had put forth shoots. Thoughts were growing, books were growing under the quiet boughs of the ancient elm trees, in the fragrant shadows of the locusts, the perfume of the daphne and the lilac. Books were springing from the Cambridge mind, thick and fast as the grass in the Cambridge dooryards. And anyone could see that Longfellow's poems, whatever their subjects were, expressed the young American state of mind.

For softly, without effort, as he sat in the vast shadow at his open window, the poems rose in his mind, like exhalations, — *Voices of the Night*. Stanza by stanza, the poems came, sometimes all at once, songs, reveries, echoes of German verses, mingling with the whispers of the summer wind, — *Footsteps of Angels, The Light of Stars, The Reaper and the Flowers, Hymn to the Night*.

In later days, when other fashions came, when the great wheel of time had passed beyond them, one saw these poems in another light. They seemed to lack finality and distinction, whether in thought or phrase. But no one could quite forget their dreamy music, their shadowy languor, their melodious charm, their burden of youthful nostalgia.

Such were the "voices of the night." The voices of the day were firmer and clearer. Longfellow's mind went back to Sweden, to the still Scandinavian woodlands. The old pagan gods awoke once more, and one heard the hammers of the Vikings, so like the hammers that one heard in Portland, building their oak-ribbed ships. That was his great discovery, after all, that was the brightest feather in his cap: other American writers and scholars were rediscovering Italy and Spain, he was the first who had visited, amply, at last, with a living imagination, the lands of the skalds and the sagas, where one found traces of one's forbears, forests like one's own New England forests, village ways like the New England ways. Influenced by northern forms, Longfellow created poems that were redolent of the vast American woodlands, the prairies, the prodigious Mississippi, and poems fragrant still with hemlock, fir and balsam, the wild brier, the salt breeze of the rocky shore.

Longfellow's tone was humble. He seemed to write for the joy of sharing his treasures, as if he were glad to be thought a mere translator, a simple story-teller, a nursery minstrel. This was both disarming and deceptive, for Longfellow had an original mind. He was an innovator in metres and rhythms; he introduced new modes of feeling; he touched his world with a magic that was mild but unmistakable.

*Longfellow as a professor at Harvard. Here he inspired his students with his tales of European travel.*

*Longfellow in the study of the Craigie house, 1847.*

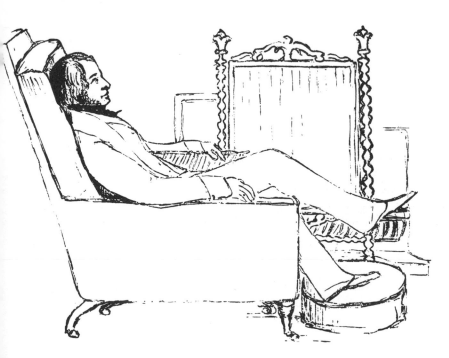

Evangeline

The Children's Hour

The Courtship of Miles Standish

The Ride of Paul Revere

Tales of the Wayside Inn

*Longfellow had married a merchant's daughter,* fair as a Portland figurehead, and the young couple had bought the Craigie house. As the years went by, there was something Goethean in the spacious simplicity of this. Never was a poet more calmly happy. Rising early, brewing his own mocha, standing at his desk by the southern window, he opened the day by translating some lines of Dante. It was like running a ploughshare through the soil of his mind.

Now and then, at almost any moment, after a morning's work on his Dante lectures, a poem rose in his mind, stanza by stanza, and whipped itself on paper with arrowy speed, — a song, a sonnet, or ballad of the seacoast, suggested by some event in the morning paper. Everything that passed into his mind turned into music and pictures. *Evangeline,* 1847, too, was a picture-poem, the roundest and the ripest that Longfellow wrote. The first King Leopold of Belgium caused to be cut on a seal the word Atchafalaya, — the name of the lake where the lovers passed each other, each unaware of the other's presence, — because "life is like that," he said. Longfellow felt this and conveyed the feeling. It was a feeling that will preserve a poem which has so much simplicity and grace.

In 1854 Longfellow had resigned from his professorship at Harvard. His college work was like a great hand laid on the strings of his lyre, stopping their vibrations. The first result of Longfellow's freedom was the Indian idyll, *Hiawatha*. This was an October poem, floating in an air of Indian summer, a haze of yellow harvests and autumnal quiet and the smoke of camp-fires and far-away lodges. He had plowed through Schoolcraft's collection of Indian folk-lore, and the Indians that emerged in the poem were not the warrior-stoics of flesh and blood. He had softened and simplified and humanized them. There was a quiet magic in the story, a golden languor as of afternoon, of corn-fields in the setting sun, purple vapours and the dusk of evening.

With his notes of domestic affection and the love of the sea, of landscape and legend, Longfellow's fame spread like the morning sun over the English-speaking peoples. During a visit to England he found that he was an English poet almost as renowned as Tennyson. He found that he was a German poet too, after another summer on the Rhine largely spent with Freiligrath, who had translated his poems. So great was the demand for his works that twenty-four English publishing-houses brought out editions in competition and ten thousand copies of *The Courtship of Miles Standish* were sold in a single day. A constant stream of well-wishing visitors passed through the Craigie house. The flood of interruptions became so great that Longfellow longed for a snow-storm to block the door. An Englishman who stopped to see him said he did so because there were no American ruins to visit.

Longfellow's soul was not an ocean. It was a lake, clear, calm and cool. The great storms of the sea never reached it. And yet this lake had its depths. Transparent as his mind was, there were profundities of moral feeling beneath the forms through which it found expression, the fruits of an old tradition of Puritan culture, and, behind this culture, all that was noble in the northern races. With all his defects, his flaccidity, flat and trite as he often was, Longfellow stood for poetry as no one else. He knew it, with a joy, a breadth of learning, a devotion that caught the imagination of high and low.

*There was something sweet and sunny in the atmosphere of the Craigie house that reflected the soul of the generous poet — he whom neither fame nor praise could ever spoil or alter.*

# Young Boston Goes to Sea

*Richard Henry Dana's "Two Years Before the Mast,"*

*a tale as taut as a rope, filled with masculine vigor.*

*Longfellow's mind was never far from* the sea. Even describing the hills he said that "the sea fogs pitched their tents there, and the "Building of the Ship" was an apotheosis of New England naval craftsmanship. Most of the writers of the period wrote well about ships and shipping. The new clippers with their graceful prows and swelling hulls were considered by many a proof of the American search for beauty. Horatio Greenough, the sculptor, when he returned from Italy, exclaimed as he looked at a clipper-ship: "There is something I should not be ashamed to show Phidias." It was out of this atmosphere that New England's first great book of the sea emerged. Richard Henry Dana's *Two Years Before the Mast,* an Odyssey of the days of the brigs and the clippers, when half the American merchant marine was manned by young New Englanders, was a prose poem about the beauty of ships. It had opened a new world for story-tellers.

This younger and bolder Dana, the son of the poet, remembering the punishments of school days, had much to say on the subject of flogging at sea. He had practised navigation on the Winthrop duck-pond and sailed away to California on the brig *Pilgrim* as a Harvard junior whose studies were interrupted by failing eyesight. Returning from his adventures in the hide trade, he had written the book, basing it on his diaries. He had read the manuscript aloud to his father and his uncle, Washington Allston, both of whom were somewhat critical. But when the book was printed, two thousand British sailors bought it in a single day, and the old connoisseur, Samuel Rogers, said that it had more poetry in it than almost any modern verse. It was the real thing, as the sailors knew, the first book written about the sea, not from the bridge or cabin, but by one of the hands.

But a reader did not have to be a sailor to be swept along by the book. One did not even have to know the meaning of a jigger, a bunt or a knighthead, a larboard or a starboard watch, a cross-jack yard or a mizzen top-sail. The "heave ho" and the "heave and pawl," the "heave hearty ho" and the "heave with a will," the "cheerily, men," while all hands joined in the chorus, blew one's mind awake. The book, like the vessel, leaped over the seas, trembling to the keel, while the spars and masts snapped and creaked; and one felt oneself in a wholesome and bracing climate, with spray and the smell of tar and salt.

No one could fail to perceive that the ship was a symbol of life, since the first part of the voyage was spent in getting it ready for sea and the second part in getting it ready for port. The book was full of overtones and symbols, and all the details of the sailor's life were noted with the bold veracity that springs from a heightened state of consciousness, a tension, well-controlled and even calm, that passed at moments into exaltation. Such were the moments when Dana, at the helm, witnessed the breaking of day over the ocean, the sighting of the

*The Boston boys hovered around the wharves and half of them wanted to go to sea. They listened to tales of Chinese pirates, greeted some cousin home from Spanish Manila.*

*Richard Henry Dana, Jr.*
*at the time of his*
*trip to California*
*on board the* Pilgrim.

iceberg, near Cape Horn, — the enormous mountain-island, with its dark cavities and valleys, its pinnacles glittering in the sun, rising and sinking at the base while its points nodded against the sky, crumbling, tumbling, thundering in the sea.

After his return from the sea young Dana had become a lawyer. For thirty years and more, in Harvard Square, promptly at eight o'clock every morning, one saw him, green bag in hand, waiting for the Boston omnibus. He was always telling tales of the sea; and everyone knew that his book had done as much for the sailors as Dickens had done

for the debtors and orphans of England and *Uncle Tom's Cabin* for the slaves.

Dana's sympathies remained with the common tar and he became known as the sailors' lawyer. His office smelled like a forecastle, crowded as it was with men from the ships. He battled like an avenging angel for the seamen's rights and alienated all his paying clients, for the lords of the sea, like the "lords of the loom and the lash," as Charles Sumner called them, did not like a man who called attention to the wrongs of sailors and slaves. Dana, an aristocrat in every sense, fastidious in all his tastes, excelled in the fastidiousness of conscience. He had compiled a seaman's manual to help the sailors in their fight for justice.

Even as one of Boston's most distinguished lawyers, Dana never forgot the tropical nights, the soft trade-wind clouds under the stars, "the seas and floods in wavering morrice moving." He said that he was made for the sea and that all his life on shore was a mistake, that he should have been a traveller, with no profession or home, roaming over the world like a gypsy.

*Even in later years as a*
*successful Boston lawyer Dana*
*remembered the sea. He should*
*have been a traveller, roaming*
*over the world, he thought.*

*Dana described the flogging of*
*seamen. All his life he tried*
*to redress the injustices*
*suffered by the sailors.*

# Transcendentalism Explores the Inner Life

*a new idealistic philosophy teaches man to*

*cultivate and expand his own uniqueness.*

*The young Dana, — before the mast, —* had once kept his crew of sailors from going ashore on the California coast by reading aloud all day from Scott's *Woodstock.* Rough as the sailors were, most of them were Massachusetts sailors, and everyone took it for granted that in Massachusetts reading had a right of way. Boston, all New England, respected learning. No New England boy was allowed to question that he was destined to succeed in life, provided he knew enough.

It was true that at first the Boston pedagogues resented the assaults of Horace Mann, who had no use for their old-fashioned ways. But no one could resist this human cyclone, the tall, humourless man in the long frock-coat, so anxious, so exacting, so dogmatic, with the will of a battering-

*Elihu Burritt learned to master twenty languages while working as a blacksmith.*

*He made lecture tours on foot, often walking 100 miles to fill an engagement.*

*New England acquired the lecturing habit. Theodore Parker, as other transcendentalists, newly evaluated the world and man's place in it.*

ram, who founded the State Board of Education in 1837.

The passion for learning on the upper levels soon spread through all the other strata. Here and there, some workman followed suit. Elihu Burritt of Worcester, the "learned blacksmith," was a typical figure of the moment. This well-known self-taught linguist who worked all day on the anvil made a version of Longfellow in Sanskrit and mastered more than forty other tongues.

At Harvard, the young men read much, too much, or so it seemed to those who had frugal minds. They were hatching very strange ideas: they said that terrestrial love was only a reflection of celestial love. They spoke of "bathing in a sea of thought." They went off mooning in the woods. They refused to talk about railroads, banks and cotton. They laughed when their fathers quoted Dr. Johnson. They smiled when their uncles quoted Burke. And if all this was not the result of reading, where, pray, had they acquired their notions?

Books of a new kind had begun to appear,

French and especially German books, even books by Englishmen and Scotchmen, who should have known better, filled with the wildest sort of metaphysics. The young men who read the new writers, — Thomas Carlyle, George Sand, Jean Paul, Schleiermacher, — were drawn to these writers because they spoke of the inner life; and this was because the outer world repelled them.

For the shape of the outer world had ceased to please the more sensitive minds of the younger generation, the imaginative, the impressionable, the perceptive, those who characterize a generation, — for the practical people never change, except in the cut of their clothes. The young had begun to explore the inner life, the depths of thought and sentiment. They were bored by the ideal of the marble statue as a pattern of social behaviour. They did not wish to "get," they wished to "be." To reaffirm the senses and the soul. To exist, expand, feel, to possess their own uniqueness. Some new and hidden fount of life was about to revivify existence. The strange, dire planet called Human Nature, hitherto so dark and almost baleful, had swum into their ken.

Coleridge propagated these transcendentalist attitudes for which the New England mind was so well prepared. He encouraged reliance on intuition, warm, perceptive, immediate. Transcendentalism referred to the self-sufficiency of the human mind, the creative powers of man. It spoke for an order of truth that transcended, by immediate perception, all external evidence. "God becomes conscious in man," as Fichte said. From various German thinkers, Jacobi and Fichte, the new generation in New England was receiving special impulsions towards heroism and towards mysticism.

Much of this German influence reached New England through the medium of Carlyle, the "Germanic new-light writer." Over the rising school of New England writers, even over the toughest-grained, Carlyle and Carlylese were to leave their traces. Even the style of Thoreau was to be tinged faintly here and there with the rhythms of a writer whom lesser minds could not resist.

He vindicated, they felt, their celestial birthright. He gave them faith in their own endeavours. A calculating age of profit-seekers was deaf, dumb, and blind; and yet the Invisible still existed, and opened itself to the inward eye, and fought on the side of the seeker of it. However, the prophet of this new credo was not Carlyle but another man who dwelt in the little town of Concord.

*Romantic German philosophy shed new light on the human mind, over which the sun of hope seemed to be rising.*

*Carlyle represented the romantic spirit on its ethical side. He had a powerful influence on the rising school of New England writers.*

# The Sage of Concord

*Emerson spoke for the active forces waiting in his hearers, eager for the word that would set them free.*

*Emerson. Sculpture by Daniel Chester French.*

*The Bostonians of the early* eighteen-hundreds had been accustomed to oratory; it filled them with exalted thoughts. At school they learned to recite the swelling strains of the *Life of William Tell:* "Friends of liberty, friends of sensibility, ye who know how to die for your independence." Deep in their hearts they believed that they could emulate these historic models and reproduce the deeds of history.

The sons of William Emerson, for instance, the former minister of the First Church, were born with these convictions in their blood. One of them, a boy of twelve named Ralph, a chubby little spouter of Scott and Campbell, who had recently trundled his hoop about the Common, where he pastured the family cow, was to express them later in his essays.

Ralph Waldo Emerson already had a mind of his own. He carried the *Pensées* of Pascal to church, to read during the sermon. At night, in his cold upper chamber, covered with woollen blankets to the chin, he read his precious *Dialogues* of Plato. He associated Plato, ever after, with the smell of wool.

Though born to be educated, Emerson was a desultory student at Harvard. Even three generations later, when people spoke of his education, they put the word in quotation marks.

It was not that he did not know his Greek and Latin, but that he was never systematic. He had read, both then and later, for "lustres" mainly. He had drifted first to Florida and then to Europe. He had drifted through many misfortunes, drifted into and out of tuberculosis, drifted into teaching and out of the Church, maturing very slowly. The trouble with him was that he seemed to like to drift. To the outer eye, at least, Emerson's life was an aimless jumble. Was he pursuing some star of his own?

Like his father he had chosen the ministry as his profession. But Unitarianism could not hold him. The walls of this temple, he thought, were wasted and thin, and at last nothing was left but a film of whitewash. Then, gradually, another faith possessed him. Channing had mentioned some recent writer who said there were two souls in the human body, one the vulgar, waking practical soul, the other a soul that never suspended its action and guided the involuntary motions. This hint of German transcendentalism lingered and grew in his mind. What was this involuntary soul, this "absolute being" of the German thinkers, but the "inner light" of the Quakers, that indescribable presence, dwelling in every being and common to all?

He felt a sudden influx of power; the currents of the universal being seemed to circulate through him. Was not all nature saturated with deity, and was he not himself a part of nature? Nature was indeed a living whole, a spiral ever ascending, and he felt that the new age of science represented a further ascent. Men would rise above their conventional notions, emerge from their belief in mere prescription, their blind and ignorant following of custom. They would learn to trust themselves, the universal soul within themselves, walking the earth at last as supermen. This was Emerson's notion before it was Nietzsche's.

In no haste to publish his reflections, Emerson, settled in Concord, "put his ear close by himself," as Montaigne had done before him, and held his breath and listened. He liked the phrase of Simonides, "Give me twice the time, for the more I think the more it enlarges." In solitude, Emerson found, his faculties rose fair and full within, like the forest trees and the field flowers.

He looked to life for his dictionary. Why should he travel for his illustrations? The people of Concord served him well when he came to make his points. It was the magic of his genius to lift the curtain from the common, showing us the divinities that are all about us, disguised as gypsies and pedlars, as farmhands and clerks.

He bought a woodlot by Walden Pond, a wild rocky ledge, and cut vistas over the water, where he bathed on summer afternoons. There he strolled and lingered, sitting on the bank, reading Plato or Goethe, writing in his journal. There he was "adjacent to the One." He had always felt like a king in the woods. It was as if he had left behind all his human relations and become one with carbon, lime and granite. The frogs piped, the leaves rustled, and he seemed to die out of the human world and enter another existence, a life of water, air, earth and ether. In this state of elevation, elation and joy, shared by all the mystics, the vision of a superhuman race becomes more real than reality. Nietzsche felt so at Sils-Maria, and so Emerson felt in the woods at Walden. There was a god in man.

Emerson's own path lay clear before him. It was to look within himself and report his own perceptions and reveal the powers that lay in the soul of man. If one paid no attention to the world's opinion, but followed one's own proprium, if one lived wholly from within, the world would come round to one at last; for one's inner voice was the voice of the "collective psyche," as later writers called the Over-soul, — the term that Emerson used. One would be acting in harmony with the laws of life, to which the phenomenal world is obliged to bow.

It was especially to the young that this new prophet addressed himself. His essays, *The American Scholar,* followed by his *Literary Ethics, The Method of Nature, Man the Reformer* and others, appealed to the younger generation more intimately than Carlyle and the German writers. These speeches and Emerson's essays, appearing at the same time, — *History, Self-Reliance, Compensation,* — were filled with their problems and dilemmas, which Emerson seemed to have shared. Unlike the professional orators, he addressed himself to the thinking classes. He spoke to the individual in each of his hearers, giving them courage to listen to the whisper of the voice within themselves. He stirred them to take life strivingly in full belief that what man had done man could do, that the world was all opportunities, strings of tension waiting to be struck, especially perhaps by thinkers and writers, to whom Emerson spoke most directly.

The effect of these essays and lectures on the younger people was like that of the sound of a trumpet. It was a high and solemn music that dissolved the knots in their minds, roused their wills, enlarged their affections, filled them with a new light. They felt themselves no longer "pinched in a corner," as Emerson described their former state, but potential benefactors and redeemers, advancing on chaos and the dark. For Emerson pictured America in a way that made them feel how much the scholar counted. This careless, swaggering, shallow nation of theirs, this great avaricious America, boasting of its crops and the size of its cities, gambling away the charters of the human race for a petty, selfish gain, this country needed them to calm and guide it, to check self-interest, to give it repose and depth. Who doubted what the mind could do, seeing the shock given to torpid races by Mahomet, by Buddha, or by Newton or Franklin? All that was requisite, at any time, was a few superior men to give a new and noble turn to things; and Emerson summoned his hearers to the task.

*Concord was plain, low, quiet.* The village had no obvious distinction, and the enterprising Yankees passed it by. The hills and woods, not too exciting, afforded a gentle stimulus to genial and uninterrupted studies. The very cattle lying under the trees seemed to have great and tranquil thoughts.

Concord was a school for the study of human nature. One learned all the trades and professions by talking with the blacksmith, the grocer, the plumber. All history repeated itself in Concord. The wealth and goods of the Indies and China streamed through the village in the trucks and wagons that carried the wares of Boston to Vermont and New Hampshire. One had only to mix a little imagination with all these sights and sounds of the common life: then one found Asia and Europe, past and future, within the circle of one's daily walks. Such were Emerson's thoughts.

To experience his genius and communicate it, to detect and watch the gleam of light that flashed across his mind from within, was Emerson's dream and hope; and this alone governed his method of living.

It was for no private ends that Emerson sought privacy. If the seeker of truth needs solitude, and almost a going out of the body to think, should a poet apologize for the isolation that breeds Olympian thoughts? Solitary converse with nature was his special *modus* of inspiration. On spring days, at summer dawns, in the October woods, by flood or field, he heard sweet and dreadful words that were never uttered in libraries.

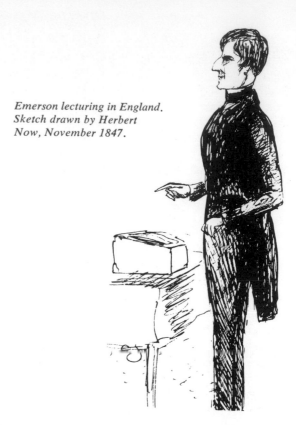

*Emerson lecturing in England. Sketch drawn by Herbert Now, November 1847.*

*Emerson in ecstasy over nature. Humorous drawing from the note-books of Christopher Cranch.*

Well he could understand why bards and solitary thinkers had been taken for makers and givers of laws, they who had stood for liberation, for courage, freedom, victory. The poets who had shown this power most clearly were the great religious awakeners, Zoroaster and Plato, the bards of the Vedas, of the Vishnu Purana and the Bhagavad-Gita. The luxuriance of the imagery, the breadth of the Eastern modes of thinking refreshed Emerson's New England imagination. The Oriental muse had an electric power that animated and unbound his mind.

Poet that he was in all his prose, he toiled unremittingly over his verses; and, in fact, he had developed a style of his own, as marked in his poems as in his essays, a lean, spare, quick, intellectual style that could only have emerged, one felt, from Concord. There was something bleached and dry, in the best of this verse, like that of an age-old wisdom, exposed for thousands of years to sun and wind, and one felt as if the mountain air had somehow blown upon it. Among partial men, he stood for the complete man. All the forms of life were in balance in him; he saw and handled that which others dreamed of, the whole scale of experience. He was the master of the dance of life, who knew that every man would begin to move when the music reached and touched his imagination.

Emerson as a young cleric at the time of his pastorate at the Second Church of Boston.

After his visit to Europe, (1847-1848) Emerson became the leader of the transcendentalists.

Emerson in 1873 when he travelled widely, "going to school to the prairies."

During his last years.

The Emerson house in Concord.

Emerson's study.

# Henry Thoreau

*he longed to write sentences that would lie*

*like boulders on the page, durable as Roman aquaducts.*

*In Emerson's white house in Concord,* Henry Thoreau had taken up his quarters. He occupied the room at the head of the stairs, a little room, but he was a little man: his nose and his thoughts were the biggest things about him. Emerson, and especially Emerson's children, had formed a warm affection for their difficult Henry, difficult, that is, for the rest of Concord but a treasure for the household of a sage.

The village people looked askance at him because he was so pugnacious. He liked to administer doses of moral quinine, and he never thought of sugaring his pills. But at boating and camping he was a master-woodsman, skilled as Ulysses, shrewd as any fox. The redskins had forgotten the arts he knew. Arrowheads and Indian fireplaces sprang from the ground when he touched it. He charmed the snakes and fishes. Wild birds perched on his shoulder. His fingers seemed to have more wisdom in them than many a scholar's head.

He wished to be a philosopher, not a mere thinker of subtle thoughts but one who, loving wisdom, lived a life that was simple, magnanimous, free. Henry liked the soldier's life, always on the stretch and always ready for a battle. Why should one be burdened with impedimenta?

Henry had plenty of acid in his composition. He had taken a few suggestions from Zeno the Stoic, — for one, that he had two ears and a single mouth, in order to hear more and speak less. He could not help taunting his fellow-Yankees. Seek first the kingdom of Heaven! Lay not up for yourselves treasures on earth! What does it profit a man! . . . "Doing a good business!"— words more profane than any oath, words of death and sin. The children should not be allowed to hear them.

For himself, he wished to live deep. He wished to suck out all the marrow of life. If the days and the nights were such that he greeted them with joy, if life emitted a fragrance like herbs and flowers, if it was more elastic and more starry, that was his success and all he asked for.

His style was to mirror the man. He had a sharp eye for the faults of phrases that had to be pulled open, as one opens the petals of a flower that cannot open itself. He liked to see a sentence run clear through to the end, as deep and fertile as a well-drawn furrow.

He wished to write well, to warrant every statement and each remark, till the earth seemed to rest on its axle. He longed to write sentences that would lie like boulders on the page, as durable as Roman aqueducts. Sentences, kinked and knotted into something hard and significant. Henry revised and revised, until his page was a mass of blots and blackness.

His poems were of a homespun kind, well-woven, but indifferently cut. The smoke obscured the flame,

*Concord River: He did not want to go to Europe,*
*since all the essentials of life were to*
*be found in Concord.*

66

but now and then a jet rose out of the smoke, and Henry wrote a line or two that shivered its way up the spinal marrow. If his poems were often disjointed, like his prose, it was because of this habit of journalizing. He jotted down his paragraphs and verses and waited for a cooler moment to patch them together, — a good way for epigrams, but fatal for poetry, and none too good for prose. His journal was a calendar of the ebbs and flows of the soul. It was a beach on which the waves might cast their pearls and seaweed.

What he gave was solid. As for friends, what were they, for the most part? Bubbles on the water, flowing together. Very few were ever as instructive as the silence which they shattered with their talk. Company, he felt with Hawthorne, was a "damnable bore."

Henry, to be sure, had friends with whom he exchanged a few words, perhaps on his way to look for mud-turtles in Heywood's luxuriant meadow. He also had some who were wilder, the breams who nibbled from his fingers, while he stroked them gently and lifted them out of the river, the muskrat that emerged from the hole in the ice. The muskrat looked at Henry, and Henry looked at the muskrat, wondering what the muskrat thought of him, — safe, low, moderate thoughts, of course. Muskrats never got on stilts, like some of the Transcendentalists. Once he conversed with a woodchuck, three feet away, over a fence. They sat for half an hour, looking into each other's eyes, until they felt mesmeric influences at work over them both.

For the sort of friends who never hurt one's feelings, one did not have to look far. He went for his daily walk, with note-book and spyglass in his pocket, and the hat with its lining gathered in the middle to make a little shelf, a botany-box.

*Thoreau at the age of 37, in his travelling outfit. From a sketch by his artist friend D. Ricketson.*

*Thoreau as a young man, painted from life by his sister Sophia. December 1839.*

*A photograph of Thoreau, two years before his death in 1862.*

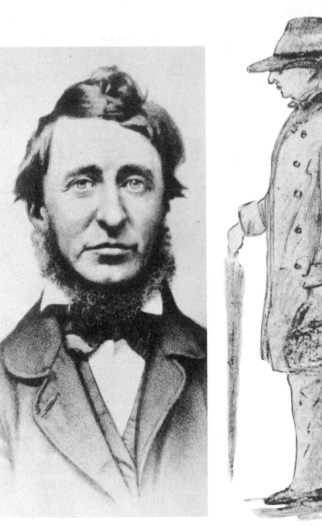

than the annual rent of a student's room in Cambridge.

He had long cherished the notion of a forest life. He felt at home in his sylvan dwelling. It made him think of some of those mountain-houses he had seen, high-placed, airy, fragrant, with a fresh, auroral atmosphere about them. There were moles living in the cellar. He had occasional visits from a hare. His average weekly outlay, for necessaries he could not supply himself, was twenty-seven cents. Why should anyone live by the sweat of his brow and bore his fellowmen by talking about it? Henry believed, and wished to prove, that the more one simplified one's life the less complex the laws of life would seem. Why all this pother about possessions? He liked to think of the ancient Mexicans, who burned all their goods every fifty years. Space, air, time, a few tools, a note-book, a pen, a copy of Homer, what could he wish more than these? What did he care for temporal interests? It was his vocation to discover God.

His life here seemed to flow in its proper channels. It followed its own fresh currents, and he felt himself lurking in crystalline thought as the trout lurked under the verdurous banks. Henry could never have wearied of the woods, as long as he could visit a nighthawk on her nest. When winter came he tramped through the snow a dozen miles to keep an appointment with a beech tree, or some old acquaintance among the pines.

All praise to winter, then, was Henry's feeling. Let others have their sultry luxuries. How full of creative genius was the air in which these snow-crystals were generated. If winter drove one indoors, all the better. Days to sit at home over one's journal, days for writing, days to speak like a man in a waking moment to others in their waking moments. For Henry was hard at work. His own book, rewritten from his journal, was the *Week on the Concord and Merrimac Rivers,* the story of the journey with his brother, never to be forgotten, when they had doubled so many capes and run before the wind and brought back news of faraway men.

Sometimes, even in the morning, usually sacred to reading and writing, the wind fairly blew him out of doors. The elements were so lively and active, and he felt so sympathetic with them, that he could not sit while the wind went by. Henry sometimes stood under a tree half a day at a time, in a drenching rain, prying with microscopic eyes into the swarming crevices of the bark. He would watch for an hour a battle of ants. He sometimes felt as if he were nature itself, looking into nature, as the blue-eyed grass in the meadow looks in the face of the sky. He could always hear in the atmosphere a fine Aeolian harp-music, like the mellow sound of distant horns in the hollow mansions of the upper air. Music was perpetual with Henry.

⚬

*Henry Thoreau had built a hut* at Walden. In March, 1845, he had borrowed Bronson Alcott's axe, — which he took pains to return with a sharper edge, — and cut down some tall, arrowy pines for the timbers, studs and rafters. The hut was ten feet by fifteen. The cost, all told, was $28.12½, — less

Henry wished to write a book that would be saturated with his thought and reading, yet one that would not smell so much of the study, even the poet's cabin, as of the fields and woods. He dreamed of an unroofed book, lying open under the ether, a book that could hardly be forced to lie on a shelf.

In the meantime, he had left his Walden cabin. Why? For as good a reason as he had gone there. He had other lives to live, and he had no more time to spare for this one. He wanted a change, he did not wish to stagnate. Walden was only a bivouac in his campaign. He had other journeys in mind, to Cape Cod, for instance, with Ellery Channing, and later a jaunt to Canada, Quebec and Montreal. (Total expense, two guide-books included, $12.75.)

On the Cape, one saw wholesome faces, well preserved by the salty air, faces bleached like old sails, hanging cliffs of weather-beaten flesh. Henry had three books more or less on the stocks: *The Maine Woods,* full of the scents of the forest, *Cape Cod,* redolent of the sea, even *A Yankee in Canada.*

Later Henry Thoreau went to live in his father's house. He had his den in the attic. There he kept his collections, the birds' nests, mosses, plants and arrowheads. If he had had to spend all his days confined to a corner of this attic, he would have felt at home there. The world would have been just as large to him, as long as he had his thoughts.

After the publication of his *Walden* in 1854,

Thoreau was in danger of losing his solitary habits. With the acclaim that followed this book, he was becoming almost a man of the world . . . and *Walden* was actually selling. It was finding the kind of friends that make a classic. He had had his name posted for public lectures, in Worcester, Salem, Plymouth, — they absolutely required his presence.

Still, as much as he could, Thoreau stayed close to the Concord woods. In 1861 he had caught cold

*Thoreau's hut, ten by fifteen feet — total cost all told, $28.12½.*

*Walden Pond . . . the cove where Thoreau's cabin stood.*

69

from over-exposure while counting the rings of some trees on a snowy day. His health failed and for a year and a half he fought valiantly against tuberculosis. He had outlived his juvenile-braggart phase and had grown more and more to seem the sage. Knowing that nothing could save him, he had settled down among his papers, with an Indian's indifference to the future, completing some of his lists of birds and flowers and finishing *The Maine Woods*. His thoughts had entertained him all his life, never so much as at present.

When Thoreau died in 1862 his friends could hardly imagine Concord without him. Solitude peered out from the dells and wood-roads, and the bobolinks seemed to sing a minor strain.

Thoreau's fame was slow in growing. Emerson and Ellery Channing brought out his posthumous books, — his poems and letters. But only his friends could imagine why anyone should wish to see his journal. Emerson was convinced that, if it was published, it would soon produce in New England a "plentiful crop of naturalists," and this proved to be true a generation later. When volumes of selections from the journal appeared, a school of lesser Thoreaus sprang up at once; and

> The happy man who was content
> With his own town, his continent,

became a teacher of wisdom, all over the world.

*Inside the cabin: Why all this pother about possessions? Space, air, time, a few tools, a note-book, a copy of Homer — what could he wish more than these?*

# Intellectual Whirlpools

*the Peabody bookshop, scene of Margaret Fuller's conversations —*

*Brook Farm . . . an experiment in transcendental living.*

Elizabeth Peabody, the
mother of the American
kindergarten, felt life
was a process of
perpetual education.

Margaret Fuller, impetuous voice of the
West Street Circle, encouraged her friends to
trust their higher selves.

*During the eighteen-forties the liveliest* spot in Boston for younger people was the Peabody bookshop at 19 West Street. There Mrs. Peabody and her daughter Elizabeth sold the German and French reviews and the writings of the continental authors whose thoughts were in the air. Elizabeth Peabody had multifarious interests. One of her passions was the gardening of children who, she felt, should be "artists from the beginning." Her second Bible was Gerando's essay, *On Moral Perfection and Self-Culture,* and no one was admitted to the circle who did not accept its teachings, — that life was a process of education of which perfection was the proper aim.

Other ideas were flying high and low from the intellectual whirlpool in West Street. Boston, hitherto so cold and formal, had begun to receive the gospel of Conversation. This was the message of Margaret Fuller. With the aid of Conversation, the impetuous Margaret wished to minister to the minds of women. What were their legitimate hopes? Why should they all be constrained to follow employments for which only some of them were fitted? Why should American women be satisfied with the common routines of living? They should look for their hidden gifts. Genius, Margaret thought, would be as common as light if men and women trusted their higher selves.

An electrical apparition was this "queen of Cambridge." She thought of herself as a princess who had been left by mistake on a Cambridge door-step. The girls raved about her. There was always something odd in the way she wore a sash or a necklace. Her simplest frock had an air of fancy dress. Margaret's own mission was to "grow." She felt that her impulses were disproportioned to the persons and occasions she encountered and rightly carried her beyond the reserves that marked the appointed lot of women.

With her chosen friends, she gathered the spoils of culture, — a little meagre still in frosty Boston, but amplified by her enthusiasm. In each of her friends she seemed to divine the law of his own interior growth. She gave them to themselves, or so they felt, drew out their unsuspected faculties. They sensed that Margaret carried a hazel twig, — for she seemed to divine their hidden springs.

# Brook Farm

*...where the poet plucked weeds*

*to the rhythm of Keats and Browning.*

*Charles A. Dana (left), later of the* Sun, *was the griddle master at Brook Farm. George W. Curtis (right), later of* Harper's, *gave lectures, trimmed the lamps.*

*In West Street, one could buy over* the counter, in exchange for a little good will, — or a thousand dollars, in case one happened to have it, — a share in the Utopian community that was rapidly taking shape at Brook Farm. George Ripley was already on the farm, at West Roxbury, nine miles out of Boston. He had always expected to be poor and rather preferred obscurity to fame. "Give me philosophy!" was all he asked. He had heard the call of "association," of the communists and Christian socialists, the Owenites and the Fourierists. In the winter of 1840-41, the West Street circle had discussed Ripley's project of a community to be run by the group.

Brook Farm came into existence in the spring, and building was added to building, the Hive, in the shade of an ancient sycamore, the Eyrie, the Nest. Of the circle of the Transcendentalists, most of the ablest members remained aloof, as benevolent neutrals and visitors. "Doing things in crowds" seemed to them too youthful. But Hawthorne, who had no theories, hoped to find at the farm a practi-

*Christopher Cranch, graceful, affable, a welcome guest. He played the flute, drew comic illustrations.*

*Orestes Brownson gave lectures on Catholicism, pounding the table truculently.*

cal basis for his married life. Charles A. Dana, fresh from Harvard, later known as Dana of *The Sun,* and George William Curtis, later of *Harper's,* were members for a longer period.

There were farmers and artists among the members, working-men and Brahmins, girls with hazel eyes and extravagant moods. Ripley, the ever-faithful "Archon," steered the unsteady ship with unwavering eye. He was up before the dawn, dressed in his blue tunic and cowhide boots, milking, cleaning the stalls, giving a Sunday lecture on Kant or Spinoza. Charles A. Dana had classes in Greek and German. George William Curtis trimmed the lamps; Charles A. Dana was the griddle-master. There was much sitting about on stairs and floors, and the conversation, — analytical often, bristling with the new philosophy, with "intuition" and "the analogous," the objective, the creative, the receptive, — sometimes assumed those painful forms of wit that flourish among the intelligentsia.

The stage from Scollay Square brought visitors, a few, at first, those of the inner circle, then hundreds and even thousands. Margaret Fuller came to conduct a Conversation on Education. Emerson often came to lead the talk; sometimes Bronson Alcott. Orestes Brownson dropped in, shouted and pounded on the table and strolled with Isaac Hecker in the grove.

Brownson was a courageous man, in the Church as well as out of it, whom the Brook Farmers learned to respect in the end; for having been too Catholic for the Yankees, he was too Yankee for the Catholics after his conversion.

Of the other guests at Brook Farm, two were especially welcome. The tall slight graceful Christopher Cranch, with his flute as his constant companion, had drawn there his comic illustrations for some of Emerson's essays. William Henry Channing was more austere. He was a self-tormented creature, earnest, hypersensitive, torn by doubts, a "concave man" who was always retreating, as Henry Thoreau remarked, like a fair mask swaying from a bough.

After eight years of ups and downs, Brook Farm came to an end, not without important consequences. Charles A. Dana and John Sullivan Dwight of the *Journal of Music* received their first training as editors of *The Harbinger,* the magazine published at the farm. But something had gone out of the life of the farm. Ceasing to be voluntary, it ceased to be poetic; and, when disaster fell, the farm fell with it.

# The Alcott Family

*Bronson Alcott "had precious goods on his shelves — but he had no show window." — Emerson.*

*When the West Street circle had* been at its most promising heights its members had embarked on another educational venture. Both Margaret Fuller and Elizabeth Peabody had joined hands with Bronson Alcott, the Socrates of Temple School. Alcott was a tall, mild, milky, passionless man, with a singular gift for understanding children. Was not every well-born child a genius? By the Socratic method, as it seemed to Alcott, by posing the proper questions, one could elicit from a group of children all the thoughts of Plato. He tried to reach his pupils from within. No forcing, no cramming, no rod or ferule. He had made the rooms of Temple School gracious and attractive and devised recreations and amusements, plays, physical exercises, even a system of self-government.

Unfortunately the school was a practical failure, and after its demise Bronson Alcott had settled in Concord. If the world was not ready for him, be it so. It was no mean surrender. He trusted in the majesty of goodness and called no man master.

To fill the little mouths of the Alcott household, to provide their bread and potatoes, their boiled rice and grated cheese, Alcott resorted to the spade and saw. He worked for his neighbors by the day, delved like any farmhand, chopped their wood.

*Bronson Alcott would be called today a child psychologist. He encouraged his little daughters to put their thoughts on paper.*

*Temple School, with Alcott teaching. He believed that children must know themselves to escape from "the tyranny of custom."*

*Louisa May Alcott had shared Concord life in all aspects, invested it in* Little Women *with the gaiety of a Robin Hood ballad.*

had built her first play-houses with diaries and dictionaries and had learned to use them both at four or five; for her father, a "child-psychologist," as people said in later years, analyzed and examined the minds of his daughters before they were able to speak and encouraged them to shape their thoughts in diaries and stories.

Miss Alcott had shared the Concord life in all its aspects. She had gathered moss for Alcott's arbours and browsed in Emerson's library, where she read Shakespeare, Dante, Carlyle and Goethe. She had roamed the fields with Thoreau, studying the birds and the flowers.

She longed to be an actress, she longed to be a novelist, and she meant to live her own life, whatever the neighbours and cousins might say. She went to the Civil war as a nurse, and she lived alone in boarding-houses, paying her way as a governess, a housemaid, a seamstress. Sewing sheets and pillowcases, neckties and handkerchiefs, she wrote plays and stories in an attic, lying awake and planning chapters of novels and sometimes working fourteen hours a day.

Miss Alcott was an experienced story-teller when she finally wrote *Little Women*. It was the author's high spirits that captivated the world in this charming book in which she invested the Concord scheme of life with the gaiety and romance of a Robin Hood ballad.

Wise and friendly eyes looked on. There was something emblematic in these labours. Dr. Channing remarked that Alcott at the chopping-block was the most inspiring object in Massachusetts.

There were those who laughed at Alcott. They said that his intemperate love of water made his mind hazy and cloudy. If he had eaten a little meat or fish, it might have had more marrow and substance. But Emerson, who knew his foibles well, loved Alcott for his copious peacefulness and for the mountain landscape of his mind.

There were precious goods on his shelves, as Emerson said, but he had no show-window.

The life of Louisa Alcott, — Bronson Alcott's devoted daughter, — spanned all the great days of Concord, for she was born in 1832, a year before Emerson settled in the town of his forbears. She

*Orchard House, scene of Louisa May Alcott's* Little Women.

Alcott's dream of education based on transcendental theory had a late fulfillment in the eighteen-eighties at the Hillside Chapel, seat of the Concord School of Philosophy. During his lecture tours to the West, Alcott had met numbers of students for whom the little town was a loadstar and who flocked thither in the summer, with their New England condisciples, to sit at the feet of the Yankee worthies and sages. Alcott and his student William T. Harris joined hands, and the Concord School of Philosophy came into being. Sooner or later, two thousand neophytes sat on the rustic settees or gathered on the grassy stretches outside the chapel.

The school was Alcott's triumph. It had sprung from a conversation at Orchard House, beside which the Hillside Chapel stood, with its Gothic doors and windows, and the hardy old philosopher was the dean and leader. The younger intelligentsia joined with the older, and the school lingered on through nine idyllic summers.

*Lecture in the Chapel,*
*Concord School of Philosophy.*

*Bronson Alcott, sitting on the step of the Chapel,*
*lecture hall of the Concord School of Philosophy,*
*of which he was dean and leader.*

# Nathaniel Hawthorne

*fate wrapped his folk tales in a Gothic darkness.*

*While Boston and little Concord* were moving forward, Salem, stricken by the War of 1812, had lapsed into quietude and decay. The waterside streets were no longer thronged with sailors with bundles under their arms from the cannibal isles, or from India or China. The great days of the port were a tale that was told, over and over, by the ancient skippers, who dozed away their mornings at the custom-house, with their chairs tilted against the wall.

Salem had an immemorial air, the air that gathers about a town which, having known a splendid hour, shrinks and settles back while its grandeurs fade. But Salem was old in spirit, aside from its faded grandeurs. Salem was still Gothic, in a measure. In its moss-grown, many-gabled houses, panelled with worm-eaten wood and hung with half-obliterated portraits, dwelt at least the remnants of

a race that retained the mental traits of a far-away past. Beside the kitchen fires, old serving-women crouched, always ready to tell the children stories. Some of them seemed to remember the days of the witches. Their stories were as dusty as the cobwebs.

Salem, like the whole New England seacoast, bristled with old wives' tales and old men's legends. One heard of locked closets in haunted houses. One heard of old maids who lived in total darkness, misers who wallowed naked in heaps of pine-tree shillings. One even heard of Endicott's dreary times, when the stocks and the pillory were never empty. In these quiet towns, where nothing happens, — except an occasional murder, — to agitate the surface of existence, history is ever-present, lying in visible depths under the unstirred waters.

The Hawthornes, who lived in Herbert Street, under the shadow of a family curse, were often troubled by an apparition that seemed to haunt their yard. The only son of the household, Nathaniel Hawthorne, who lived like a ghost himself, haunting a little chamber under the eaves, appearing only at nightfall, could not count the times he had raised his head, or turned towards the window, with a perception that somebody was passing through the gate.

All day long, every day, or almost every day, for twelve years, he sat in his flag-bottomed chair in his little room, beside the pine table, with a sheet of foolscap spread out before him. He was writing stories that rose in his mind as mushrooms grow in a meadow. He had lapsed into this solitary life, half through inertia, and half, — he had always known he was going to write, — as if to protect a sensibility that was not yet ready to yield its fruits.

He felt like a man under a spell, who had somehow put himself into a dungeon and could not find the key to let himself out. His mind was bathed in a kind of *chiaroscuro* that seemed to be a natural trait; and yet it was a trait that he cultivated, half by instinct, half by deliberation. He had a painter's delight in tone. He liked to see a yellow field of rye veiled in a morning mist. Dissolving and vanishing

77

objects. Trees reflected in a river, reversed and strangely arrayed and as if transfigured.

Sometimes, in summer, on a Sunday morning, he stood by the hour behind the curtain, watching the church across the way. The sunrise stole down the steeple, touching the weathercock and gilding the dial, till the other steeples awoke and began to ring. His fancy played about this conversation carried on by all the bells of Salem. At twilight, he would still be standing there, watching the people on the steps after the second sermon. Then, as dusk set in, with a feeling of unreality, as if his heart and mind had turned to vapour, he ventured into the street.

Often, when he set out at dawn, he rambled over Endicott's Orchard Farm, over the witchcraft ground and Gallows Hill, exploring the coast from Marblehead to Gloucester. During the day he would sit on the top of a cliff and watch his shadow, gesturing on the sand far below.

He would stop at a farm for a glass of milk or linger in the market-place at Pittsfield. Opening his note-book in the evening, he jotted down his observations. He had seen a tame crow on the peak of a barn. A half-length figure had appeared at a window, with a light shining on the shrouded face. Was it worth his while to record such trifling items? To Hawthorne they were anything but trifling. Every one of these notes possessed for him a golden aureole of associations, traits of New England life, aspects of New England scenery.

*All around the town one heard old maid's tales of witches and ghosts.*

*He had a massive head. His eyes were black and brilliant. Picturesque, he appeared vaguely foreign.*

78

Most of Hawthorne's journeys, to be sure, were journeys *autour de sa chambre*. He was never away from Salem long. His notebooks, however, were precious memorabilia. They gave his ideas a local habitation. One saw this in the stories he was writing, sketches of actual life, historical tales and allegories. As for his recent stories, they had, he felt, the pale tint of flowers that have blossomed in too retired a shade. It was a new creation, this world of Hawthorne.

What traits, or rather, what fears did these tales reveal in the mind that conceived them? Hawthorne had lived too long in this border region, these polar solitudes where the spirit shivered, so that the substance of the world about him hung before his eyes like a thing of vapour. He felt as if he had not lived at all, as if he were an ineffectual shadow.

Luckily, Hawthorne had another self, a sensible double-ganger. This other Hawthorne, this prosaic Hawthorne, the son of a Salem skipper, was interested in his own self-preservation. Twelve years were enough in a haunted chamber, filled with thoughts of suicide and madness. In 1836, this other Hawthorne entered the publishing house of "Peter Parley," wrote his "Universal History" for him and edited his *American Magazine*. Then, having broken the spell and gone to Boston, this matter-of-fact, substantial, physical Hawthorne accepted a position at the custom-house.

*To the end of Hawthorne's life,* separate personalities, the practical and the poetic, dominated his destiny in turn. Both these personalities, meanwhile, had focussed themselves on a single object. Hawthorne had fallen in love. He had become involved with the Peabody family.

It was Elizabeth Peabody, on one of her visits from Boston, who had disinterred Hawthorne from his living grave. With her unfailing scent for remarkable minds, she had followed his work in the magazines. She drew Hawthorne out, induced him to see Sophia, inveigled him into the Transcendental circle. The ever-active Elizabeth called upon her friend George Bancroft, the historian-collector of the port of Boston, and obtained for him the post at the custom-house. Meanwhile, Sophia drew pictures for one of his stories, in the style of Flaxman's outlines.

After his marriage to Sophia in 1842, Hawthorne, the helpless victim of his twilight mood, had come to Concord by a natural attraction that

*Sophia Peabody became Hawthorne's wife. She was witty and charming, a clever linguist.*

*An illustration drawn by Sophia in the style of Flaxman for Hawthorne's story,* The Gentle Boy.

seemed to reside in the tranquil atmosphere. He too had his Eden at the Manse, under the silvery mosses, where he was writing, — living as he wrote, — *The New Adam and Eve.* Sophia, with her ever-busy paint-brush, had worked a miracle there. The dim, dusty, dismal, priestly dwelling had vanished at her touch, under the floods of morning sunlight. At night, in the soft rays of the hanging lamp, the lovers read their Shakespeare or gave each other lessons in German.

As Hawthorne went for his early stroll in the winding wood-paths, happy visions coursed through his brain. He was writing stories of a larger sweep than his earlier tales and sketches, and some of them were equally sombre, filled with a pervasive sense of evil, the snake that lurked even in Concord gardens. The human heart, — there was the sphere wherein the original wrong subsisted of which the crime and misery of the world were merely outward types. Was not any plan, ignoring this, destined to prove a chimera, a masquerade, as Brook Farm itself was, dissolving before one's eyes like a summer cloud? He had joined the Brook Farmers in all good faith. He had toiled like a dragon, as Ripley said, until he had begun to ask himself what part in his own economy these feats of the barn and dungheap represented. He had brooded, brooded, sitting by himself in the hall of the Hive. There was a worm in the rose-bud of life. If the human heart were purified, then, and then alone, the evil shapes that haunted the outer sphere would vanish.

After three years at the Manse, Hawthorne went back to Salem with a heavy heart, as the new surveyor of the custom-house. The mud, the dust, the east wind, the petty trickeries of the politicians, the chilliness of the social atmosphere, — benumbed and befogged his senses. He went about his work with the dogged and silent practicality that always characterized his mundane life, testing the rum that was sent to the Guinea Coast, while the poet slept within him.

At the end of three years, he moved to Lenox. He had written *The Scarlet Letter* in Salem, the book that had won his freedom; for under his mask of insensibility the poet had been alive and brooding there. In this winter of his discontent, he had also written a few fables and sketches. The tone of *Main Street* and *The Great Stone Face,* like that of *The Snow-Image,* was of a dove-like innocence that often cloaked the wisdom of the serpent.

*Scenes from* The Scarlet Letter.

*Hester led to the Market Place*

*The Minister's Vigil*

*The Minister's Confession*

Tanglewood Tales, *told in a wild spot in the woods near Lenox, where Hawthorne and his children went for picnics.*

The Snow Image — *of dove-like innocence that often cloaked the wisdom of the serpent.*

The Marble Faun *grew out of Hawthorne's trip to Italy in 1858. It dealt with the life and problems of the American art colony in Rome.*

*Lady Elinor's Mantle* from Twice Told Tales

Septimus Felton, *Hawthorne's last unfinished novel.*

*Lenox as Hawthorne saw it. Everything happened in Lenox — and everyone came there. Close by lived Fanny Kemble and at Arrowhead Herman Melville was writing Moby-Dick.*

*At Lenox, the air was scented* with sweetgrass and clover; and there, in the little red cottage on the lonely farm, Hawthorne had his year of wonders. There he wrote *The House of the Seven Gables* and planned *The Blithedale Romance;* while his wife made tracings of Flaxman's outlines on the dull-yellow painted chairs and tables, he told the children stories that explained the drawings, *The Wonder Book* and *The Tanglewood Tales.* Tanglewood, as the children called it, was a wild spot in the woods close by where they all went for picnics in the summer and autumn.

Never quite at home away from the seashore, he still had hours at Lenox on summer evenings when he felt as if he could climb the sky and run a race along the Milky Way. Free at last after the leaden years he had spent at the Salem custom-house, his mind was at its fullest flood. His bones were astir, even to the marrow. Salem, dust of his own dust, and with it the Boston of Puritan times, pressed

*Hawthorne photographed by Mathew Brady after his return from abroad.*

*In the library of Wayside at Concord Hawthorne often read to his family.*

The Old Manse in Concord, where Hawthorne lived after his marriage to Sophia Peabody.

Hawthorne's birthplace, 27 Union Street, Salem.

The Wayside, which Hawthorne had bought from Alcott. Here he lived with his family to the end.

against and filled his consciousness. The dam had burst, in Salem, with *The Scarlet Letter*. The overflow was *The House of the Seven Gables*. To see the world with a side-long glance, by a certain indirection, was second nature with him; and this was the mood his romances conveyed. It was this that gave him his effect of magic and made these beautiful books, with their antique diction, something other than novels and, if not greater, more intimate in their spell than novels can be. They clung to the mind like music, like Gluck's mournful strains of the land of shades or the solemn joy of Mozart.

After a long stay in England and in Italy, Hawthorne took up his life again in Concord, at Wayside, the house he had bought from Alcott, where a man was said to have lived who believed he was never to die. Hawthorne built a tower over the house, a reminiscence of the Italian villa in which he had lived in Florence. There he had his study, reached by a trap-door, with a standing desk fas-

tened to the wall. With England still fresh in his mind, he composed from his note-books the beautifully rounded chapters of *Our Old Home*, a book that was somewhat unhappily named; but a sudden change seemed to have come upon him with his return to America, a blight as of winter, a deadly estrangement even from his own imagination. The sight of a friend or a stranger approaching his house drove him up the hill into the woods. Seventy-five years later, one could still trace the path that Hawthorne's footsteps wore on the tree-covered ridge.

Then, one day in 1864, the news reached Concord from Plymouth, New Hampshire, that he had died in his sleep at the village inn. For years, he had been in the habit, while idly scribbling, of writing the number 64, which had, he felt, some fatal meaning for him. He had not disappeared, but he had wandered away with as little purpose, knowing perhaps that he would not return.

# The Anti-Slavery Writers

*poets and literary men, always in search of a*

*cause, welcomed once more the sound of a trumpet.*

*Out of the depths of the country,* far from Beacon Hill and Brattle Street, one "heard as if an army muttered."

> And the muttering grew to a grumbling.
> And the grumbling grew to a mighty rumbling.

The Anti-Slavery movement was on its way. It was the village centres that grumbled and rumbled, the back streets of the manufacturing towns, the tailors' shops, the Quaker farms and solitary homesteads. There dwelt, unchanged, the spirit of the Puritans and the Friends, the stiff-necked sectaries of Cromwell's army, men who had fought for the right to wear their hats when others stood uncovered, fought for a beard as they fought for a principle. Such were the readers of *The Liberator*. In their bones, as Garrison spoke, stirred the fires of the days of Pym and Hampden. "I am in earnest, and I will be heard!"

This was very far from the tone of Boston, far from the tone of Cambridge. It was the voice of the ploughman, the mechanic, the humble cottagers. Under the Boston mind worked the same leaven, but much more complicated thoughts restrained it. The fears of the "cotton interest" inhibited many; so did the social ties of the merchant families, which bound them to the families of the planters.

Even in Boston, however, the abolitionist question worked like madness in the brain. Channing's little treatise on slavery had made a measure of opposition to it almost a condition of self-respect. The book showed, as no writer had shown before, the disastrous effects of slavery, both on the slaves and on the masters. Officially both Church and press took sides with the merchants and lawyers; but the abolitionist cause made rapid progress even among those whose tastes and feelings Garrison most offended.

*Anti-slavery meeting on Boston Common. To the voice of William Lloyd Garrison Boston was obliged to listen.*

*Mast Head of The Liberator*

*Vignette from The Liberator*

The conflict of conscience animated generous minds. While the bankers and politicians grew colder and colder, the poets and the literary men, always in search of a cause, a just and proper focus for their feelings, welcomed once more the sound of a trumpet. Some of the lawyers joined them. Richard Henry Dana, the sailors' lawyer, whose natural instincts and interest were all on the conservative side, threw prudence to the winds. He never lost an opportunity to act as counsel for the runaway slaves.

In this abolitionist campaign, which was dividing households, the orators especially had found a cause. Eulogies of Washington and Adams, profitable to Edward Everett, rang hollow in the ears of the new generation. The ancient art of oratory, the pride of ancestral Boston, had become an abuse. It was breathing out its vacant life in words, and suddenly, as if by a blood-transfusion, its slow pulse began to beat again. Oratory once more possessed a function. It touched the springs of action,

for the voices of Charles Sumner and Wendell Phillips were voices to which Boston was obliged to listen.

A century later, reading Phillips' speeches, one could still feel the moral passion that seemed to rekindle the eyes of the watching portraits when he invoked the fathers in Faneuil Hall. One could still feel the electric excitement that played about the speaker's head. With his patrician air and his flashing wit, his volleys of historical allusions, he magnetized the crowd, although he carried his life in his hands when he walked home after a stormy meeting.

Whatever in the way of stimulus the movement afforded the poets, the poets repaid tenfold. Even the angular Garrison wrote sonnets, in the gravest style of Milton, composing them in his midnight walks across the bridge to Cambridge; and John Greenleaf Whittier, his lieutenant, had long had cause to know that words, in times like these, had consequences.

*William Lloyd Garrison lived with his printing press beside him in a dingy room, a table for his bed.*

*Wendell Phillips' mind was like a Gatling gun, raking his hearers with his sallies.*

*Charles Sumner, a lecturer rather than an orator, piled his precedents mountain high.*

85

# Whittier, Poet~Laureate
# of New England

*his idylls of the village and the farm brought back to countless readers the world of their childhood.*

*The lithe Whittier, tall, eager, with burning eyes, had a force of moral passion and feeling.*

*John Greenleaf Whittier's passion* for abolition was fired by a tragic personal experience. He had written an anti-slavery pamphlet "Justice and Expediency" and sent it to his friend Dr. Crandall in Washington. Merely for lending it to a brother-physician Dr. Crandall had been put in prison, where his health had given way in the dampness and darkness, and he had died. In fact, in the Whittier of these feverish years, there was more "deed" than "word," strangely in a Quaker non-resistant who clung to the old Quaker ways that enabled him to get "into the quiet." But the lithe, quick Whittier, tall and eager, with his black hair and burning eyes, was anything but passive. He liked to face a mob. His black Quaker coat had been pelted with eggs, and he had seen his newspaper-office, the office of the *Pennsylvania Freeman,* burned over his head.

Whittier was a shoot of the oldest New England. His family had lived in the Haverhill farmhouse since 1688, and no one had known, or was ever to know, the lore of the Merrimac Valley better than he. His mind was steeped in local associations, tales of witches, tales of the Indian wars, the gossip of wandering farmhands and gypsies.

Discovered by Garrison as an abolitionist partisan, Whittier's reputation became that of a newspaper-poet. His associations had never been literary. His active life had been spent with orators and reformers, editors, propagandists and politicians. He was regarded as an unlettered rhymester, an antislavery journalist in verse. Spirited improvisation was his special gift.

The girls had snubbed him for his poverty and rustic manners and teased him to the brink of suicide. He had had his compensation, for his virginality fed his poetry. But he was a philanderer all his days and could scarcely hold back the flood of "pilgrims" that threatened to engulf his later years, the lady-poets who sent him snips of their dresses, begged him for intimate souvenirs, proposed to marry him. These were the days when he always put on his hat before he answered the door-bell so that he might appear to be going out.

As time went on, he returned to the scenes and subjects that had characterized his early verse; and, while he continued to write for the abolitionist cause, he became more and more the rural poet.

Whittier's longest prose-piece, *Margaret Smith's Journal,* was a picture of the New England settlements in the days of the Salem witches. Through the bedevilled air, one caught the scent of the mayflower, the trailing arbutus, the symbol of springtime innocence.

This was Whittier's element, and more and more the "wood-thrush of Essex" sang the summer pastorals and the songs of home that had so much of New England in them. In rudely vigorous ballads, he told the old legends of the seacoast, *Skipper Ireson's Ride, The Dead Ship of Harpswell;* and his husking-poems and corn-songs, his idylls of the village and the farm, *In School Days, The Barefoot Boy, My Playmate,* redolent of sweet-fern and clover and meadows ripe with corn, brought back to countless readers the world of their childhood.

*The farmhouse at Haverhill, Massachusetts, homestead of the Whittiers since 1688, where the poet was born in 1807.*

*Interior of the Whittier house with the kitchen hearth immortalized in* Snowbound.

*Whittier's study at Oak Knoll, Danvers, Massachusetts, where he spent his last years.*

Snowbound, *a winter idyll, had much of New England in it, like Whittier's summer pastorals and songs of home.*

# Uncle Tom's Cabin

*in all the history of the printed book, the*

*Bible alone had appeared in so many versions.*

Uncle Tom's Cabin
*from a series of old time lantern slides.*

*Harriet Beecher Stowe was one of* the volcanic souls whom the abolitionist movement brought to the front. As the daughter of Lyman Beecher, she had lived through the days of her father's "Revival." She had studied at Hartford, at her sister's school. At twelve, hearing of Byron's death, she had wandered off to a lonely hill-side, laid herself down in a field of daisies, looked up at the sky and wondered about Byron's soul. The vehemence and intensity of Byron's feeling fascinated all the Beechers. Her father, who did not approve of novels, made an exception of Scott, whom his children had to read; and Harriet found the *Arabian Nights* in a barrel of sermons in the family garret. She dreamed of some heroic cause, some mission or crusade, that would call out her powers of devotion.

When the Beechers moved west to Cincinnati, Harriet married Calvin Stowe, a teacher in her father's seminary. The capital of the West was half made up of New England people, with a literary club and a magazine. She began to write stories and essays, often on the kitchen table, surrounded by pots and pans, with half a dozen children asking questions.

It happened that her father's seminary was an abolitionist centre. Runaway slaves who appeared there were kept and passed along to the north, and just across the river, in Kentucky, were large slave-plantations. Mrs. Stowe spent several days on one of these plantations, which she afterward described as Colonel Shelby's; and, although she had never lived in the South, she heard so much about it and met so many Southern men and women that she was prepared to picture it as no Southern writer had ever done.

The moment for this came later, when she moved to Brunswick, Maine, where her husband was asked to teach at Bowdoin College. The Stowes lived there in a house in which Longfellow had lodged as a student. The Fugitive Slave Law had just been passed, and letters came pouring in upon Mrs. Stowe describing its tragic consequences, the separations of husbands and wives, the scattering of mothers and their children. Her mind became suddenly incandescent. She felt she had an apostolic mission to put an end to slavery once and for all; she felt that it was not herself but God who wrote the tale of *Uncle Tom's Cabin*.

If this book was not the cause of the Civil War, as Lincoln said later, it was at least one of the major causes, for it blocked the operation of the Fugitive Slave Law. As a literary event, it was the greatest since Prescott's *Ferdinand and Isabella*. It was a world event, in fact. Macaulay, Heine and George Sand reviewed it. Three Paris newspapers published it at once, and Uncle Tom's Cabins rose all over

Europe, as restaurants, creameries and bazaars. It appeared in thirty-seven languages, and three times over in Welsh, into which Scott and Dickens had never been translated; and it sent Heine back to his Bible and made such an impression on Tolstoy in Russia that, when he came to write *What is Art?,* he took it as an example of the highest type, with Dostoievsky's *House of the Dead,* and much of Victor Hugo. In all the history of the printed book, the Bible alone had appeared in so many versions.

Was Tolstoy right in his opinion? On the whole, yes. Mrs. Stowe's mind had the swing and rhythm of the great story-tellers, like Dickens, Cooper, Scott and Victor Hugo. Her characters were real, boldly conceived and presented, and they were involved in situations of a crucial and primary kind. She had a panoramic eye and a just and truthful feeling for human relations that carried her out of the sphere of propaganda. There was no disposition to blame the South; she made one like the Southerners more than ever, and she chose a native Vermonter, Simon Legree, to symbolize all that was worst in a national evil.

Mrs. Stowe's New England novels, written with the same rude strength, established a school and a method. It was her New England, not Hawthorne's, that gave later writers their point of departure. She set the stage for Sarah Orne Jewett.

A triumphant reception awaited Mrs. Stowe when she visited England. Hundreds of thousands, like the Queen herself, had been stirred and moved by Uncle Tom. Mrs. Stowe found her portrait in English castles, and crowds trooped after her carriage as if she had been a prima donna.

*HARRIET BEECHER STOWE*   *A volcanic soul, stirred by an apostolic mission.*

*Henry Ward Beecher, famous Brooklyn preacher, with his sister Mrs. Stowe in 1868.*

*Mrs. Stowe in 1852, when* Uncle Tom's Cabin *was first published.*

*Mrs. Stowe in later years.*

His verse was good
with its charming
air of literary
breeding.

# James Russell Lowell

*compact of incongruities, he was a bookman*

*without compare in all America.*

*The solid chunky frame housed a
substantial Yankee.*

*Of all the Cambridge literati,* none perhaps joined
the abolitionist cause with as much gusto as young
James Russell Lowell. This was one of his many
tinges, for he was a polychromic nature. There were
various reasons for it. His father and his grand-
father had had the Boston Negroes on their conscience, and Lowell's young wife, Maria White, a
poet like himself, — one of the Watertown girls, a
pupil of Margaret Fuller, who had belonged to the
"band," — was deep in all the democratic movements. Lowell was full of the zeal of the convert.
He was in a state of exaltation and found it exhila-
rating to have an object that was outside and beyond his art. His literary facility was surprising.
*The Biglow Papers, A Fable for Critics,* scores of
shorter pieces in verse and prose were pouring from
his mind at once. Four volumes of his work appeared together, in the "year of revolutions," '48.
He could hardly write slowly enough to develop
his thought; he could hardly write fast enough to
record his impressions. Moreover, he was a lion at
twenty-nine. He was the "best launched man of his
time," as N. P. Willis said.

Of all the younger writers, he was the most adroit
and the most accomplished. He seemed to be a
master of all the poetic forms, ode, song, epigram
and sonnet, the narrative poem, the elegy, the idyll.
Everyone knew *To Perdita, Singing, The Rose* and
*Rosaline, An Indian-Summer Reverie,* with its
charming scenes of Cambridge, especially *The Vision of Sir Launfal.* Longfellow and Poe alone,
among the American poets, wrote with the colour
and music that Lowell exhibited in all these verses.

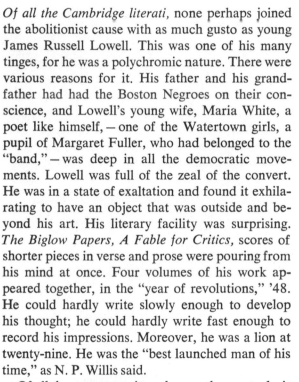

Sir Launfal, *a touching
popular poem in the
Tennysonian manner.*

The Biglow Papers
*expressed aversion
to war. Lowell here
reached the depth
of the popular mind.*

90

His artistry was highly conscious. He had studied all the current models. His poetry, undoubtedly good, seemed to be largely at second hand. His titles, like his poems themselves, savoured of other poets, — so much so that one asked if Lowell's writing was not wholly prompted by his reading. For each and all of his poems, except *The Bigelow Papers,* one found a model somewhere in England's Parnassus, in *Locksley Hall,* in *Don Juan,* in *English Bards and Scotch Reviewers.* In fact, to the end of his life, in Lowell's verses, lines cropped out and passages appeared that obviously belonged, in style and feeling, to Tennyson, Wordsworth or Keats.

Lowell was scarcely the "maker" he longed to be. He was even a little presumptuous, saying of his "kind of winged prose" that it "could fly if it would." That he was a rhetorician was closer to the truth. The fact remained that one forgot his poems. One read them five times over and still forgot them, as if this excellent verse had been written in water.

He produced his solidest writings in his radical phase. It was no doubt Maria White's influence that aroused his passion for the abolitionist cause. Under its sway he wrote *The Biglow Papers,* a book which had the impact of a folk creation. That literate and illiterate in New England met on a common ground of feeling, that they were at one in essential matters, religious and political alike, that their regard for human rights, their hatred of war and false ideas of empire, sprang from their common principle, — this was the burden of *The Biglow Papers.*

Something new too under the Yankee sun were Lowell's critical essays. No one could know how good they were, how fresh and perceptive, who had not read the critics of the eighteen-forties. Whatever were Lowell's limitations, no one could deny that he, with Poe, had opened a new era in critical practice: he and Poe were the first American critics to exercise their judgment freely.

Aside from this, and *The Biglow Papers,* his descriptive poems were the best. A book of American verse could scarcely omit *An Indian-Summer Reverie.* Everything that was rich and sunny, all that was loving, strong and true, in Lowell's heart and talent, spoke through his *Under the Willows* and *The Fountain of Youth,* the "June" of *The Vision of Sir Launfal,* — with every leaf and blade "some happy creature's palace."

*Elmwood, the hub of Lowell's Cambridge. He liked to pitch hay in its meadows.*

*Lowell at Elmwood, Cambridge. Photograph by Oliver Wendell Holmes.*

A Fable for Critics *the first judicious appraisal and self-appraisal of American literature.*

*"There comes Poe, with his raven, like Barnaby Rudge,
Three fifths of him genius, and two fifths sheer fudge.*

*"There is Hawthorne, with genius so shrinking and rare
That you hardly at first see the strength that is there.*

*"There is Lowell, who's striving Parnassus to climb
With a whole bale of isms tied together with rhyme.*

*Tremont Street, Boston, in 1860.*

# Literary Boston

*it excelled in the*

*machinery of culture*

*as in culture itself.*

*The founding of The Atlantic Monthly,* in 1857, marked the high tide of the Boston mind. Lowell, the editor, assembled for the first number contributions from Emerson, Motley, Holmes, Longfellow, Whittier and Mrs. Stowe. It seemed, from a distance, like a family party, in spite of the diversity of these minds. Lowell scarcely had to look for his contributors beyond the Boston, Cambridge, Concord circles.

The note of *The Atlantic* was not self-conscious, in spite of Lowell's tendency to be so. The magazine was born mature. It was observed that, sooner or later, almost everything *The Atlantic* published, essay, poem and story, found its way into a book and had at least a measure of permanent interest, and as time went on, the scope of the magazine grew broader and broader. It became a national institution. The supremacy of *The Atlantic* was unquestioned. To have published a poem in it was to

*Mrs. Julia Ward Howe, whose* Battle Hymn of the Republic *first appeared in the* Atlantic. *She had written it in half an hour.*

*Edward Everett Hale published* The Man Without a Country *in the* Atlantic. *His Philip Nolan became a folk figure like Rip Van Winkle.*

be known among writers all over the country. In the rural towns, as in the Western cities, thousands of eager faces, by the evening lamp, scanned each new issue of *The Atlantic,* thrilled by a new poem of Whittier or Lowell, perplexed by Emerson's cryptic rhymes.

With its magazines, booksellers, editors, Boston excelled in the machinery of culture as well as in culture itself. Writing in New England could not have flourished without the backing and coaching of astute and sensitive publishers; and the well-known house of Ticknor and Fields was the publishing centre of Boston. William D. Ticknor, the senior partner, a cousin of George Ticknor, had built up a large business with English authors by paying for their books, an act of justice that was not required by any law of copyright.

The younger partner, James T. Fields, a man of letters in his own right, was a big, jovial creature, always dressed in Scotch tweeds, with a full beard, abundant hair, keen, twinkling eyes and a hearty manner. The Old Corner Bookstore in Washington Street, where Fields sat behind his green curtain, laughing and manufacturing reputations, was already an institution. There was always some author in Fields' cozy nook, Longfellow, Mrs. Stowe or Emerson, sitting on the window-seat in a litter of books and papers.

That the New England mind had crystallized, that there was a renascence in Boston, — one of those "heats and genial periods" of which Emerson spoke in *English Traits,* "by which high tides are caused in the human spirit," — had not escaped the firm of Ticknor and Fields. In fact, they were the practical centre of it. The publishers of Emerson, Hawthorne, Holmes, of Longfellow and Mrs.

Stowe, were able to feel that they were creating classics; for their authors were becoming national and even international figures. Their little brown editions were known wherever books were read. In Russia, even in India, even in China, all these names were favourably known, and lecturers in the West, like Alcott, found that they had an almost sovereign reputation. Seen from a distance, the New England writers appeared like fixed stars in a constellation that grew more brilliant with every decade.

*John Bartlett owned the University Book Shop at Cambridge. He knew the phrase when anybody wanted a "familiar quotation."*

*(above left) Washington Allston showed in one of his paintings the poor author treated condescendingly by the rich bookseller. (below right) When professional publishers appeared, authors reaped rich profits. Typical was Hawthorne's relationship with his friends and business managers, the Boston publishers Ticknor and Fields (right).*

93

# Oliver Wendell Holmes

*Dr. Holmes had* named *The Atlantic Monthly* as Alcott had named *The Dial.* He was the first contributor. As an anatomy professor he had little time, — though his life as a poet had started far back when he was still a student at the Harvard Law School. In those days he had written a poem called *Old Ironsides.* He had composed it with a pencil, standing on one foot in the attic of his old house in Cambridge, the house in which the battle of Bunker Hill had been planned. One still saw the dents of the muskets on the floor. The frigate *Constitution,* in the Boston navy-yard, was about to be dismantled and abandoned. The poem, reprinted on handbills from a newspaper in Boston and scattered about the streets of Washington, saved the ship and made the poet famous.

After he had won his degree at Harvard, in the class of 1829, and after dropping the law for medicine, he found his father eager to send him abroad, to study for a year in Edinburgh, the favourite training-school for American doctors, and two years in Paris. The years in Paris sharpened the wit of this ingenious Yankee. They also had their effect on a mind that loved attractive living and was to claim the rights of attractive living on behalf of his somewhat frost-bound countrymen.

After returning home, the doctor liked to lecture alike in verse and prose. A corrective, lecturing, for a mind a little too ready always to think too much of its own time and place. One of the doctor's whims was to consider all New England, and even all America, as a large and friendly boarding-house,

*Dr. Holmes in his office,*
*photograph taken around 1865.*

a house with an ample breakfast-table, at which, for a number of years, he found himself appointed to preside. Here he was in a position to study his fellow-boarders, and this gave him an opportunity to take them into his confidence and plant in their minds a few well-chosen seeds, — seeds both of moral etiquette and worldly wisdom.

The boarders listened, all America listened, as the Autocrat unfolded his amusing wisdom, unrolled that inexhaustible scroll which only those possess who have kept their wits alive by constant use. The schoolmistress pondered this wisdom and presently passed it on to her flock. All Young America, sooner or later, heard her say that "those who ask your opinion really want your praise and will be contented with nothing less."

There were men wiser than he, and well he knew it; but in all America there was none more witty. No one else could have written *The One-Hoss Shay, The Morning Visit, The Moral Bully,* or *How the Old Horse Won the Bet.* Talk was his native element. He rejoiced in every kind of conversation, even the kind that floated over the shallows. His talk was the eighth wonder of the Boston world. In later years, on a certain occasion, Henry James the elder said to him, "Holmes, you are intellectually the most alive man I ever knew." And the little doctor replied, and he almost danced as he spoke, "I am, I am! From the crown of my head to the sole of my foot, I'm alive, I'm alive!"

*Holmes, the anatomy professor, cartoon drawn by himself.*

*The One Horse Shay, a symbol of old-time Calvinism.*

*The Boarding House: a microcosmic mirror in which all America found herself reflected.*

The summer home at Beverly, Massachusetts, where Holmes spent the last years of his life. Here he wrote the prophetic poem, The Last Leaf.

*What was the mission of* Oliver Wendell Holmes? It was very simple: to set thought free by conversation. Was it not very bad to have thoughts and feelings, which ought to come out in talk, *strike in,* as people said of certain diseases? There was the great American evil, morbid introspection, class-distinctions that were unconfessed, scruples of conscience, secrets that ought to be exposed to common sense, forms of speech and phrases, ugly and distorted, the outward and visible signs of a twisted life within. Fruits of unconscious living. Out with them, and talk them over!

The boarders listened like a three-years' child. Everyone else was prepared to listen when the doctor wrote a novel, *Elsie Venner;* for he had long believed that every intelligent man had the stuff of a novel in him, and therefore why not he? In fact, he wrote three novels, as he wrote three books about the breakfast-table.

His novels were "medicated novels"; and, as the doctor was always a talker, he strolled about from page to page, airing his views about his characters, dismissing them at times with a turn of the hand as if they were so many cases at a medical meeting. His composition was very untidy. But he always had a new story, even when it was only a ghost of a story. Although *Elsie Venner,* of all these later books, was the only one that seriously counted, the doctor knew so much about human nature, and had such a tang of his own, that one could read him at his worst with pleasure.

He was always putting two and two together, and *Elsie Venner* stood for a large sum in this species of multiplication. He imagined the beauti-

ful, cold girl with the glittering eyes who was destined for a tragic end, the gliding, sliding Elsie, with diamonds on her breast, and her asp-like bracelet. She was still and dangerous, and the village folk believed that she was able to twist herself into all sorts of shapes and tie herself in a knot. In short, she suggested the rattlesnake that Dr. Holmes kept in his cage; and the story was that a snake had bitten her mother, just before Elsie was born. The doctor was interested indeed in the subject of pre-natal influences, but not in quite so simple a way as this. He wished to test the doctrine of original sin, which was still raging in New England. The rattlesnake's bite was only a figure of speech for any kind of untoward circumstance, — a couple of drunken grandfathers or abuse in childhood, — that might explain anyone's aberrations of will. If one saw this clearly in Elsie's case, what about all the other unhappy creatures who were born with poison in their system?

With *Elsie Venner* Holmes had discharged a thunderbolt that fairly rocked the walls of Philistinism. Who, after reading this novel, could talk about "total depravity?" Who was to condemn? Who to judge? Dr. Holmes, perhaps unwittingly, had played into the hands of Dr. Darwin. He had played into the hands of Dr. Freud. He had played into the hands of another doctor of whom perhaps he had never heard, Dr. Marx. One never knows how far a doctor's table-talk may carry him.

*"The Long Path" on Boston Common, a famed Holmes landmark.*

Elsie Venner: *his only novel that really counted.
He had such a tang of his own that one could
read him at his worst with pleasure.*

*Holmes in his study.*

*Holmes in later years resting during his daily walk around
Boston.*

Some Prominent Members

# The Saturday Club

*a group strung like a harp with a dozen intelligences.*

*When Thackeray wrote to Fields,* "I always consider Boston my native place," he was referring to the temperature, the warm and genial air of the Yankee Athens in these days of its later efflorescence. Agassiz's beaming face at the Saturday Club, and Longfellow, benign, all unconscious of the spell he wove, at the other end of the table, set the pitch of the gatherings. If the Saturday Club had not existed, Dr. Holmes would have invented it, for such an association, in his opinion, — a club strung like a harp, with a dozen ringing intelligences, each answering to some chord of the macrocosm, — was the crown of a literary centre.

It was one of the doctor's convictions that a handful of men, at any given moment, carry in their brains the ovarian eggs of the future, and that one should talk with them in order to seize in advance these germs of thought, not yet developed, germs that are moulded on new patterns which have to

be long and closely studied. For no fresh truth ever got into a book: an egg once hatched was already old. There were jobbers of thought and retailers of thought; but he wished to know the producers of thought. That was why he loved his club so dearly. One could listen to Asa Gray on botany, Peirce on mathematics and Lowell on language, Agassiz on geology and fossils, Motley on history, Norton on cathedrals. If one followed for a dozen years any line of knowledge, every other line would intersect it; and here all the lines intersected, the doctor was happy to find, — in this carnival-shower of questions, replies and comments, axioms bowled over the table like bomb-shells from professional mortars, while wit dropped its explosive trains of many-coloured fire and pelted everyone who exposed himself. Emerson enjoyed the club for much the same reasons. Of the lonely men of Concord, he was the only member. But Emerson, who said he fed on genius and who liked to see feats of every kind, feats of mathematical combination, of memory and the power of abstraction, Emerson sat like a child at the meetings. Every word that was dropped set free his fancy. He talked, but rarely; he preferred to listen. His was Goethe's gift, the "highest to which man can attain," wonder. When Emerson spoke at all, he spoke slowly, feeling for his phrases and epithets, — looking about and at last seizing his noun or adjective, — the best, the only one which would serve the need of his thought.

The club had dinner meetings. The Porterhouse steak at the Porter House, the Parkerhouse rolls at the Parker House, guinea-fowl and venison on all occasions, and wine, "the grand specific against dull dinners," as Dr. Holmes called it, sped the festive enterprise.

In days to come, the Saturday Club reflected all the changes of the Yankee mind. Consisting chiefly of authors, at first, acknowledged leaders of national thought, it altered when it alteration found. Local worthies, eminent men, but eminent mainly as men of Boston, replaced the original members, who possessed an all-American sanction. As the scope of the membership altered, so did the types, and lawyers and judges, professors of science, economists, physicists, chemists largely supplanted the men of letters, who had spoken for the soul as well as the mind of the race.

*Charles Eliot Norton, a friend of Rossetti and Ruskin, awakened in his Harvard students a sense of the beauty of Italian art. He preached the gospel of taste, — taste as a means of salvation. He made a translation of Dante in masterly prose. Norton's crusade coincided with the foundation of the Museum of Fine Arts in Boston.*

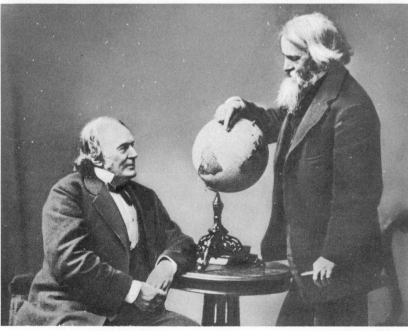

*Benjamin Peirce, for 50 years professor at Harvard, the outstanding mathematician of his time, demonstrates a geographical problem to Louis Agassiz, seated. This Swiss professor, a sort of Johnny Appleseed of Science, talked with enchanting verve, — leaving ample spaces for applause. Watching him draw on a blackboard, one saw insects and fishes bursting from their eggs.*

# Epilogue ~

*The Civil War brought to a* head, however inconclusively, a phase of American culture that later times described as the New England "renascence." This movement of mind continued in the generation that followed, and many of the writers who embodied it long outlived the war. Some of them produced their best work, or work, at least, equal to their best, during this later period. But all had given their measure before the war, and several had disappeared before it. That they stood for some collective impulse, exceptional in the history of the national mind, no one questioned then or questioned later.

If they found themselves "done up in spices, like so many Pharaohs," as Dr. Holmes remarked in later years, it was because they were looked upon as classics, —

> In whom is plainest taught and easiest learnt,
> What makes a nation happy, and keeps it so.

Meanwhile, the more the ancient rural life receded into the background of men's lives, the more it roused their feelings of romance. The farm, the village ways, harsh enough in actuality, seemed, to the barefoot boys who had gone to New York or were making their fortunes in State Street, merry and jolly. They liked to remember their school-days,

the snow-bound evenings under the lamp, the swimming-hole, nutting-time. Sawing wood in the frosty air had surely seemed less dull than adding figures. This was the theme of a hundred poems and stories that multiplied with time, as the farm became a universal symbol, — the farm, the barn, the orchard. No New England boy or man could ever forget the country, the cider-making days of old, the heaps of golden apples. The new generation of city-dwellers longed to be reminded of these rural scenes, and the popularity of the "household poets" rose with the exodus from the "household" setting, the homestead and the farm. This was the secret of Whittier's fame. His poems were the touchstone of their past. The pioneers going west carried Whittier with them as emigrant Scotsmen carried the poems of Burns. *Snow-Bound* was their image of home, the safeguard of their memories. When two or three New Englanders gathered together on the Western plains, or a houseful of scattered uncles and aunts and cousins, he brought back the pumpkin pies of old and the painted autumn woodlands.

And New England men were scattering far and wide, — not only in the American West. In the South Sea Islands, in China, in Burma, they were planting churches and mission-centres, writing their versions of the Bible in half the tongues of Asia. They remembered Thanksgiving Day in the Himalayas and read their *Snow-Bound* on the Yang-tse River. New England seemed romantic in the distance, as Shanghai and Canton had seemed in their barefoot boyhood.

Of the popular writers, Longfellow, Whittier, Holmes, something seemed destined to survive in the general mind of the nation, when the life of all the regions, taken together, formed a final synthesis. These authors, whom every child could understand, remained as classics indeed, but mainly for children; while the handful of esoteric authors, — Hawthorne, with his cloudy symbols, whom one could only see through a glass, darkly, Thoreau, who "listened behind him for his wit," and Emerson, came more and more into their own. Whatever doubts the country at large felt regarding the other New England authors, Hawthorne, Thoreau and Emerson were clearly of the main stream, with Poe, Emily Dickinson, Whitman and Melville.

*The Larch Walk at Concord. The trees were planted by Hawthorne from slips brought from England. This walk connected Bronson Alcott's house with Hawthorne's Wayside.*

# Book Three

# The
# Times of Melville and Whitman

*More and more, as the century advanced,* and the cities grew larger and larger, the immemorial rural life that had formed the American point of view lost its hold over the imagination. The earlier writers had loved the forest, — Cooper, Bryant, even Irving, whose *Rip Van Winkle* was a tale of the primitive woods. Thoreau had been at home in the depths of Maine, and Emerson's "wood-notes" were characteristic even of the author of *The Scarlet Letter,* with its "wild heathen" forest scenes. Now the rural type of mind, fashioned on the farm, in the village, was fading, along with the woodsman's, into the background of the picture. In the fifties, Greeley, Barnum and Beecher, the three great worthies of New York, had all maintained the character of the *rus in urbe.*

But now the life-hungry natives of the backwoods communities, the sons and daughters of the farm, were pouring by hundreds of thousands into the cities, caught by their glamour and their lights, their crowds and shows.

With the growth of the cities the power of money had also grown in a sinister way and poverty was increasing along with this. New York was becoming the almshouse of the poor of half the planet, and foreign countries were deliberately dumping their paupers and criminals in the United States, — their blind, their crippled, their insane. Several of the European nations were making the town a penal colony, and its slums were rapidly approaching the European level.

Many writers were alarmed by the growing division of classes and the spread of poverty along with the increase of wealth, — Melville, for one, who had been deeply aware of the poverty of England in *Redburn* and was one of the first to be aroused in the United States.

Melville and Walt Whitman were ardent Jacksonians both, as long as the true line of democracy, — respect for the rights of the less privileged classes, — lay with this party. But when the Jacksonians entangled themselves with the Southern slave-holders and the new Republican party appeared with Frémont, the writers bet on the "mustang colt," — Stephen Foster's phrase for him, — as four years later they flocked round Abraham Lincoln. Emerson, Whittier, Longfellow, Irving, Bryant and Whitman alike were all for the candidate Frémont and the Republican party, as long as this party's concern was for human, not property, rights. This marked the American imagination and set it off from others. It constantly dwelt on the "plain" man, who remained in Europe the under-dog, and who had been freed and enlarged by American conditions.

This simple type of man possessed the American imagination in a hundred forms as the type of the gentleman possessed the English mind, as the military martinet possessed the Germans, and it explained the old feeling of Americans that the world was beginning afresh with them, that they were appointed to liberate the masses of mankind.

In this age of Melville, Whitman, and Mark Twain it became the object of innumerable writers to reveal the hero in the ordinary man, the nobility in the least prepossessing. With what pleasure Mark Twain made much of the "lightning" quickness of the river-pilots, as Bret Harte dwelt on the adroitness of Yuba Bill. So Mark Twain chose Huckleberry Finn, a little ragamuffin, to embody his conception of truthfulness, loyalty and goodness. These writers drew their characters as the diamond-cutter shapes the stone in a way to produce the greatest lustre, feeling that the characters themselves were intrinsically precious, as Whitman felt when he said that the men in the mountains, in the mines, on the plains of the West were equals of the Homeric gods and heroes. And was not Melville's Captain Ahab a creature formed for noble tragedies?

Such characters only appear in books at moments when they exist in life, or as images that are vitally present in the general mind, and there actually existed in the older America, imbued as it was with the Bible and the classics, "ungodly godlike men" like Ahab, the whaler.

These were no "common shallow beings found on soundings or near shores" but "ponderous and profound," like the sperm-whale of Melville, types in their love of space and freedom of the great mid-century American years, full-blooded, magnanimous, genial, large and deep.

By the mid-century it was apparent that literature was firmly established in the United States, in every section of the country, with the new generation. This literature was young still, but much had happened since Joseph Dennie remarked that becoming an author in America was as hopeless as founding an academy of science in Lapland. In the train of Washington Irving and Cooper and the poets of New England, a literature had appeared all over the South and the West, and Emerson's "rank rebel party," destroying the old, building the new, had given birth to continental writers. Mark Twain, for one, writing of Europe, had cut the umbilical cord that united the still infant nation to the mother-culture, and in Melville and Whitman, with two or three others of comparable weight, America as a whole had found its voices.

*Broadway in 1850. At left Barnum's Museum. On opposite side Brady's Daguerrotype Gallery, St. Paul's and the Astor House. The bookshop of this famed Hotel was a gathering place for many of New York's literati.*

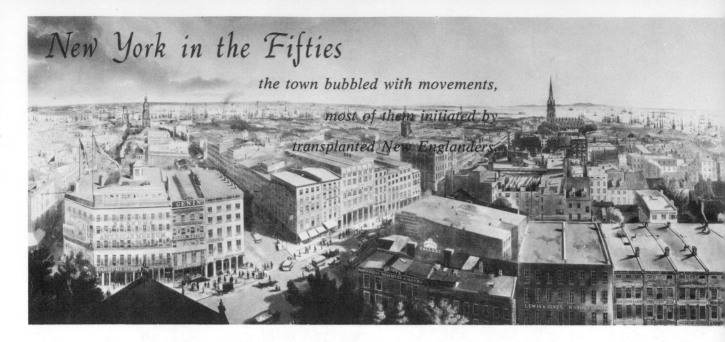

# New York in the Fifties

*the town bubbled with movements,*

*most of them initiated by*

*transplanted New Englanders*

*When the Brook Farmers disbanded,* in the autumn of 1847, a number of the brightest spirits settled in New York, where *The Tribune,* Horace Greeley's paper, welcomed them to its staff. New York in the middle of the nineteenth century, almost as much perhaps as Boston, bubbled with movements of reform, with the notions of the spiritualists, the phrenologists, the mesmerists and what not. One could scarcely recognize the old town of the Knickerbockers in this turmoil of movements and groups and exotic ideas.

At Robert Owen's "World Convention," held in New York in 1845, many of the reformers' programmes had found expression, and, since then, currents of affinity had spread from the Unitary Home to the Oneida Community and the Phalanx at Red Bank. The Unitary Home, a group of houses on East 14th Street, with communal parlours and kitchens, was an urban Brook Farm, where temperance reform and women's rights were leading themes of conversation.

There was a Phrenological Cabinet in Nassau Street, where one could have one's "chart of bumps" made out, and perfectionists, itinerant

*Barnum symbolized a time when the masses delighted in wonders.*

*Beecher, a country minister turned metropolitan, had a tremendous following.*

*Greeley advised others to flee the city, but he stayed in New York.*

The Lorgnette, *a weekly, scrutinized New York Society (above). The Potiphar Papers by George Curtis described in a similar vein the foibles of the rich in a time of quick money-making: (below)*

*Autograph party (1852). New Yorkers cornering a literary lion.*

healers and advocates of all manners of cults addressed the excitable New Yorkers from a dozen platforms. The temper of the American people was exuberant and more than ever uncritically sanguine, now that the republic had all but absorbed the continent.

Walt Whitman and Herman Melville, two young men of the same age, were in and about New York in the later forties. They had no doubt observed some of the new cults in town, with which Walt Whitman was rather intimately connected. He was not merely an "expansionist" editor who had preached Manifest Destiny, he was taking part in many of the movements of the time. He had written on temperance and abolition.

In the early eighteen-fifties, three men, Greeley, Beecher and P. T. Barnum, had largely ruled the New York mind, which remained predominantly rural in tone, as the characters of these three men showed. In certain respects, the acutest, sharpest-witted men kept their greenness and their rustic tastes. Many of them responded to Greeley's abhorrence of over-crowded streets and his constant advice to young men to flee from the city.

Of the new generation, meanwhile, the most popular writer of the fifties was another transplanted New Englander, George William Curtis. His later association with the Concord Transcendentalists set the key of his career as an orator and writer. Emerson had touched his spirit for good and all.

As a literary publicist later, as a mentor of the young who reminded them constantly of the "duty of the American scholar," Curtis was perhaps the foremost of Emerson's apostles. He was a moralist who grieved over "our best society" and presently wrote *The Potiphar Papers* to show how "unspeakably barren," as he said, it was. He satirized the parvenus of a time of rapid money-making whose only idea of behaviour was extravagance and display.

There was little cohesion among the writers of New York, which differed in this respect widely from Boston, while the New York writers were far less scholarly as well. Literature in the metropolis was never a learned profession. Cooper had been removed from Yale and Irving had little formal education. Still less had Whitman and Melville, two great writers of their age in America and, one might say, of the world.

107

*Bayard Taylor in Arabian garb.*

# Tales of the Travellers

*Globe-trotters and explorers bring*

*to America news of far-away regions.*

Florence, and who read the poems that he was writing, gave him letters to her publishers in London.

His animal spirits were exceptionally high, he was variously learned, he was competent or more than competent in several fields, in poetry, the drama, fiction, translation, reviewing, and his books of travel were lastingly readable.

For a quarter of a century Bayard Taylor filled a large space in the American scene as a rival or rather a companion of the New England authors, as a poet but especially as a writer of travels, of a long series of books in which he surveyed the world from China to Peru.

*View of a Russian clothes-market.*
*A drawing made by Taylor during one*
*of his trips.*

*As the American cities multiplied,* hopeful and busy and shining with fresh bright paint, the imagination turned to the primitive towns of ancient peoples. Readers delighted in scenes of temples and tombs lost in the deserts and jungles of the old world and the new. This interest in primitive civilizations brought to the fore a number of travel writers who explored unknown cities and lands, describing their foreign adventures with brilliance and verve.

The youthful Pennsylvanian Bayard Taylor, an assistant on the *New York Tribune* since 1848, was a rather special protégé of Horace Greeley, who discovered his gifts as a writer on foreign lands. Taylor, at that time twenty-three, was already well known as a traveller. The author of the popular *Views Afoot,* he had wandered with a knapsack for two years in Europe, plodding through Germany, Italy, Switzerland and France. In the middle forties, simple accounts of foreign cities and details of travel still interested a multitude of readers, and this young man found himself famous when he came home. Five editors offered Taylor posts, so energetic he was, so competent and willing and moreover so skilful and ready as a literary craftsman. Greeley was lucky to capture him.

In the summer of 1845 he was wandering along the Danube at the time when Thoreau was building his hut at Walden. Everyone helped him and passed him along, and Mrs. Trollope, who had settled in

108

John Lloyd Stephens

*Stephens crossed Central America
finding in its forests ancient
altars rivalling in beauty
the finest sculpture of Egypt.*

## JOHN LLOYD STEPHENS

Between 1839 and 1841 the greatest of American travel writers, John Lloyd Stephens, had twice explored the teeming forest of Central America. Several years before this he had travelled through Egypt, the Holy Land and Arabia. Stephens' books passed rapidly through many editions.

For this admirable writer was a popular writer as well, largely perhaps because of the contrast between the scenes that he portrayed and the nervous energy and bustle of American life. Besides, there was something extremely attractive in the character of John Lloyd Stephens, the frankness and manliness of feeling that one found in his books.

When Stephens travelled through the little republics of Central America, following trails and bridle paths, he cut his way into the crowded ruins, among the sculptured stones that were strewn through the woods, stopping to remove the boughs and vines that concealed the face of a monument and digging out fragments that partly protruded from the earth.

In his own way, John Lloyd Stephens, like so many other artists and writers, was one of the discoverers, in the forties, of the American scene. He revealed, at least in part, the visible past of a Pan-America that was scarcely as yet aware of its own existence.

## ELISHA KENT KANE

There was one other travel book of the fifties that lay on countless parlour tables, acclaimed by Irving, Bancroft, Prescott and Bryant, the *Arctic Explora-*

*tions* of Dr. Elisha Kent Kane, who had reached the highest latitude, the farthest north. A surgeon in the navy in Oriental waters, he spent two winters in the arctic zone, encountering with his comrades the utmost of hardship and danger that men can endure, beset by darkness, cold, scurvy and the perils of lockjaw. Dr. Kane's record of these adventures, describing their daily arctic life, revealed a world that was hitherto all but unknown. Readers were entranced by Dr. Kane's descriptions of these "icy halls of cold sublimity." Two of them were young men, Samuel Clemens and Bret Harte, who were both in California when the book was published.

Dr. Elisha Kent Kane

*He sketched pen-pictures of
arctic nights that Dante
might have created.*

# Herman Melville

*in his mind there loomed early*

*a tragic sense of life, — with the sea*

*a symbol of the enormity of evil.*

*Herman Melville before he wrote* Moby-Dick, —
*a proud man, with something in his face
that said "hands off."*

*One Sunday, in church, as a boy* in New York, Herman Melville saw John Lloyd Stephens, the "wonderful Arabian traveller" whose adventure stories he had read with relish. Melville's own imagination was already full of remote and barbarous countries and the big eyes of Stephens haunted him.

Twenty years later, in 1850, Herman Melville, "the man who lived among the cannibals," was also famous. His book *Typee,* the adventure story of the young whaling men Tom and Toby on the Marquesas islands, had produced a great sensation. Hawthorne and Whitman reviewed the book, Longfellow read it aloud at home as Irving had had the manuscript read to him, while Thoreau and Emerson referred to it in their journals.

The fame of the author had spread to England and he had published four more books, *Omoo, Mardi, Redburn* and *White-Jacket.* One of these, *Mardi,* puzzled and disturbed his readers, who thought of Melville as a writer of adventure stories. In this book he discussed, under a thin disguise of Polynesian colours, topics of the day, slavery, the abolition movement, the Mexican War, expansionism, the social revolution in Europe.

His three years and more at sea had awakened in Melville a feeling for the mysteries and marvels of the ocean that recalled the old maps of the days of Columbus and their portents and monsters of the deep. No writer had ever more fully conveyed that sense of the awfulness of the sea which, as Melville said, "aboriginally belongs to it," while his account of a savage society that missionaries and traders had scarcely disturbed had struck the American mind at the psychological moment. With his great power of description, he offered lovely primitive landscapes, bluffs and glens, green orchards of banana and palm, gently rolling hillsides rising to majestic heights and crags pouring over with leafy cascades and vines. One witnessed the pagan *hevar* there, the feast of calabashes and the gatherings of the talkative elders in their club, the nymphs always ready for a frolic.

The signs of growing introspection were hardly visible in the Melville of this period, — a lively agreeable young man. Yet in his mind there loomed already a tragic sense of life, — a gloomy view of man, no doubt implanted by certain experiences of his earlier years. As a young boy he had set out from home, dressed in his brother's cast-off shooting jacket, and feeling, as he said, like an infant Ishmael. Stout as he was in muscle and bone, with physical courage to spare, he had never imagined a forecastle and the horrors that occurred in that gloomy hole where sailors burrowed like rabbits in a warren. The eager, romantic, sensitive boy, friendless and alone, was shocked to the core. Murder, suicide and syphilis throve among these rogues of all nations who were shut up together with the cockroaches and the rats, and he saw suffering on every hand and evil at war with the good.

All this barbarity of civilization, its vices and its cruelties, had made the savages seem all the more admirable in contrast. He saw them innocent and happy, in the light of the baseness of the inmates of ships, those sons of adversity and calamity, the offspring of sin, and no wonder the savages impressed him as amiable, delightful and humane.

As for the Polynesian isles that attracted so many writers in time, Melville was the first artist to represent them, and the picture he drew in *Omoo* and *Typee* was objectively true in the main, although many of the details were invented or borrowed from others. Later he was to borrow much of the whale lore in *Moby-Dick* from histories of the whaling industry and other writings, for he "swam through libraries" also after whales, as he drew from Smollett in *White-Jacket*. This book was a romance, and yet there was never a truer picture of the actual life of an American man-of-war, of the sailors and their way of living and sleeping, how they died and were buried at sea, their superstitions, their friendships, their tastes and their talk. Melville was right in suggesting that the book would be taken for history in time.

*The Gansevoort house near Albany, home of the family of Melville's mother. He spent much of his youth in this house, which he described in detail in his novel* Pierre.

*Melville at the age of 23 went to sea on the whaler* Acushnet. *He deserted the ship and took refuge on the Marquesas Islands.*

*Illustration from Browne's* Whaling Cruise, *one of the sources used by Melville for* Moby-Dick.

*A portrait of the whale "Mocha Dick," renowned among sailors who greeted each other: "Any news of Mocha Dick?"*•

# Melville's Moby Dick

*a planetary book — the ship*

*"Pequod" an emblem of the world.*

*After living in New York and* Boston, Melville had married a daughter of the Chief Justice of Massachusetts. He settled with his family in the Berkshires in 1850. He had bought a farm called "Arrowhead" on the outskirts of Pittsfield, and there he planned to raise beans and corn as a part-time husbandman, living by the hoe and the spade as well as the pen.

Six miles away, Nathaniel Hawthorne, at work on *The House of the Seven Gables,* was living with his family in a little red cottage at Lenox; and Melville and he were soon walking and talking together.

While Melville could not be sure that his new friend shared all his views, he was overjoyed when Hawthorne praised his work. Hawthorne's influence became marked in a number of Melville's sketches as well as in a novel he soon wrote, called *Pierre.* Hawthorne's "blackness" excited Melville's imagination, like the dark characters of Shakespeare, whom he had read, in whom he had immersed himself, shortly before. The romance *Moby-Dick* was half a Shakespearean play at times in its characters, soliloquies, stage-directions and all. For the rest, Melville, with his taste for what he called "oldness in things," developed a style reminiscent of the painters who wished to achieve the amber patina of age, the sombre harmonious richness of the old masters. In cultivating the antique style of the writers whom he loved, Melville used literary bitumen in a similar fashion.

It was in the Berkshires in the autumn of 1851 that Melville arrived at the height of his powers. It was during this brief period when he was at work on *Moby-Dick* that he asked a friend to send him fifty assistants, "fifty fast-writing youths with an easy style," to carry out the multitude of literary projects that swarmed in his mind. He longed for a condor's quill to write with, — "Give me," he exclaimed, "Vesuvius's crater as an inkstand!" During this surge of creative power *Moby-Dick* was born, — "broiled," as Melville said, "in hell-fire."

He must have known that *Moby-Dick* was his masterpiece, the token, the final expression of his own uniqueness, the "mighty book" that owed its greatness largely to the mighty theme. The innermost meaning of the book was "the enormity of evil," and he sustained its mood with astonishing skill, from the first words of Ishmael, with November in his soul, to the last wild spin of the ship in the vortex of the sea. Even the black picture of the foundering whaler that Ishmael saw in the Spouter Inn struck the note of the *Pequod's* tragic voyage.

The book began with mysterious intimations of doom, the "loomings" that recurred with the rumours at sea, the news picked up from passing ships as the legend of the white whale grew in the minds of the sailors, the turning of the compasses when the needles went awry, the stories of crying seals and drowning seamen.

Though the book abounded in digressions, these were all a part of what Melville called his "careful disorderliness." The style was governed by the "large and liberal theme" and the powerful rhythm was in harmony with it.

All the world was in *Moby-Dick* with the "several races" of mankind that appeared on the whaler, Lascars, Chinese, Tahitians, and the Negroes whom Melville always drew with a special delight and tenderness, full of admiration as he was for their "great gift of good humour." His ship, the *Pequod,* with its babel of tongues, was an emblem of the world, traversing the seven seas and all sides of earth, and the book was a planetary book, like *Leaves of Grass.* One gave the dark side of the planet, the other the bright.

*Father Edward Thompson Taylor, famed preacher of the Seamen's Bethel in Boston. His sermons, full of the imagery of the sea, were reproduced in the sermon of Father Mapple in* Moby-Dick.

*Captain Ahab faces Moby Dick: Melville, like no other writer, described the sea with its watery immensity of terror.*

er in Boston or New York, with the single exception of Hawthorne for two or three years. What he lacked especially was an interest in society, in actual people in all the concreteness of their lives, that objective feeling for human nature, the foundation of a novelist's life, which alone could have corrected his tendency to the abstract and the subjective.

A decade later, during the Civil War, Herman Melville left Pittsfield and returned to New York. His literary life had virtually come to a close. At last, in 1866, like Hawthorne long before, he had received an appointment as an inspector of customs. For nineteen years, every day, Melville was to plod back and forth between his house and the pier on the Hudson River, all but forgotten as a man of letters, for New York seldom remembered its own and New England, now in the ascendancy, had small interest in him.

Melville, whose fame in his own country passed into a long eclipse, continued to be read in England for a number of reasons, — among others, that the English never lose interest in the sea, — and more than one reader in England connected him with Whitman. In their sympathy with all ordinary life and common occupations, together with their feeling of brotherhood for all rough workers, the two were much alike, as they were alike in their sense of the American mission.

With all his reservations Melville admired America, my "forever glorious country." His early books *White-Jacket* and *Redburn* too, — books that he wrote about the same time as *Mardi,* — asserted his belief in America as the "Israel of our time." With his own "unconditional democracy in all things," he largely shared Whitman's notion of the American "idea," and he too felt, as he said in his essay on Hawthorne, that America must have powerful writers to forward this idea. Like Whitman and Emerson, moreover, he loved "grand individuals," especially those whom he called the "kingly commons." For the "august dignity" of which he was to write in *Moby-Dick* was not, he said, "the dignity of kings and robes, but that abounding dignity which had no robed investiture. . . . Thou shalt see it shining in the arm that wields a pick or drives a spike, that democratic dignity which . . . radiates without end from God."

*Melville's active writing time* was a great deal shorter than the fifteen years that Sainte-Beuve allotted to the normal career, but he had foreseen at its highest moment that "shortly the flower must fall to the mould." His health no doubt had been undermined by the hardships of his life at sea; he had exhausted his nerves and his imagination. Melville's literary life died of inanition, for another, and a better, reason along with the rest, the excess of the subjective note or the note of speculation that all but extinguished the creative power in him. All the great traits of the writer withered in him, the gifts of character, humour, style, even the art of shaping a book or maintaining the unity of mood in a composition. He was an instance of the well-known fact that when artists take to theorizing it is often because their creative power is gone.

*The Confidence-Man* was his last attempt to write a book. The opaqueness of this laborious satire resulted from his obvious inability to draw characters any longer that were vivid enough to support the burden of thought.

As the joy of an evolving craftsmanship might have sustained his waning powers, so also a few literary friendships might have served him well; but Melville was indifferent to other writers, wheth-

# Walt Whitman

*Walt Whitman and Melville had* more than a few tastes in common, although they may indeed never have met. They were exact contemporaries, born in 1819, of the same typical Dutch-British New York stock, big, vigorous, ruddy men with spacious views of life who had lived in close communion with the sea and the earth. While Melville's family was aristocratic and Whitman's the plainest of the plain, both were profoundly democratic in their outlook and feelings and both were essentially genial in temper, despite Melville's deep reserve and the vulnerability of his nervous organization. The "great power of blackness" in him distinguished his note from Whitman's sunniness or whiteness.

For a dozen years before 1850, Walt Whitman had sauntered about New York with a curious eye, charmed by the living panorama of the myriad-headed city, the crowds, the shops, the stages, the theatres, the wharves. A farm-boy from Long Island who had become a Brooklyn editor, Whitman had written for many of the magazines, but he was scarcely known in literary circles, though his figure was familiar enough on the ferry-boats and streets. Tall and rather heavily built, with a fresh pink skin and a lounging air, — his beard was already touched with grey, — he had, as he said, an unusual capacity for standing still, rooted on a spot, at rest, for a long spell, to ruminate. He had written a facetious paper on loafing, in praise of the "genuine inbred loafer" and the calm steady "son of indolence," and this appeared to be his role, though in truth he was living intensely: at moments he felt like a god walking the earth. Merely to move at these times was a pleasure to him; it made him happy just to breathe and see. For his physical health was superb, he was strong and buoyant. He felt as if no other mortal could enjoy this show as he did, as if it had been especially arranged for him to observe.

While he shared some of the tastes of his Quaker forefathers, he preferred the "healthy this-worldliness" of his Dutch mother. His family, all of them farmer-folk, had lived for five generations or more on the north shore of Long Island, thirty miles from New York, and Whitman's later memories were all of green corn-fields, flourishing orchards, sailing-parties and clambakes on the shore of the Sound. He roamed the island in all directions from Brooklyn to Montauk, where one looked out over the Atlantic from the bluff by the lighthouse. He fraternized with fishermen and farmers, bay-men and pilots, and with dancing Negroes and boys with flutes like those of William Sidney Mount, who was painting his Long Island scenes at just this time, — Mount, who, as a friend said, "made Long Island his Italy."

Meanwhile, until he was forty or more, Whitman rambled over Long Island, where he had once edited a newspaper and taught country schools, at Babylon, Jamaica, Whitestone, Woodbury and Flushing, boarding round at neighboring farms and always more impressed by the self-reliance and native good sense of the people. He liked to read the great poets in the open air within sound of the sea, and at Coney Island, in mild seasons, on the long bare unfrequented beach, declaiming Homer and Shakespeare to the surf and the gulls. He first read the Iliad thoroughly in a sheltered hollow of the rocks, in the full presence of nature, with vistas of the sea rolling in, and he remembered feeling once that he must write a book expressing what he called "this liquid mystic theme." The rhythms of the sea were in his blood. The poetic form that he gradually evolved was oceanic, as he sometimes said, with verses that recalled the waves, rising and falling, often sunny, now and then wild with storm, scarcely two alike in length or measure.

Whitman had written verses
for Leaves of Grass as early as 1848.

From third edition, Boston 1860.

Carpenter's cottage in
Brooklyn, where Whitman
worked on Leaves of Grass.

*It was about 1840 that Whitman* became active in the Democratic party, living in New York, meanwhile, almost as much as in Brooklyn. He also had plunged with zeal into most of the movements of reform, for restrictions of the slave-system, the abolition of capital punishment, the humaner treatment of animals, and especially free trade. Jefferson for him was the "greatest of the great," and the doctrines of the rights of man, the evils of privilege, the absurdity of rank were bred as it were in his bones.

When later, in his poems and his prose alike, he dwelt on the soundness of the common people, Whitman spoke from an intimate knowledge of them, for his real occupation for years was to mingle with crowds. The ferry-boats gave him, as he said, inimitable, streaming, living poems. He delighted in all the New York types that had not yet found their Hogarth or Dickens, young men, shipbuilders, cartmen, firemen, butchers, whose looks and movements were free and picturesque.

As early as 1848 Whitman had written some verses that later appeared in his great book, and perhaps he dimly foresaw already his role of the American poet-prophet, the "new man" of the nation that was to be. But this grew slowly in his

mind to form in good time the immense exuberance of *Leaves of Grass.*

For two or three years in the early fifties, Whitman, still living in Brooklyn, worked with his father as a carpenter, building small houses, while ever since 1848, when he returned from New Orleans, he had been trying his hand at a new kind of verse.

Whitman, whose ear was attuned to the time, had heard the voice of Mazzini, the apostle of brotherhood and progress, and he also absorbed the discoveries of science and the dawning conception of evolution. Tough-minded as he was, Whitman, the most impressionable of men, absorptive as a sponge in the fertile waters of the time, sooner or later made his own, remodelled for his peculiar ends, whatever he received from other writers.

He felt a call, as clear to him as the "inner light" of George Fox, to abandon the conventional themes of earlier poets, with all the stock poetical touches, the plots of love and war and the high exceptional personages of old-world song. He was to embody in his verse nothing whatever for beauty's sake, neither legend nor myth nor romance nor euphuism nor rhyme, but only the broadest aver-

116

*He saw a symbol of democracy in the summer grass.*

*From a lithograph by Lewis C. Daniel.*

age of humanity in the ripening nineteenth century with all its countless examples in the America of the day.

This was the new verse, stripped as a Quaker meeting-house, into which he had been groping his way for a number of years, the verse that he finally put to press, setting it up in type himself, and published in 1855 as *Leaves of Grass*. At intervals throughout his life he was to add to this first book "some eight hitches or stages of growth," as he called them, with one or two "annexes" (finished in 1891), adding here, omitting there, retaining his first conception of the "leaves," for he saw a symbol of democracy in the summer grass.

Seeking a perfect transparent clearness, he clung to common modes of speech, a language that was always homely and idiomatic, renouncing rhyme and metre too, following the rhythms of nature. Whitman's style was one of the great original styles,

while his motive was not aesthetic, it was religious. This he believed was the rhythm to capture America. From Montauk to California, from the Saguenay to the Rio Grande, he wished to present America, the country and the towns, the ploughman plowing, the sower sowing and the factories as well as the farms, the joys of the engineer and the clean-haired girl in the mill.

Thus in his way Whitman was one of those prophets of new dispensations who abounded in the middle of the century, proponents of the idea that nations have missions, roles of their own to perform for the good of mankind. He was convinced that America was one of these nations, and the greatest of them, the "custodian of the future of humanity." It was to become not a conqueror nation but rather the grand producing land of nobler men and women, healthy and free, the friendliest nation, the nation of peace, the composite nation, formed from all, and reconciling all as children of an equal brood.

With much prosaic realism that reminded one of the Dutch genre-painters and sometimes flushed with an exuberance that brought back Rubens, he seemed in his ardour the personification and the voice of a happy young country. His "trumpet-note ringing through the American camp," — Thoreau's phrase for *Leaves of Grass,* — expressed the vitality of the Americans and their expanding nation, their thirst for liberty, their homogeneity, their pride and their compassion, while it offered the world good will in America's name.

*Civil War Sketch by Winslow Homer.*

*Towards the end of 1862* Walt Whitman went to Washington to find his brother George, who had been wounded in the war, and there he remained for eleven years until he moved to Camden, for he never again returned to live in New York. Almost at once he found himself involved as a volunteer nurse working in the vast war-hospitals with the disabled and the dying, occasionally watching for nights together when he was concerned with some special or critical case.

In the three remaining years of the war, constantly thrown with these young men from all the states, North and South alike, Whitman measured as never before the American people *en masse,* of whom he had countless intimate and re-

vealing glimpses. Sometimes he dressed wounds, sometimes he found that his personal presence accomplished more than medical nursing.

He carried a little pocket note-book and took notes as he went along, sometimes while one of the soldiers was telling his story, jotting down other memoranda in the crowded streets and working them out more carefully in the evening at home. In this way he wrote *Drum-Taps* and many a passage in *Specimen Days,* under a big old cherry-tree, in the hospitals, in the fields, for all he saw and heard aroused undreamed of depths of feeling in him and quickened his fervent faith in the future of the country.

He felt he had never realized before the majesty and reality of the people in the mass, — it fell upon him, he wrote, like a great awe. Never could anyone speak in disparagement of Americans, whether of the North or the South, to one who had witnessed these hospital scenes in the war, and more than ever he felt that humanity could depend upon itself alone with its own inherent, normal, full-grown traits.

Whitman had never met Lincoln, though he saw him twenty or thirty times and almost every day during one season, when the President, who was living out of town, rode by on his grey horse surrounded by a squad of cavalrymen with sabres drawn. He had an air, Whitman thought, of a pioneer Michael Angelo and a look of great tenderness and goodness underneath the furrows. There was a story that Lincoln in Springfield had read the second *Leaves of Grass* and even read passages aloud from these "chants of the prairie."

In his way Whitman had prophesied the advent of Lincoln at the time of Frémont's candidacy in 1856. He had said then it would please him to see some bearded pioneer, shrewd, healthy, well-informed, appear in the West, stride over the Alleghenies and walk into the White House. As it happened, Lincoln, like Whitman, was the son of a carpenter and farmer.

Lincoln was a great story-teller, like David Crockett, who knew the boatmen's lingo and the river-lore of the Mississippi, the tales about Boone, Mike Fink and Simon Kenton. He largely transacted the nation's affairs with anecdotes of frontier circuits, for, having small use for abstractions and

*In* Specimen Days *he pictured the surgeons at work in a field at night.*

118

*When Lincoln died on April 15th, 1865, Whitman wrote several poems to honor his memory.* O Captain! My Captain *soon became his best known piece which he often recited.*

*Lincoln was to Whitman the symbol of the Union which he saw in turn as a symbol of the future of mankind.*

*John Burroughs, the nature writer of later days, and Whitman became friends during their period of work at Washington. Burroughs saw in Whitman one of the primary bards whom nations could build upon.*

theories, he loved the concrete, as artists love it, and spoke and taught, like a poet, in parables and fables. He liked the homespun Western humour because it relieved the melancholy, the fear of madness and suicide, that weighed on his mind, and, besides, it kept him closely in touch with the frontier people he represented, the loungers round the stoves in country stores.

Lincoln, a Southerner by family and birth who was grafted on the West and who had remained unchanged as a man in the White House, had long since become for Whitman a symbol of the Union, which he saw as in turn a symbol of the future of mankind. Whitman shared Lincoln's sympathy with peoples everywhere that were struggling to be free.

In all these political matters Whitman and Lincoln fully agreed, and one might have said that in public life Lincoln represented what Whitman was expressing in poetry in *Leaves of Grass*. They stood for those "axioms of a free society" that Lincoln found in Jefferson and that Whitman touched with emotion and developed further.

The so-called "Christ portrait" taken in the early 1850's. Whitman was prematurely gray.

# Whitman ❧ The Image of the Poet

"The very best thing about Walt was his godlike face and mien, and this will die with the generation which was blest with the sight. I once went up to him when I saw him on Chestnut Street and said that I must personally thank him for being so handsome, adding that I hoped he didn't mind. 'No, Horace,' he said, 'I like it.' " — *Letters of Horace Howard Furness*.

The "carpenter portrait" which accompanied the first edition of "Leaves of Grass", 1855.

Photograph showing Whitman during his editorship of the "Brooklyn Eagle".

At Pfaff's, the meeting place of New York's Bohemia, Whitman welcomes young William Dean Howells, fresh from the West.

*Walt Whitman photograph taken by Sorony in 1879.*

*Whitman in contemplation. Pencil study by Herbert Gilchrist, his Camden friend.*

*During his last years in his Camden, N. J. home.*

*Max Beerbohm cartoon Walt Whitman, inciting the bird of freedom to soar.*

*Whitman's favorite portrait of himself taken by Pearsall, Brooklyn 1876.*

*Near the Camden Wharf in a wheel-chair, a gift of his admirers.*

STEAMER DAY IN

*Steamer day in San Francisco. Lithograph by L. Nagel*

*The gambling saloons were the largest buildings in San Francisco.*

# The Far West

*unravaged by the Civil War, the region flourished and attracted new writing talent from the East.*

While the North, the South *and* the Middle West were occupied with the Civil War, the regions beyond the Rockies were at peace and thriving, largely thanks to the war which had driven a multitude thither and thrown California upon its own resources. Mining had more or less given place to cattle-raising and fruit-growing, the chaos of the fifties had resulted in stability and order and the new stream of Nevada silver pouring in from the Comstock lode added to the steady prosperity of San Francisco.

With magazines and libraries increasing through the war-years, San Francisco had become the literary capital of all the vast country west of the plains and the mountains. There a singular group of writers rose and flourished for a while. Others appeared and joined them as birds of passage.

The centre of literary San Francisco was the *Golden Era,* the "miner's favourite," eleven years old in 1863, when Joaquin Miller came down from Oregon, Mark Twain arrived from Virginia City and a number of other writers passed through the town.

Charles Warren Stoddard was already writing the poems that Bret Harte collected when he was himself the best-known writer on the Coast, the adviser and critic not only of Stoddard but of Joaquin Miller and Mark Twain. In this group Bret Harte was the master-craftsman. "To his criticism and encouragement," Stoddard said, "I owe all that is best in my literary efforts." Mark Twain later wrote, "Bret Harte trimmed and trained and schooled me patiently."

It was not long before Harte himself became famous through his poems and stories of the new strange wild California, the world of Roaring Camp, Poker Flat and Sandy Bar, of "partners," gentlemanly gamblers and lucky strikes.

He had struck its more idyllic note in his first tale *M'liss* in 1860, prompted by his life as the master of a pioneer school in a little mining camp in the lower Sierras, but, busy as he was at other tasks as late as 1867, he scouted the "grand gold-hunting crusade" as a subject for writers. What he later called the heroic era of the California Golden Fleece he saw as "hard, ugly, unwashed, vulgar and lawless," while he turned his mind to other themes, legends of the Spanish past and the brilliant series of parodies that he called *Condensed Novels*.

Dickens was the decisive influence one saw at once in Bret Harte's tales, in their play of humour and sentiment, their mannerisms, their style. Dickens had prepared the way for him in his treatment of outcasts and rough men in vividly drawn surroundings of slum and country, together with a feeling for the goodness of heart that so often exists in the rudest. For the rest, the miners were only one of a dozen aspects of the Western life of which he was a capital observer, — politics, ranching, newspapers, schools, religion, business, lawyers and the law and the glittering and varied scene of San Francisco.

The gambling saloons were the largest buildings in the town, the scene of many a tragi-comedy when the "successful miner on a spree" was reduced in ten minutes to the status of a crossing-sweeper. Bret Harte knew these gaudy halls and the restaurants where, as often as not, the waiters were noblemen or Sicilian ex-bandits.

*Bret Harte was the master craftsman of the San Francisco group. He "trimmed and trained" Mark Twain and other young writers (left).*

*Joaquin Miller, the "Byron of the Sierras." His rough-hewn poems evoked life in the mountains and on the plains (right).*

# The World of Bret Harte

*his stories were the prototype of*

*all the Westerns, with brawls, holdups*

*and romantic idylls in the woods.*

*This was the secret of Harte's success: he showed the good in the heart of the outcast.*

*It was a world in transition* that appeared in the stories of Bret Harte. The notorious abuse of coincidence, one of the weaknesses of his art, might almost have been due to the region and time he pictured, a chaos that crystallized in the brilliant Bret Harte heroines who expressed as they reflected this atmosphere of excitement and risk. These were the frank direct young women who were always ready to "lead the way" in the "trackless, uncharted *terra incognita* of the passions."

In one or another of his many stories Bret Harte sketched first or last virtually every phase of the California social scene. But the Bret Harte country proper was the mining country, approached by the Stockton boat or the boat to Sacramento. This was the land of straggling shacks, yellow ditches, and crumbling roads where the Argonauts of the Sierras pursued their quest, the land of Red Dog, One Horse Gulch, Blazing Star, Lone Pine Flat, Nip and Tuck, Sandy Bar and Rough and Ready. Some of the camps were moribund, others were alive with expectation, swarming with red-shirted miners and the waifs and strays of played-out gulches and bars on some neighbouring river, and occasionally a gang of bully-boys.

Whence and how had they come to the mines? Often this question remained unanswered, but sometimes Bret Harte drew the curtain that hung between them and their past and revealed their background in Virginia, Kentucky or New England. Practically all of Bret Harte's stories were drawn from events that really happened, as most of his characters were based upon actual persons, and he was nowhere truer to life than when he revealed the deep civilization that so often underlay the rough crust of the hardened frontiersman.

What made these stories important was that they served as the prototypes of all the "Westerns," with all the stock characters that appeared in the later tales, — characters, fresh with him, that were "stock" in time, — the pretty New England schoolmistress, the sheriff and his posse, the bad man, the gambler, the heroic stage-driver, the harlot with the heart of gold. His holdups, lynchings, barroom brawls and romantic idylls on mountain ranches were the models that hundreds of writers followed in the future, few of whom ever compared with him in workmanship, style or refinement, for Bret Harte was not only original, he was an artist.

With the opening of the Overland railroad in 1869, a brief bright epoch ended in San Francisco. It no longer stood for the unique frontier that captivated the mind's eye, it had lost its earlier appeal to the imagination, and one by one the writers who had reached it by clipper or steamship, by stagecoach or covered wagon, left by train. Like Mark Twain, who also left, and the Oregonian Joaquin Miller, all these writers presently appeared in England, where the leader of the circle, Bret Harte, was to stay for the rest of his life, fading forever from the American scene.

*The First Family at Tessahara.*

*The Luck of Roaring Camp.*

*In the Carquinéz Woods.*

*Devil's Ford. The camps were hardly more than disorganized raids on nature.*

*The Iliad of Sandy Bar.*

*Let out on Storm Star Mountain.*

127

# Cowboys, Bandits and Books

*the dime-novels, like the movies later,*

*mirrored the struggle of the plains*

*to establish law and order.*

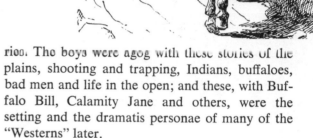

*On his first real visit* to the West in 1879, Walt Whitman rejoiced in the limitless spread of the plains, the untrammelled play of nature, the large, calm, able men he met who seemed to be illustrations of his own poems. He found his earlier thoughts confirmed in the boundless prodigality of this farmland of the future.

It was virtually a *tabula rasa* now in its further-western stretches where traditions were forgotten and conventions were all but unknown. The plains were the scene of a struggle now to establish law and order that brought peace-officers and bandits to the fore alike, and these were the days of the famous plainsmen, the heroes of novels and movies later, who followed Kit Carson, Jim Bridger and the men of their time. Some of the bad men, like Jesse James, the first train-robber, were graduates of the border banditry of the Civil War, when guerillas were licensed to commit all manner of crimes.

But even the desperadoes honoured the peace-officer Wild Bill Hickok and the great "gun-fighting" marshal, Wyatt Earp Hickok was the deadliest shot that had ever been seen on the Western plains, (or so at least Buffalo Bill, his follower, said). He was one of Frank Harris' three lifelong heroes. After Harris had accompanied him on the long drive to Chicago, Wild Bill ranked in his mind with Cervantes and Shakespeare.

America at large and especially America's youth shared in the fresh stream of adventure through a flood of "dime" sto-

ries. The boys were agog with these stories of the plains, shooting and trapping, Indians, buffaloes, bad men and life in the open; and these, with Buffalo Bill, Calamity Jane and others, were the setting and the dramatis personae of many of the "Westerns" later.

Meanwhile the desert lands to the south were inspiring studies of Indian life and Major Powell had explored the Colorado River. His *First Through the Grand Canyon* was the record of the expedition through the only region west of the Missouri River that had never been investigated

*Calamity Jane*     *Wild Bill Hickok*     *Billy the Kid*

by trappers before 1869, the thousand-mile series or chain of canyons, the so-called river of mystery and fear, that led by falls and rapids to Arizona.

Virtually more distant than China or Norway from San Francisco or New York, Arizona had been wild enough in 1868, when Ross Browne discovered that a trip from Germany to Iceland and back was easier and cheaper than a journey from San Francisco to Tucson. One saw fresh Apache tracks on the main roads everywhere and felt the constant presence of murderers and robbers. Billy the Kid was often there before he was killed in 1880 after killing a man for each of his twenty-one years. "Straight as a dart, light as a panther," this child of the gambling-houses and mining-camps made most of the popular dime novels seem meagre and tame. He had spent his boyhood in Santa Fé, where General Lew Wallace, the governor of the territory from 1878-'81, was finishing *Ben Hur* in the governor's palace. Working at night, he was warned to close his shutters so that the light of his lamp would not be a mark for Billy, who had threatened to kill him.

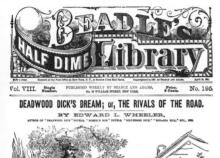

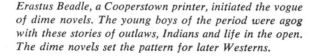

*Erastus Beadle, a Cooperstown printer, initiated the vogue of dime novels. The young boys of the period were agog with these stories of outlaws, Indians and life in the open. The dime novels set the pattern for later Westerns.*

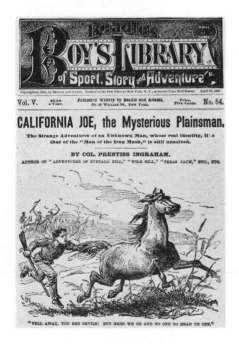

*Major Powell, first to explore the Colorado River. He focused attention on the wonders of the Grand Canyon.*

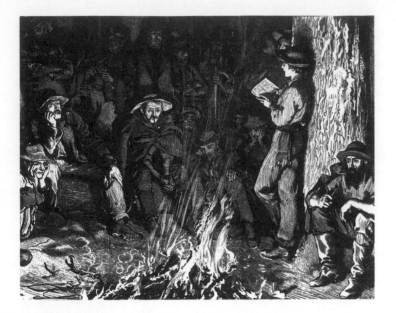

*Artemus Ward, the Hoosier-Yankee,*
*used the Barnum technique*
*in his lectures.*

*When the young John Hay, whose* father was a
frontier doctor on the Mississippi, returned home
from studies in the East he was struck by "the
dreary waste of materialism" that prevailed in his
old home town. Though Hay later returned to live
in Ohio, — in the mid-fifties, — the Middle West
struck him as "barbarous." William Dean Howells,
born in Ohio a year before Hay, was filled with
similar apprehensions and he expressed "a morbid
horror of going back."

Life on the Middle Western frontier in the
eighteen-forties in Ohio, Indiana, Minnesota and
Illinois was undoubtedly grim. E. W. Howe was to
recreate a picture of it in his *Story of a Country
Town*. This book showed how hard and loveless
the pioneer life could be — with women pale, fret-
ful, always overworked and the men rough and
harsh. It conjured up the mood of toil and aridity
of the frontier existence, its loneliness and charm-
lessness, the gracelessness that weighed on the
mind.

In the raw mushroom villages of these regions,
the desperado was ever-present, and there were
horse-thieves, border-ruffians, grafting politicians
and land-sharks speculating in imaginary titles to
claims. It was thought sinful in these bubble-towns
to take a bath on Sunday or shave or brush one's
boots or walk in the woods, and the best fare in the

*Vaudeville minstrels sung*
*their way through many*
*frontier settlements.*

*The New England schoolmistress*
*was ubiquitous in the West.*
*Culture followed the plow,*
*however slowly.*

*its life was hard and drab. As John Hay observed,*

*there was as yet no room for a genius in this region.*

sod-built taverns consisted of salt pork floating in lard, bread that was only half-baked and water-logged potatoes. The mud and the pigs were ever-present, and there were odd do-nothing characters, misfits haunting the river and the stores, who suggested Sherwood Anderson's people later. The frontier was generally stagnant in its formal culture. One would scarcely have looked for ideas here.

There was, however, a thin trickle of "culture" or at least entertainment that reached the West in various watered-down guises. An occasional circus and minstrel show, the visit of a circuit rider or humorous lecturer helped to relieve a humdrum existence. The most famous purveyor of Western humour was Charles Farrar Browne, who created the character of Artemus Ward, the Hoosier Yankee of the backwoods.

In Artemus Ward's make-up there was something Barnumesque. In other respects, however, he seemed an authentic product of the land of the Hoosiers, a land that was supposed to abound in the odd and the quaint, and one might have encountered his travelling show on any of the Western roads, — the wax-works and the snakes and the kangaroo and a leg of Pharaoh's daughter, the one that rescued the infant Moses in the Nile. The will to believe was active on the frontier, where the persons and places of the Bible were vividly real.

Earlier there had emerged from Cincinnati a new form of entertainment in the minstrel shows. It may have been there that Daddy Rice, the father of American minstrelsy, first sang and "jumped" Jim Crow. Rice had sung and danced his way through most of the frontier settlements of Ohio, Tennessee and Kentucky. So had Dan Emmett's Virginia minstrels, Christy's minstrels and various others that were well established by 1850 all over the West and the South. Some of the songs they spread through the country, Emmett's *Old Dan Tucker,* for one, *O Susanna* and Farrell's *Old Zip Coon,* were heard before long even in the remotest regions.

The city of Cincinnati contributed considerably more than minstrelsy to the life of the West. It was the region's liveliest centre of culture. It had its own magazines and publishers and a hundred thousand people, many of whom were transplanted New Englanders. With them had come the New England schoolmistress, who was present even in the remotest hamlet. Her work acted as a definite leaven for cultural pursuits, and before long one heard on occasion the frontiersman's daughters discuss, — over their milk-pails, — Longfellow, Dickens and Scott.

*John Hay, returning from studies at Brown, found the West a dreary waste of materialism.*

*William Dean Howells, born in Ohio, went to Cambridge and expressed a morbid fear of going back West.*

*E. W. Howe saw in the frontier town a symbol of the toil and aridity of pioneer existence.*

The Hoosier Schoolmaster. *a crude provincial classic with a pungent local quality.*

If *"there was as yet no room in* the West for a genius," — there were indeed a number of good writers in the Mississippi Valley states or eastward in Indiana or northward in Wisconsin. One found their most typical note perhaps in Edward Eggleston's homely novels, which reflected the common life of the northern frontier. Eggleston, born in Indiana, the son of an emigrant Virginia lawyer, may well have read Bret Harte's California stories, but he owed his interest in regional writing largely to the influence of Taine, whose lectures on *Art in the Netherlands* stirred him deeply.

Later, as a circuit-rider, he travelled through the West on foot in a pair of Indian moccasins. Sometimes he virtually lived on a lazy old horse, reading, as he rode along, his Greek and Latin books. Before he abandoned the ministry and went to New York in 1870 he had also spent several years in Minnesota, observing the rise of the mushroom towns in the land-boom of the fifties.

This frontier world of Indiana, Minnesota, and Illinois appeared in several of Eggleston's homespun novels, with the sharp contrasts of a settler's life that witnessed camp-meetings and barbeques, corn-shuckings, revivals. His best novel, *The Hoosier Schoolmaster,* published in 1871 and based on his brother's adventures as a pioneer teacher, was a crude provincial classic of a sort,

full of Dickensian mannerisms, with a pungent local quality that was sometimes impressive.

Eggleston defined his purpose in writing this novel and the others that followed: it was to "represent the forms and spirit of our own life" and "free ourselves from habitual imitation of that which is foreign." He was the first of a long line of Middle Western realists who were truthful and honest as he was and sombre as well.

While Eggleston and other Western writers took flight for distant parts, a number of the Hoosiers remained on their own home-ground. Lew Wallace had lived as a boy in Indianapolis when his father was governor of Indiana. He had served as an officer in the Mexican War and spent two years in Mexico, where he studied the history of the conquest. In 1873 he published *The Fair God,* a romance full of minute and varied pictures of the Aztec world.

Wallace had great vitality as a story-teller, as one saw in *Ben-Hur,* the best of his romances. The Bible worship of the West found much to like in this book and its classical note, the drama of the sea-fight, the chariot-races, made it a prodigious and perennial success.

Ben Hur. *Its scenes were based on research in the libraries of Constantinople.*

In the Hoosier poet James Whitcomb Riley, the Middle West meanwhile expressed the "folksy" note that characterized it, the neighbourly spirit of so many of the settlers, their genial optimism, their homely domestic affections, their pastimes and tasks. This "poet of the people," as he came to be called, — or "poet of the schoolchildren," — reflected the tastes of a thoroughly settled West, a village world which was very unlike the wilder world of the Mississippi that appeared in Mark

In A Child's World *he vividly evoked the ways of the pioneers.*

*James Whitcomb Riley, the "Hoosier Burns," considered all his readers his personal friends.*

Twain's *Tom Sawyer* and *Huckleberry Finn*. It rather resembled in many ways the rural New England of Whittier's poems with its husking-bees, barn-raisings and barefoot children. Riley continued, in point of fact, the line of the popular New England poets and Longfellow for thirty years was his travelling-companion, the mascot he carried in his bag on all his reading-tours, the poet of childhood as Whittier was the poet of the farm.

There were echoes of Dickens in *The Raggedy Man*, in *Little Orphant Annie*, in the travelling professor of phrenology, an American type that one found in Henry James, Mark Twain and Melville, and Riley perhaps had Dickens in mind when he became a public reader who was almost as famous and as versatile in his actor's role. This was in the day of the "platform kings" who appeared in Indianapolis, — Wendell Phillips, Josh Billings, Mark Twain and Bronson Alcott. Riley was described as a great comedian impersonating some little girl, a boy in a watermelon patch or a Hoosier farmhand. Like Dickens, he felt that his hearers were all personal friends.

His poems were all of old times, old favourites, the rustic beauty of the Western scene, pets and children, happiness, friendship and grief, with a constant reference to "you and me." With his prodigious facility, Riley combined a remarkable skill, while he resembled Stephen Foster in the note of a constantly personal feeling that explained his vogue with a multitude of homespun readers.

*Like Dickens, he became famous as a lecturer. He liked the actor's role.*

*There was no one like Riley for conjuring up the Saturday chores or the Old Swimming Hole.*

133

# Sidney Lanier

*strong and genuine in his poetic force, he became
the first real voice emerging from the South.*

*After the holocaust of the war,* many writers from the South found that there was no place at home for men of their complexion. Some of them went to New York. Others flocked to Baltimore, "that almost sole harbour of refuge." Richard Malcolm Johnston, who had lost the whole of his large estate, settled there as a schoolmaster in 1867, and Sidney Lanier joined him there a few years later to teach at the new university, Johns Hopkins.

With a present that one could scarcely face and without any visible future, only the past was tolerable to the Southern mind. The so-called "plantation tradition" bloomed afresh with the younger writers and with Southern novelists for decades to come who were under the spell of the cause that was lost with the war.

Thus for years the Southern writers were marked by a curious unreality that led to a kind of revenge on the part of their successors, who seemed to take a savage joy in tearing the veil from the picture of life that others had created so fondly in this heyday of illusions. What Mark Twain called the "Sir Walter disease," which had, he said, so large a hand in making the Southern character before the war, — so that "in great measure" Scott was "responsible for the war," — this disease raged still in the unreconstructed South in manners, names and customs as well as in books.

Sidney Lanier, a Georgian, brought up on Scott and Froissart in his father's house, thought of himself as a mediæval knight. He saw in himself, a troubadour wandering about the world, with a lute and the ribbon of his lady-love slung on his back. The fact that the lute was a flute did not alter the vision.

When, two years before his death, he addressed the "knights" in the Shenandoah valley, charging them "to do after the good and leave the evil, and ever to live nobly in the service of their fair ladies." was he not still living in the fantasy-world in which he had drilled the Macon boys who thought of themselves as English bowmen of Crécy? Still,

Lanier's poetic force was so strong and genuine that he became the first real voice emerging from the South.

Imprisoned during the war as a sailor in the Confederate navy, he had smuggled his flute into the camp. There his playing elated his fellow-prisoners, for he was a musical prodigy who as a child was an organist, a pianist, a violinist and a guitarist also. Joel Chandler Harris, hearing him later in Macon, described his playing as "ravishing, enchanting, mysterious and weird."

Already known as a poet, Lanier was a victim of the tuberculosis that he had caught in the war as a result of exposure, and his life was a desperate race with death, — he was to perish at thirty-nine, — as well as a dreary struggle to make a living.

Lanier was a Georgian bred in the bone and one of the Georgian group of writers who dominated the Southern mind in letters for a while. Georgia itself, of all the states, had received the harshest treatment in the war, but it was the first to recover and rise from its ruins. It was, moreover, the first state to sink the local in the national spirit, as the so-called "New South" was first conceived in Georgia. The problems of the post-war readjustment were less grave there than elsewhere and the burdens of reconstruction were less severe.

Loyal as he was to Georgia, the scene of *The Marshes of Glynn* and *Corn,* Lanier found in Baltimore the companionship that he had missed further South where there was "not enough attrition of mind on mind" to "bring out any sparks from a man."

Pale, dark, slender, nervous and eager, with a passionate belief in his mission in the world, Lanier was the ideal of the bard to many in his time. Brought up in a strict Presbyterian household, he was in grain as much of a Puritan as Emerson ever had been, while he shared belatedly the New England delight in the German romantic writers. His novel *Tiger Lilies* was all compact of Novalis and Jean Paul Richter.

*Lanier as a young man.*

With these tokens and tastes of the older South, Lanier combined more recent notes that gave him distinctly the character of a voice of his age, in some respects an important voice of the nation as well as the South with a faith in America as a whole that suggested Whitman's. With the nation as well as the section in mind, he felt that the republic needed large farms in order to achieve its "mighty works," but that it needed the small farm too to foster manhood and self-reliance, the farming that was not a business but a way of life. This was the thought that underlay Lanier's first long poem *Corn* and some of his dialect verses of the Georgia crackers.

What made Lanier, for the rest, important, especially for the South, even more than his poems, was his feeling about them, the sense of the high vocation of the poet and the dignity of poetry in a region where previously it had been regarded as a pastime. Good or bad, his poems were new, or some of them at least, where most of his American contemporaries were shadows and echoes, in all that made them poets, aside from their themes. There was much that was moving and beautiful in the longer poems, *The Psalm of the West, The Symphony* and, above all, *The Marshes of Glynn,* with its real feeling for the Southern scene, the winding creeks, the marsh and the sea, the live oaks with their clouds of hanging moss.

# Negro Folklore Charms the Nation

*it took the genius of Joel Chandler Harris*

*to make the Southern folk-tale immortal.*

*Eastman Johnson had studied Negro ways for his* Old Kentucky Home.

*It was in Lanier's dialect poems* that one heard for the first time the actual talk of Negroes on the printed page. Irwin Russell followed him with dramatic Negro monologues that were suggested by the ballads of John Hay. Other writers explored the richness of Negro lore, largely because of the curiosity the Negroes were exciting in these years of their emancipation after the war. After Thomas Wentworth Higginson had written about their spirituals in *The Atlantic Monthly* in 1867, Winslow Homer had painted them and Eastman Johnson had travelled South to study the Negroes for his "Old Kentucky Home." An interest in their folk-tales and folk-songs had spread far and wide.

It was just at this moment that Joel Chandler Harris appeared, the other Georgian who, as a boy, had heard Lanier perform on his flute and who was to charm the world with the "Brer Rabbit" stories.

Born in Georgia among the poorest of the poor, Harris had lived with his mother in a one-room cottage, a shy little homely stammering red-headed boy who looked like one of the piney-woods Georgia crackers. He made friends with the Negroes, with whom he always felt at home, hunting 'coons, 'possums, rabbits and foxes with them, spending much time as a little boy with Uncle Bob Capers, a teamster, who told him tales of the creatures of wood and field. At Forsyth, as a young reporter, he knew an old gardener named Uncle Remus, and he had had a great friend called Uncle George, a widower who lived in his cabin alone and told him stories by the evening fire in which Brer Fox and Brer Wolf were usually the villains.

*Corn-husking chants and stories were the source of Harris's Uncle Remus series.*

As time went on Harris was to know every by-path in the woods. He hunted foxes with the hounds, treed 'coons with the Negroes, and, lingering in the quarters, spent hours watching the dances and listening to the songs and the stories that had often come from Africa. He heard ploughman's songs, the Christmas and corn-husking songs and the melodies and spirituals that Higginson had been the first to gather.

*Uncle Remus, the venerable, noble old man, bubbling over with stories.*

*Joel Chandler Harris illustrated through animal legends the Negro's ingenuity in outwitting his master.*

When Harris was turned adrift after the war, he worked as a printer all over the state, and settled in Atlanta in 1876 as Henry Grady's colleague on the *Constitution*. The name of Uncle Remus appeared in the paper in 1876 in one of the sketches that Harris had begun to write. These were finally collected as *Uncle Remus: His Songs and Sayings*, the first of a number of volumes, in 1880.

Brer Rabbit was always the hero of the tales, a mighty man in those days, as Uncle Remus called him, much bigger than at present, whom nothing could scare and no one could fool and who always got away.

All the creatures, said Uncle Remus, had to look out for themselves, especially if they had no horns or hoofs, since, like Negroes, they were helpless. In fact, these animals were Negroes in disguise, just as Brer Rabbit was the Negro Hercules. He was as much their mythical hero as Paul Bunyan was of the lumberjacks.

For the motto of the tales was St. Augustine's, to "spare the lowly and strike down the proud," and the Negroes in these fables got even with their overseers and masters. The weaker creatures, in every case, discomfited the stronger, as the Negroes wished, by their mischievous arts and cunning, — the cow killed the lion, the rabbit got the better of the wolf, and the terrapin of the bear; and Brer Rabbit was permitted to strut about proudly when he humbled Brer Fox before Miss Meadows and the girls.

Even before Harris, these Negro tales of the "animals and creeturs" were universally known in the South. Theodore Roosevelt was brought up on them by his Georgian mother and aunt in New York, where one of his uncles had published them in *Harper's Magazine*. There they "fell flat," as he remarked, for this later friend of Harris' was aware that it required a "genius" to make them immortal.

*Brer Rabbit was always the hero whom even Mr. Wolf could not fool. The weaker creature in every case discomfitted the stronger.*

*During the Civil War a million* soldiers had travelled from section to section who had previously known only their farmlands in New England or the South; and, aware as they were of the general scene, their interest had also been aroused by the unknown regions and people they had encountered, — Americans of whom they had never dreamed before. The writers in all the sections became suddenly conscious of the local life, which they wished to record and describe before it was too late.

*Constance Fenimore Woolson was drawn by the charm of Southern ways.*

## MISS WOOLSON

As the South was beginning to find itself, the North, too, focussed its interest on the lands below the Mason-Dixon Line. Northerners swarmed over the South, journalists, agents of prospective investors, speculators with plans for railroads, writers anxious to expose themselves to a new environment.

One of these was Constance Fenimore Woolson, a young woman from New Hampshire, a grandniece of James Fenimore Cooper, who like many Northerners, was drawn to the unhappy South by affection, compassion, admiration or the charm of the life there. With her singular gift of minute observation and a talent for analysis, her imagination lingered over the relics of the ancient South, the quaintly emblazoned tablets and colonial tombs, the wrecked old mansions that stood near by, perhaps in ruined rice-lands, amid desolated fields and broken dykes. Such was the dwelling on the Georgia sea-island that sidled and leaned in *Jupiter Lights* with one of its roofless wings falling into the cellar. After St. Augustine, Charleston especially attracted Miss Woolson, crumbling as it was but aristocratic still.

In a later novel, *Horace Chase,* one of the best of all her books, she anticipated Thomas Wolfe in describing Asheville, in which the young capitalist from the North who falls in love with the Southern girl sees the "Lone Star" of future mountain-resorts.

Miss Woolson was a highly conscious writer, careful, skilful, subtle, with a sensitive, clairvoyant feeling for human nature, with the gift of discriminating observation that characterized Howells and Henry James. She was surely best in her stories of the South, fascinated as she was by its splendour and carelessness, its tropical plants, flowers, odours and birds, and the pathos and beauty of the old order as she saw it in decay.

*She studied the relations of Southerners with the visitors arriving from the North.*

*following the lead of Bret Harte, writers*

*endeavored to convey the colour and speech of*

*people in little-known regions.*

*Up in the mountains, families still
lived in an eighteenth-century world.*

## MISS MURFREE

*In a story called Up in the Blue Ridge,* published in 1878, Constance Fenimore Woolson had written of the people whom Mary Murfree, — "Charles Egbert Craddock," — began to describe in a series of tales the first of which appeared in the very same year. Miss Woolson had observed them at Asheville, the scene of her novel *Horace Chase,* when they straggled into the village for the Saturday market and the mountain-women in their deep sun-bonnets rode up and down the street while the men sat on their heels in a row by the store.

There in their little clusters of cabins, with walls of rough logs and chimneys of mud, mysterious, unkempt, lank, and unknown outside, lived an uncouth and fierce race of men. No one had observed the mountaineers, who were living in the eighteenth century still a life that was even more timeless than that of the plantations. They might almost have been wild clansmen in Scotland still, living by barter largely, without trades or professions, with every man his own cobbler, carpenter, gunsmith and miller.

Miss Murfree, the daughter of a Tennessee planter, was drawn to the mountain-folk when she heard others ridicule their outlandish manner of speaking and their barbarous ways. She set out presently on a horseback journey far into the mountains, visiting huts with witch-like women smoking pipes, hovels with a pack of a dozen or a score of hounds. Almost at once Miss Murfree began to chronicle the life of the mountaineers. Like all the world, she had read Bret Harte, who set an example for so many writers by focussing his mind on a regional scene and its people, and she must have noted at once the surface similarity between his domain of the Sierras and her Tennessee mountains.

In her many stories, long and short, the same characters reappeared that one met in her first book, *In the Tennessee Mountains,* but this and *The Prophet of the Great Smoky Mountains* revealed an unknown human sphere in a way that was singularly real, impressive and poetic.

The stories were vibrant as often as not with the violent feelings of the mountain-folk, whether anger, love, loyalty or resentment. But, interesting as much of it was, the best of this writing was scarcely readable two generations later, because of its abuse of dialect, so typical of the time, and as fatal as the abuse of bitumen in the work of the painters.

*Miss Murfree described life in the
Tennessee backwoods regions.*

139

## GEORGE W. CABLE

*For the writers who were attracted* by regional colour and dialect, New Orleans proved a true bonanza. The New Orleans writer George W. Cable was one who cared deeply for the local life. He was enchanted by the musical patois of the French-speaking ruling class, which had its effect in the shaping of his own literary style, as well as the language of the French-speaking Negroes, with whom he took great pains to talk.

Cable, an engineer, had joined a surveying party in the swamps and bayous of the Atchafalaya River. His observations in camp in the delta country figured in many of his novels and shorter stories, scenes in which he had roamed surveying the great gulf marshes and reedy isles, the haunts of alligators, wildcats, racoons and serpents.

As a boy he had spent hours on the levee watching the Negro gangs that sang as they pressed the cotton-bales, and since then he had studied the uncanny side of the Negroes too. Cable had picked up the story of the Negro chief Bras-Coupé which he related afterward in *The Grandissimes,* the giant, like Harris' Blue Dave, who had escaped to the swamp and become the terror of hunters, slaves and children.

Cable also studied the folk-ways of the Acadians who were small farmers still, illiterate and poor,

*He was intrigued by the Creoles, their history and character. His novels reflect the romance of old New Orleans life.*

140

though, for good or ill, they were catching the spirit of progress. Cable soon pictured these people in *Bonaventure*.

But, with all his feeling for the Acadians and the Negroes, Cable's great interest was the Creoles themselves and their setting in old New Orleans, which always charmed him, the city whose history he explored for sketches in the *Picayune,* reading old newspapers, ransacking the municipal archives.

A lover of Creole antiquity, he dug up strange true stories that exhibited the romance and picturesqueness of the New Orleans life, stories of the twice-married countess, the haunted house in Royal Street, the young aunt with white hair and the white slave Salome. His imagination dwelt on everything that gave its uniqueness to a town where one felt "further away than elsewhere from everywhere else in the world." As for the French quarter and its balconied façades and cool flagged flowery inner courts, Cable had known it from his earliest boyhood in the town, with the dazzling white walls of the St. Charles Hotel where the nabobs of the river-plantations had come in the heyday of the quadroon balls at the Salle de Conde.

Cable was all eyes and ears for these shifting phases of the life of the town, as he was for the Choctaw squaws who sold sassafras and bay, the Spaniards and Cubans in the cafés, the Sicilians with their violent gestures, so energetic when they worked, so composed when they were at rest.

In regard to the equality of the races, Cable's feelings were pronounced. There were times when he seemed to justify miscegenation, although he opposed it strongly in his political essays. There, speaking as an ex-Confederate soldier and a son and grandson of slave-holders, he defended the right of the Negroes to education, to legal equality, to being "citizens" in every sense. His feelings in this matter partly explained the unpopularity that sent him North in 1885 to live for the rest of his days at Northampton in New England.

Of all his types the New Orleans Creoles were the most important in Cable's stories. It was the goodness of the Creoles themselves that Cable especially singled out, that he treasured and extolled in his novels and tales about them. His style was half French in his earlier books, light, precise and epigrammatic, with an air that seemed to mirror the Creole mind.

*As a boy George W. Cable had observed the Negroes who sang as they pressed the cotton-bales.*

*Scene from Cable's* The Grandissimes, *a story of Creole life.*

*Mark Twain and Cable, both writing about their native regions, were close friends. They often shared the lecture platform.*

# Mark Twain

*the serio-comic Homer of the river world. He made the Mississippi a focus of the national mind.*

*He dreamed of becoming a pilot — the ambition of all village boys.*

*Mark Twain at the time when he was a Mississippi pilot, ca. 1859.*

*There was no one in all the* Western regions with a livelier eye for the shows of things, together with their insides and undersides, than Samuel Clemens, aged fifteen in 1850 and already setting most of the type on his brother's paper at Hannibal, Missouri. He was charmed by the lordly packet-boats that passed Hannibal every day when the Negro draymen shouted "Steamboat a-comin'!" and the streets came alive with a clatter of trucks and men hurrying to the wharf. He dreamed of being a pilot on one of those boats, the permanent ambition of all the village boys.

The river was a multitudinous world and all sorts and conditions of men were found already on the Mississippi steamboats, with their sunny balconies, domed saloons, galleries and smokestacks cut to look like clusters of plumes. There, as a pilot before the Civil War, Mark Twain said that he had encountered first or last all the types of human nature one met in biography, history, or fiction.

With his books Mark Twain was to make the Mississippi a focus of the national mind, as Washington Irving earlier had made the Hudson, on a scale incomparably larger and richer than Irving's. Through him this greatest of the American rivers became a dwelling-place of light, one of the enchanted countries of the imagination, a world, uncolonized hitherto, where the mind had never been at home and where henceforth it was always happy to rest. Broadhorns from Pittsburgh floated past side by side with enormous rafts, acres of boards with long sweeps and flagpoles fore and aft, with wigwams scattered over the expanse of white sweet-smelling timber and a campfire blazing in the middle. They moved so slowly that a boy could swim out and ride with the fiddling, dancing crew, listen to their Crockett-like stories and tremendous talk and watch them jump, cracking their heels together.

But the heart of the magic for Mark Twain had always been the steamboats. He had been enchanted as a boy by their white wooden filigree work, their gilded acorns and deerhorns and chandeliers and pictures. The pilots were treated with exalted respect whenever they appeared in the village and they always expressed their wishes in the form of commands. Their skill was a legend along the river, for they followed blind channels that were choked with logs and grazed invisible wrecks in rushing water. That was "gaudy" piloting, "gold-leaf, kid-glove, diamond-breastpin" piloting, and Mark Twain had finally rivalled the best himself. He loved the river in a hundred ways.

This was the summer world, bright and fresh, brimming with life, where Mark Twain had spent part of every summer, where he made friends especially in the Negro quarters. There Mark Twain learned how to ward off witches and nip spells in the bud, as he learned the many bad-luck and the few good-luck signs; he heard the stories that were later told by the Georgian "Uncle Remus" and tales that he himself was to recount about runaway slaves.

All these scenes appeared in the books that Mark Twain wrote about the river, along with the camp-meeting, the funeral, the circus, the auction and the characters, drawn mainly from the Hannibal people, who were to suggest in turn innumerable figures in later books by others. Mark Twain was the serio-comic Homer of this old primitive Western world, its first pathfinder in letters, its historian and poet.

*Piloting — an enviable profession, freer than that of the writer, manacled forever to his public.*

*The town was abruptly awakened by the cry "Steamboat a-comin' . . ."*

*One encountered on the river all types of human nature.*

*Mark Twain was twenty-nine years old* in 1864, when he came to live in San Francisco, and he had seen much of the country already as a Mississippi pilot and a wandering printer. Ever since he was a boy he had longed to "get away." A Southerner on both sides, like Lincoln, — his father was Virginian, his mother, Kentuckian, — he had been for two weeks a lieutenant in the Confederate army, and before this, at seventeen, leaving home to see the world, he had visited St. Louis, Philadelphia, Washington and New York. He lodged in mechanics' boarding-houses, paying his way. At loose ends when the Civil War destroyed the river-traffic, he followed his brother to Nevada across the plains, mining for a few months in Washoe, as the territory was called, and later on the Stanislaus over the California border. Then he had become a journalist in Virginia City. He was soon well-known as the "Washoe Giant," the author of a series of burlesques and hoaxes who was presently also described as the "Moralist of the Main" when he censured the abuses and corruptions of San Francisco.

Mark Twain was "from Missouri," — a phrase that arose in later years, — and something new under the sun of letters. He had to be "shown" things that others accepted on faith, he had a strong feeling for the actual as opposed to the sham.

*Roughing It,* written a few years later, described Mark Twain's Far Western life, beginning with his overland stage-drive from Missouri to Nevada, spinning through Kansas and a part of Nebraska over the "great American desert," where one trod on a bone at every step. He related the oft-repeated story of Horace Greeley and Hank Monk, the famous stage-driver on the road to Placerville, whose tally-ho with six horses was the first that had crossed the Sierras and who was "always on time" at any cost.

Mark Twain revealed in *Roughing It* a masterly grasp of an American scene. Along with his chapters on the mining days he included a few on the Sandwich Islands, for, to report on the sugar-industry, he had gone to Honolulu where the Hawaiian king sat on a barrel fishing on the wharf. Charles Warren Stoddard had visited the islands two years before Mark Twain, charmed by the pagan elements that disturbed this "brevet Presbyterian," as he called himself. Mark Twain was shocked by the island girls, and he found their native dances "strange and unpleasant."

This little touch of prudery recurred in other books in which Mark Twain was to record his impressions of travel; he could not contain his fury, for instance, at one of Titian's Venuses, which he called the "vilest," the "obscenest" picture in the world. Mark Twain was the true frontiersman, like David Crockett, in an earlier day, who was shocked by the mild goings-on in the theatre in Philadelphia and "blushingly retired," as he wrote.

*Mark Twain became suddenly famous when he wrote the sketch* The Celebrated Jumping Frog . . . *(1865)*

*Greeley shooting through the ceiling of Hank Monk's stage-coach, imploring the driver to slow down. From* Roughing It.

*When the Civil War destroyed the river traffic, Mark Twain became a journalist in Virginia City.*

*Mark Twain's first important book, The Innocents Abroad,* was a singularly complete expression of the frontier culture. He wrote, or rewrote, this for a paper in San Francisco, for he returned there after the voyage, the first modern luxury cruise, in 1867, on the "Quaker City." He wished to "squeeze some of the wind and water" out of the letters he had written on the ship. While convinced of the superiority of his own country, he confronted the European scene in the mood of a "debunker." He "galloped through the Louvre," and this ex-Mississippi pilot remarked that the Arno, a "his-

*Mark Twain writing his first important book,*
The Innocents Abroad. *(1869)*

torical creek," would have to have water pumped into it to become a river. He was amused by the foreign tongues, especially the "awful German language," which he later described: "Whenever the literary German dives into a sentence, that is the last you are going to see of him till he emerges on the other side of the Atlantic with his verb in his mouth."

Mark Twain's intention in this book was to see the old world with his own eyes, not as other and earlier American tourists had seen it, — to tell what he had seen, not what he had read. The rhapsodic reaction of the American tourist to Europe had struck him as too often conventional, sentimental and false. In his efforts to "get a natural focus" on things that he observed, he struck the first note perhaps of the tourist mind that flourished in American writers fifty years later, when they were determined not to be fooled by "culture," but he also resembled too many of them in throwing out the baby with the bath, in rejecting the "truth" of culture along with the "shams." Really believing, as he later wrote, that a "chromo" was as good as a "Raphael," that the "august opera" was no better than the hurdy-gurdy, he attacked the legitimate claims of culture. Teaching writers to be honest in their vision, he also sanctioned the bad taste, the provincialism and philistinism and ignorance of the American masses.

Yet just in this, oddly enough, Mark Twain performed an essential role, distressing as this was at the moment to cultivated people. Did not Mark Twain, in his negative way, do almost as much as Walt Whitman had done to clear the path for an American culture of the future, as the Vandals of old prepared the way for another new culture in the north of Europe because they were insensitive to the Mediterranean culture? For ignorance and incomprehension are the womb and the cradle, as often as not, in which new states of mind are conceived and sheltered, new cultural variations, new human types. Ignorance, *not* independence, was Mark Twain's contribution, in *The Innocents Abroad,* to the growth of an American culture; and was not Mark Twain's active ignorance on the side of growth? His defiant Americanism destroyed the subservience of Americans to the local ideals of the mother-lands, — it broke the umbilical cord that attached them to Europe. This was an indispensable step in the process of building ideals that were not derivative but native and in time universal.

In its fathomless naiveté, The Innocents Abroad, prepared the ground for a new and unique American art of letters. Mark Twain contributed to the establishment and fostering of this native art in much of his western writing. For *Huckleberry Finn,* with *Tom Sawyer* and the first part of *Life on the Mississippi,* — books that were all composed

before 1885, — were germs of a new American literature with a broader base in the national mind than the writers of New England had possessed, fine as they were. As the literary centre of gravity of the country shifted slowly westward and the Western writers in time came into their own, one found traces of Mark Twain in their rhythms, in their vision, in their choice of themes, in their mode of seeing and recording what they heard and saw. *Huckleberry Finn* with its panorama of river-towns and river-folk was the school of many a later Western writer; the imaginative world of Sherwood Anderson was largely based upon it and the style of Ernest Hemingway owed much to it as well. There was a measure of justification in Hemingway's remark that "all modern American literature comes from *Huckleberry Finn.*"

Mark Twain's great books on the West were all written in the East. For several years before 1880, he had been living at Hartford, half-way between New York, where he was to live in later years, and the "Indian summer" Boston of William Dean Howells. He had married, he had visited England twice, he had taken the journey of *A Tramp Abroad,* he had written Mississippi sketches and the romance of *Tom Sawyer.* He had become so famous that letters reached him quickly which bore his name as their sole address, and "as Mark Twain says" was a universal phrase. In Washington, where he had spent a few months after the voyage of *The Innocents Abroad,* all the members of the Cabinet had read his book. Senators gathered about him and offered him appointments as minister or consul.

While the world acclaimed him as the greatest folk-writer of the time, a social philosopher rather than a humorist, Mark Twain thought of himself as a journalist, writing for money. He was not going to "touch a book unless," as he said, "there was money in it." His motives were seldom those of an artist whose primary concern is to do good work. His commercial and his literary motives were inextricably mingled. When he spoke of the "possibilities" of his literary work, he meant possibilities in dollars, not in form or in style. He did not respect

146

his writing, and nothing was ever more haphazard than Mark Twain's ways in composition, the hit-or-miss methods that resulted so often in failure. Many of his books were confused and involved, infantile, half thought-out, inane, and even his great stories, with their brilliant beginnings, ended badly, — *Tom Sawyer* in the commonplace melodrama of juvenile fiction, *Life on the Mississippi* in a welter of statistics. Indeed, as an artist, Mark Twain was just what Arnold Bennett called him: he was the "divine amateur" whose two great stories, "episodically magnificent," were inferior as "complete works of art."

What was he, then? — for Mark Twain was without doubt a writer of genius. He was the frontier story-teller, the great folk-writer of the American West, and he raised to a pitch unrivalled before him the art of oral story-telling and then succeeded in transferring its effects to paper.

It was true that in *The Gilded Age* Mark Twain was also a pioneer, striking out for new themes. The book was one of the earliest novels that tried to come to grips with the movements and events of the post-war American years. Few writers at that time imaginatively grasped the nation as a whole, the conception of a unified America was still vague in men's minds. This made the adventure of *The Gilded Age,* written in collaboration with Charles Dudley Warner, all the more courageous. While the novel was a failure, like other books of his, it had a largeness of conception and feeling that was Mark Twain's own, — a "magnificence" of imagination, as Howells called this. It was vague in its point of view, for its object was to satirize and condemn the speculative spirit. This was the source of the evils of the time and Mark Twain was too involved in it, too busy living his age, to see it with detachment.

Later in *A Connecticut Yankee in King Arthur's Court* the "capitalistic" Mark Twain had his innings, the inventor, the promoter, who hoped to control the carpet-weaving industry, the lover of machines and schemes for making money. The Connecticut Yankee set out to make mediæval England a "going concern." The book celebrated without reserve the "booming" nineteenth-century civilization, — the "plainest and sturdiest and infinitely greatest and worthiest of all the centuries," as Mark Twain called it. Here Mark Twain squared accounts with Scott and his magnification of the Middle Ages. He extinguished "this nonsense of knight-errantry" by making it absurd and grotesque.

*The Connecticut Yankee wanted to make mediaeval England a going concern.*

*The Prince and the Pauper: "Monarchy, the grotesquest of all swindles invented by man."*

*Mark Twain greets Colonel Sellers (John T. Raymond) in the dramatization of* The Gilded Age.

*Always in the centre of the stage, he was the foremost of story-tellers, an art he had learned as a boy from the Negroes.*

*The Return of the Native. Hannibal remained for him the measure of humanity. Here his mind was at home.*

*As a traveller he wanted to see the world and tell what he had seen, not what he had read about foreign lands.*

*In his old age Mark Twain did most of his writing in bed with a mind that was almost as relaxed as his body.*

*Always by choice in the centre* of the stage, Mark Twain was a symbol of the new America. Fresh, arresting, ebullient, his tastes, feelings and interests expressed those of the nation. As a writer he had somehow struck the key-note of his epoch, the boisterous geniality and self-confidence of the triumphant nation, unified by the Civil War, aware of the resources it was rapidly exploiting, good-naturedly contemptuous of the Europe it had once revered. He was irreverent, like many Americans, but only irreverent regarding things which the mass of Americans agreed were not worthy of respect. Typically American too was his impulsive humanitarianism. Early in his career he showed a deep concern with religion and morals, compassion for the under-dog, and a hatred of political corruption.

In dozens of other respects as well, Mark Twain's personality was an all but unparalleled emblem of the country and the time, to such a degree that his name evoked in the minds of his contemporaries a picture of America itself in this post-war age. He was the natural democrat who wrote the story of the prince and the pauper to show that they were identical when one removed their clothes; and who was more interested than he in money-making, inventions, machines at a moment when the capitalist system was approaching its zenith?

With all the buoyant hopefulness that was also a typically American note, he was drawn to money-making schemes as a fly to a jam-pot, although he lost fortune after fortune. He was the first author ever to use a typewriter and he had the first telephone that was used in a private house.

It was certain that a few of Mark Twain's writings were destined to live with the best in America. He was to be remembered also as the type of his epoch, the humorist and the gambler, dramatic, shrewd, compassionate, impulsive and boyish, the "man from Missouri" who became an American legend.

# Book Four

# New England : Indian Summer

*In July, 1868, Charles Francis Adams* and John Lothrop Motley returned to Boston. For many years they had lived abroad, in the diplomatic service. Both had reappeared to recover their bearings in the new American world. Adams' younger son, Henry Adams, who had spent the Civil War years in London, acting as his father's secretary, recorded their first impressions in words that were famous later: "Had they been Tyrian traders of the year B.C. 1000, landing from a galley fresh from Gibraltar, they could hardly have been stranger on the shore of a world, so changed from what it had been ten years before."

The energy and daring of New England, once devoted to humanitarian causes, to literature and statesmanship, were turning to the developing West, and the capitalists of Boston were building railroads. The coming generation, as Henry Adams saw, was "already mortgaged to the railways" and everything they implied, capital, banks, machinery, mines, together with new ideas and habits, social and political, to fit the new scale and suit the new conditions. The country had turned into a "Bankers' Olympus."

The elements of change in this long-settled country of New England were not as marked at first as in other regions; nor were they ever as marked as they were in the West . . . but they were marked enough, with the war, the growth of the railroads and the factory system, the spread of wealth, the spread of immigration, which implied the spread of poverty.

The war, in a measure, uprooted the native population, with whom wandering habits had been growing for decades. The West attracted them. With the opening of the transcontinental railroads, the economic centre of the country gradually shifted westward; and New York, with more and more of the Western trade, increasingly drew the foreign trade from Boston.

In the mad scramble for wealth the old idealism, New England's precious heritage, had been burnt away. The war, with its fearful tension, draining the national vitality, had left the mind of the people morally flabby.

The most popular men, in all walks of life, during these decades, Ben Butler, Beecher, Barnum, D. L. Moody, when they were not venal, were singularly coarse, as compared with the earlier leaders. Money and "numbers" governed all their thoughts. They thought in terms of quantity, very seldom in terms of quality, and Barnum's "publicity methods" characterized them all.

These changes in the New England scene were reflected in literature almost at once. The stories of the younger writers, whose books were already appearing, abounded in the problems of the moment, the shifting population, the abandoned farms, the evils of immigration and the factory-system, the increasing corruption in politics, the rise of the newly rich, the feeling that the region was declining. Gone were the days when Yankee boys aspired to be sailors or missionaries or poets. All these occupations had stirred the imagination, and so, in its way, had the life of the farm and the forest. The business life was hostile to all these interests. It encouraged the reading of newspapers and occasional books on engineering, but the world of thought and feeling impeded its action. The decline of culture, marked throughout the country, was visible almost at once throughout New England.

Longfellow and Norton deplored the dwindling away of literary interests. Higginson remarked that nine lectures in every ten were merely stump-speeches. Parkman said that flatulent writing was growing at the expense of pregnant writing. Boston, Henry Adams thought, had ceased to believe in itself any longer and many a sign of the times confirmed this feeling. On the intellectual level, Boston was less and less the port of call it had been in the days of old.

New England had lost its political leadership, and many of the New England men had lost their connection with the soil. They were uprooted and adrift in a world they did not understand and found more and more uncongenial, and even some of the older men who had been ardent patriots were uncertain of their moorings and their bearings.

No wonder the young men with literary ambitions were even more apprehensive. They knew they were doomed to fight their fights alone, in a world that was more likely to divide and destroy them. Some, like Henry Adams, were all but born discouraged. Others, like Henry James, were to spend ten years trying to solve the question where to live. William James was also to pass ten years consumed with a sense of futility, although in the end he developed a faith like his father's. William James and Howells, who had come from the West, retained the buoyant mood of the early republic; but most of the others were cautious and conservative, cool and disillusioned on the surface, with the knowing air of men who expect to be swindled, who cannot trust the society in which they live.

In reaction against a public life that had grown corrupt and vulgar, they cultivated the "private life" and deliberately sought the unpopular. They exaggerated the "little" to shame the "big." These were a few of the traits that characterized the generation, producing its anomalous effects.

*America was to dispense with statesmen like John Quincy Adams, and cast its lot with the politicians.*

*Henry Adams needed time to realize that the day of the Adamses was over.*

# *Henry Adams*

*a restlessly introspective probing mind, he pictured*

*his time with a unique power of suggestion.*

*The adventures of Henry Adams* in a world transformed by the recent war were to take place largely outside of New England; but no one observed his age more keenly, whether in New England or elsewhere. A shy self-conscious little man, inordinately proud, with a restless introspective probing mind, he had taken it for granted, as an Adams, that he had a career before him, the sort of career that Adamses always had. It had never occurred to him, till his return from England, that the days of the Adamses were over. He had never supposed that America would dispense with its best-trained statesmen and cast its lot with politicians who took their orders from bankers.

Charles Francis Adams, his father,

as Minister to England, had raised to its highest pitch the prestige of American policy; but the bankers had prevailed in his absence. They had won the war for the North and demanded their pound of flesh, if they had to kill the country to obtain it.

With some such thoughts as these, and such misgivings, Henry Adams returned to the homestead at Quincy, the retreat of all the Adamses for three generations in times that called for study and meditation. The old order had passed and his dreams of power passed with it. He would have to make his way as best he could in a world in which his quality scarcely counted.

*Henry Adams had hoped that, like other Adamses, he was destined to sit in the White House.*

152

All the Adams' idols had been statesmen, and this was a family inheritance that he could not escape. He had grown up in the shadow of presidents; he had visited the White House at twelve; he had lived among politicians all his life, whether in Washington or London, and some sort of connection with politics was inevitable for him. He tried to arrange to buy the Boston *Advertiser*, to start an independent-liberal party. His "vast and ambitious projects for the future" took him to New York and Washington often. However, he was unsuccessful in entering the political world. An Adams, he would not stoop to conquer. Every hope or thought which had brought him to Washington proved to be absurd. No one wanted him, and so he turned in disgust from President Grant whose manifestations "outraged ordinary decency."

But if Henry Adams could not make history, he could write and teach it, — and so he became, in 1870, a professor at Harvard.

American history was in Adams' bones. Part of it was Adams history and most that was not Adams had reached him through a thousand early channels. His happiest hours in childhood, in the farmhouse at Quincy, were passed as he lay, in summer, reading Scott, on a heap of congressional documents,—he day-dreamed on musty documents as others on hay. Along with the materials, he had the models. Henry and his brothers, Charles Francis and Brooks, had all read history more than anything else.

Adams found history "wildly interesting," and he seemed to be a happy and successful author. Behind this mask, however, another life went on. Adams was deeply dissatisfied. He had not wished to be a professor, and even historical writing, which he enjoyed for a time, soon palled upon him. His history was a masterly performance. With its easy and confident style, its wealth of portraits, this monumental work was beyond all praise. But Adams wearied of the task before it was finished. Later he explained this lapse of interest by saying that he could "make life work" no longer. Evidently, to write fine books was not to be a "success" for him. What was his standard, then? What did he wish?

What Adams desired was power. The Adamses had possessed power, and the will-to-power was a family trait that governed Henry Adams' every instinct. Did he wish for office? He sometimes said so. But, generally speaking, what he desired was

to rule from behind the scenes; and this was his motive in writing, — it had always been so. Literature, beside politics, was small beer for Adams; he wished to exercise influence and govern opinion.

He had never felt that he was a true Bostonian, — Boston, for him, was a "bore." As early as 1860 he had affirmed, "I shall make up my bed in Washington, perhaps for life." It was natural for him to return there, "as stable-companion to statesmen." Here he hobnobbed freely with senators, generals, ambassadors, in whose hands the political history of the present lay. He was at home in Washington as never in Boston.

There, in 1884, he built a big red house. His friend John Hay, at work on the life of Lincoln, built an adjoining house in a similar style. Both were designed by H. H. Richardson, Adams' vigorous friend of his Harvard days.

The Adams circle was unique in the capital, — the embassies and the White House were dull beside it. Richardson and John La Farge and Alexander Agassiz occasionally joined the Adams circle, together with Henry James, when he happened to be in the country. Hay was Adams' constant crony. Hay had advanced from triumph to triumph, sailing before the wind with the party in power, while his friend, the saturnine Adams, whom he called "Oom Hendrick," fought against the political stars in their courses.

Adams, who had longed for power, had known for several years that he could not hope to exercise power directly. But he liked the feeling that he was near it. The statesmen and politicians in Washington sometimes followed his advice.

❧

*Before he moved into the great* red house in Washington, Adams had written his two novels, *Democracy* and *Esther*. Nimble in style and light in tone, these novels resembled in many ways the earlier works of Henry James and Howells, and in both, as so often in James and Howells, the leading figures were women, who presented Henry Adams' point of view.

Suddenly, a blow fell from which Henry Adams never recovered. His wife committed suicide one Sunday morning, while he was out for a walk. The mainspring of his life, he felt, was broken. He seemed to himself as dead as a ghost or a mummy.

*John Hay holding a copy of* Democracy, *Henry Adams' first novel. It appeared anonymously in 1880.*

*John La Farge the artist joined Adams on various trips and awakened his interest in art.*

toric sense," La Farge said, "amounted to poetry," and even Adams' reasoning was full of suggestion. His deductions set La Farge's mind sailing into new channels. On the other hand, Adams developed new faculties under La Farge's influence. He had left the world of public affairs behind him. The author of the *History* underwent a transformation, and the Adams who wrote *Mont-Saint-Michel and Chartres* was, in a measure, at least, La Farge's creation.

It was in Paris during one of his journeys, — consumed as he was with restlessness,—that Adams rediscovered the twelfth century and made the preliminary studies for the finest of his books. Saint-Gaudens took him to Amiens and La Farge to Chartres. Adams spent whole summers in Champagne and Touraine, visiting parish churches, "collecting spires," till he felt he was a "twelfth-centurian."

He had begun to realize a prophecy of his earlier years, that art was to give him his greatest advantage and pleasure. His contempt for the present grew with his love for the past. In the present he saw nothing and he wished to see nothing, and he uttered at the Paris Exposition his ironical prayer

*Clarence King, like Adams a symbol of this restless generation.*

*Brooks Adams, Henry's brother, also foresaw a civilization propelled by greed.*

Then began for Henry Adams a life of restless wandering that carried him round the world for twenty years. He was drawn especially to the lands of Buddha; he felt a longing for the East which proud people often share, when, as Kinglake said, they are "goaded by sorrow." On the first of his expeditions he went to Japan with La Farge.

Like many of his contemporaries, Adams was enthralled by Oriental thought; he was a seeker of salvation in the Buddhist way. The travels of La Farge and Adams, soon to be continued, left traces in the lives and work of both. Adams' "his-

to the Dynamo because he found nothing else in his time to respect.

When *Mont-Saint-Michel and Chartres* was published, Adams was astonished to find himself a "leader of a popular movement." A younger generation had risen who shared his despair of the present, and thousands who, like him, had lost their faith, were turning, as he turned, to the Middle Ages. "Running madly through the centuries," he had brought up at an age that he had known from the beginning and that had come to seem to him a symbol of the believing community in which he might have lived to some effect.

Adams, as a writer, had verified another prediction, made in his youth to his brother, — that he was going to "plunge under the stream" and remain under water and come up at last "with an oyster and a pearl." If the *Education* was the oyster, *Chartres* was the pearl. After so many deaths, Adams had triumphed. He had worked himself into the Middle Ages, grasping so many aspects of them that *Chartres* was destined to live as a history and a classic; while in the *Education* he had pictured his time with a force and a power of suggestion that were surely unique. It appealed to the younger generation, who felt themselves adrift, and who were in revolt against their past. The *Education* revealed a phase of American history with an unparalleled boldness and measure of truth.

155

# Practicality Triumphant

*the colned more and more to technical subjects. The classics were neglected, to the detriment of first-rate writing.*

*Observing the success of the* iron-clad ships during the Civil War, Henry Adams wrote to his brother Charles: "I tell you man has mounted science, and is now run away with. . . . Some day science may have the existence of mankind in its power and the human race will commit suicide by blowing up the world."

The trend towards practical science at the expense of the humanities became obvious immediately in the sphere of education. Charles William Eliot, an energetic chemist, had turned Harvard over "like a flapjack." The higher education of the country was largely remodelled on his ideas, for no one knew better than he what the country desired. The cry had been going up for instruction along special, vocational lines. Technological schools were rising to meet the new demands, with

*President Eliot wished to train specialists. He turned Harvard over "like a pancake."*

chairs of geology, engineering, mining, schools for bridge-builders and railroad-builders, chemists to work in the factories, geologists to develop the mineral wealth of the West. In the colleges, where the "man of thought" had always ruled as a matter of course, the students debated the question, "Resolved, that the man of action is more important." Eliot replied with a new regime that marked the decisive change, a change that was soon reflected in the minds of writers.

Eliot's elective system opened a great new epoch in science, medicine, engineering. But one saw the total effect in time, as the other universities followed Harvard and lost sight of human ends in means. Then it became apparent that civilization was losing its soul, as education had lost its soul already.

This marked, in literature, the greatest of possible changes. Particularly striking was the change in literary style. Disregarding secondary writers, all

*Cartoon from* Puck *glorifies the man of action — the victor in a match with a college graduate emaciated by "culture" studies.*

*Fiske gave a lucid exposition of Spencer's positivism, which became the prevailing philosophy of the time.*

tion of facts and rules, with no coherent body of governing truths, while the new conception of the unity of nature bound all these facts together in a web of causation.

Such was the great Spencerian vision that Fiske expounded at Harvard. As a lecturer, this hirsute, bespectacled mammoth with his hearty manner, with his gift for elucidation, was a master performer, and the "Fiske season" with popular science lectures delivered all over the country rivalled the feats of Barnum in the years to come.

*Why study? Even Ragged Dick can become a millionaire, if he is aggressive enough, and sets his cap at worldly gains.*

the first-rate writers of the later age, even those who knew the classics well, suffered as regards their style. Few of their books had the authentic ring that marked the best pages of Thoreau, Dana, Hawthorne, Motley, who were steeped in Greek, Latin and the Bible. The "vices" of their style were almost as marked as the "beauties": the thin facility of Howells and the earlier Henry James, the obscurity of the later Henry James, the excessive colloquialism of William James, the perversity of Emily Dickinson. The study of the classics had always been connected with accurate linguistic training and the study of form, while the modern tongues were loose in their construction; but, what was even more important, the classics had made spacious men and men prepared to meet great problems, most of whom were steeped in Plutarch's lives and the legends of Greece and Rome.

Meanwhile, at Harvard, the coming age was represented by a number of Eliot's appointments. Perhaps the most representative of these was John Fiske, who lectured on positivism and Darwinism, the most engrossing topics of the moment. His methodical, orderly mind moved like a stone-crusher, reducing the boulders of thought to a flow of gravel that anyone could build a mental road with. He simplified the knottiest points, he made the most difficult abstractions as lucid and easily grasped as a nursery-story, and all without any sacrifice of substance. The big, warm-hearted, exuberant Fiske, whose wit was somewhat elephantine, was vehement and cheerful in manner, both in writing and speaking. A first-rate popularizer, he was filled with the zeal of a propagandist. Evolution for him was a new religion.

Up to that moment, science was a mere collec-

In the new business world, to make a fortune became the epitome of success, and no idealism was required to achieve this goal. There was no need to improve one's mind: all that was required was a course in the school of hard knocks. Harvard, prolific in leaders, provided an exponent even of this philosophy in the Unitarian minister, Horatio Alger. Living in New York's Newsboy's Lodging-House, he set to work on his *Luck and Pluck* series, to show Ragged Dick and Tattered Tom how easily they might rise to fame and fortune. For many who began their lives as bootblacks and newsboys, the Alger theme was a joy and a solace.

Alger was one of the men who all but effaced the New England tradition, for he vulgarized Emerson's *Self-Reliance* and turned it into a laughing-stock. Alger wrote for city boys whose only motive was self-advancement. The "bitch-goddess Success," — wealth and power, — was all that counted in Alger's stories.

157

*Howells when he arrived in Cambridge, a reverent pilgrim who wanted to be "the linchpin" in the literary hub*

# The Rise of Realism

*William Dean Howells, a great observer of America. He chronicled the life of her people with charm and insight.*

*Howells at the age of 24 as Consul in Venice.*

*The publisher Ticknor pays Howells for his first poem published in the* Atlantic.

*In the early spring of 1866,* a young man named William Dean Howells had slipped into Boston. He was twenty-nine years old, slight, with a black moustache, mild in his manner and modest in appearance. One saw that he had delicate perceptions and a shrewd gift of observation, and he gave one a marked impression of will and purpose. The brooding look in his eyes betokened a future.

Howells's talents and predilections characterized the moment. The spread of science expressed in Spencer's positivism had attracted the mind to the world of outer experience and all the wondrous fruits of observation. Science revealed the importance of environment. It trained the eye to observe the types and classes of men as botany exhibited plants and animals. Balzac and his realistic successors gradually brought the novel to terms with science, and along the same lines Howells paved the way in America for the advance of realism.

Howells was a realist before he ever heard the word, — he had written realistic sketches as a boy in Ohio, sketches "as natural as the toothache," his father called them. His own personality ordained his method. The realistic view of life, which he drew as it were out of the air, appealed to his democratic instinct.

Encouraged by the Boston Olympians, Howells had moved to Cambridge in 1866, — the year of his first pilgrimage to the East. Here he became "sub-editor" of the *Atlantic*. Cambridge, when Howells settled there, was still the hub of the literary universe.

The population consisted of authors, or so it was supposed in other regions. You could not shoot in any direction, a visitor from the West remarked, without bringing down the writer of two or three volumes. When one little girl said to another, "Your grand-father is a poet, is he not?" the natural reply could only be, "Why, yes, isn't yours?"

With his gifts of observation and perception, Howells was a fit recruit for literary Cambridge. The new age, dawning in the country, seemed to him one of peace, prosperity and content. The scandals of public life, the abuses of business were remote from the little world in which he dwelt. Coming from the West, he had found a haven in Cambridge and Boston when the young men who had grown up in this region were most inclined to feel its limitations. If others were restless and anxious, he was tranquil. Even the Civil War was vaguer in his mind than it was in the minds of Boston men who had seen its woes at close range. He was prepared to accept the "true American gospel," that everything was coming right in time. Years later Howells questioned this gospel. In his earlier career he was predisposed to trust his country, and he re-joiced in the lull that followed the war. He rejoiced in his work, he rejoiced in his countrypeople. He rejoiced in the noble realities he found about him. Were not the poets and scholars as real as Wall Street? As the wife said in Tennyson's *Sea Dreams,* "Let all evil sleep." He felt as if the troubles of the world were settled.

While New England, for a number of years, was Howells' central *mise en scène,* his mind from the first was continental. If he had a purpose, this was to reconcile sections and classes in a broadly democratic feeling for life; and, in order to bring them together, he often presented his people as travellers, who meet in hotels, in stations, on trains, on steamboats. One gathered from his novels that Americans were always moving, always going or coming, abroad or at home; and, in fact, in this respect, these novels reflected the post-war years and Howells' own habit as a constant tourist.

The scenes of all these wanderings soon appeared in Howells' stories, the harvest of an all-perceiving eye. At the beaches, he observed the ladies, with their needlework beside them. The young ladies were most in evidence, perhaps on the croquet-ground in front of the hotel or out in the rowboats on the river; for all these summer resorts abounded in loverless maidens, enough to provide a novelist with heroines forever. They were always doing something to their hair, and all of them seemed to be prepared for what were called "attentions." They were the summer girls of the summer hotels, and it always seemed to be summer in Howells' stories.

Owing to Howells' extreme aversion to melodrama, nothing dramatic happened in his novels . . . but this "nothing" was the best of all. That he made something out of this nothing was the marvel of his mind and art; and moreover the something in question was highly important. It was love, in its American phases, love in the American form; and what, for American readers, was more im-portant? Wherever he looked there were brides who were charmingly dressed. Howells shrewdly noted the trifles of behaviour that so often carried the day in his game of love.

*He mostly presented his people as travellers.*

*Loveless maidens looking for attentions.*

*Love in the American form.*

*What for Americans was more important? . . .*

159

*The Americans in Howells' novels* were all a natural family, and family loyalty was his favourite theme. His stories were full of loyal households, the Maverings and the Coreys, the Gaylords, the Laphams, and Howells delighted in testing the bonds that held them together, conjugal, maternal, paternal and filial.

As Howells advanced, his more serious novels reflected, one by one, the changing conditions and phases of American life. *The Undiscovered Country* described the rise of spiritualism at the time when Mrs. Eddy was settling in Boston. Egeria and Dr. Boynton were types of the moment, as Marcia Gaylord was in *A Modern Instance. The Rise of Silas Lapham* was the best of all the pictures of the new self-made millionaires, and *A Woman's Reason* presented another type of the eighties, the girl setting out to make a living in open competition with the world of men. Through decade after decade, Howells followed the life of the nation, and he caught so many of its phases that as a social historian he had no equal.

*Howells in search of pastures new forsook Boston and went to New York. He liked the huge kind noisy city.*

Although literary Boston heaped him with all its honours and crowned him with laurels, Howells grew restive. He felt an insistent need for pastures new.

He had moved from Cambridge to Belmont, and at last into Boston itself. There he had bought a house on "the water side of Beacon Street." In this house he had written *The Rise of Silas Lapham,* and the story of the house that Lapham built was drawn from his own experience here and at Belmont. But he had had his "twenty years of Boston," and the basis of his New England life was broken. He had gone abroad for a year and seen his country once more in perspective. He withdrew from New England reluctantly and slowly. He sometimes returned to Boston for a year or a season, and many of his later summers were passed in Maine. But henceforth New York was his centre. The world was still full of novelty and interest for him, and he liked the huge, kind, noisy, sprawling city. Its multitudinous life appeared in *A Hazard of New Fortunes* which caught the note of New York as *Silas Lapham* conveyed the feeling of Boston.

There was another reason for his change: the growth of his sociological interests. He was alarmed by the growing division of classes, the rift between poverty and wealth. Along with the millionaire, the tramp had appeared on the scene, and the streets were full of beggars and hungry workmen, while the papers recounted the scandals and rascalities of business. He felt he could no longer trust his country. His optimism had been mistaken. He felt that writers and artists should ally themselves with the toilers of shop and field. The old Howells lived on, the sunny, cheerful happy man who believed in his countrypeople as much as ever. But the new Howells continued to live with the old. His social consciousness never deserted him. It remained the burden of much of his work, alike in verse and in prose.

For a number of years, in a series of novels, the question of social reform overshadowed everything else in Howells' work. He pictured in Dryfoos, in *A Hazard of New Fortunes,* the new kind of despot-financier. The rascally manufacturer in *The Son of Royal Langbrith,* who had gone through life as the hero of the town, was another proof of Howells' distrust of business; and this novel, which appeared in 1904, was one of many proofs that Howells' mind responded to every change in the mood of the nation.

As he passed into this later phase, Howells' style lost much of its sparkle, the gaiety, brilliance and wit of his earlier novels; and the novels themselves all but lost their old compactness, the perfection of organization they had once possessed. Still, even his later border-line stories dealing with psychical mysteries and hallucinations were touched with an exquisite spirituality; and, indeed, this lover of all things human, truthful and benign, was a poet. Was he shallow? Was he narrow? Here and there, undoubtedly; and he never sounded the depths of the minds that are oceans. He was rather like some great fresh-water lake. If these lakes have their shallows, they are transparent, and if they have their narrows, they are also large; and all manner of living things forgather in them, as they forgathered in Howells.

*Howells' home at 225 Beacon Street, the scene of* The Rise of Silas Lapham.

*The dean of literature. As an all-American mind, he was sensitive to new talents. There was scarcely a good new American writer whom Howells was not the first to acclaim and encourage.*

161

# Writers Strive for A Better World

*ideas of social reform find a voice in the writings of Henry George*

*as in the utopian stories of Bellamy.*

*Tolstoy, Howells said, "remade" his mind and awakened his social conscience.*

*Henry George wrote the most popular book of economics ever published:* Progress and Poverty, 1879.

*Howells' social consciousness,* — so marked in his New York years, — had been awakened by Tolstoy, who, as he said, remade his mind. He was drawn to the author of *Anna Karenina,* and it was not merely the artist that drew him. Tolstoy's Christian socialism appealed to him still more and had a profound effect on his life and writings. As he pondered the questions of the day, he felt that socialism alone could save the nation. All his major views passed through a sea-change, and even his own success smote his conscience. This change, — or this resurgence of Howells' original feeling, — was part of a widespread movement of the eighteen-eighties. Projects of reform were in the air.

This whole movement was fired in no small measure by the writings of one man. Henry George had returned to New York to stay in 1880, after writing *Progress and Poverty* in San Francisco, the most widely read book that had ever been written on economics, a book he had partly set up himself in type. By birth a Philadelphian, he had early been impressed on a visit to New York by the contrast of poverty and wealth and the slums of the city, a misery that appalled and tormented him, he said, and would not let him rest for thinking of what caused it and how it could be cured. A masterful, energetic man, short, bald, erect, with a reddish beard, he had had an adventurous life as a sailor and a printer. Desperately poor in San Francisco, with a family to support, he wrote for *The Californian* with Mark Twain and Bret Harte, studying the art of composition and the qualities of style for which he was widely known as an economist later, For, like Thorstein Veblen, Henry George was one of the few economists who counted as writers.

*Puck, the comic weekly, lampooned Henry George's taxless millennium.*

Why was it that the increase of wealth was invariably accompanied by an increase of want? And what was the cause of the recurrent industrial depressions? His answer came to him one day suddenly as he checked his horse on a hill over the water in San Francisco.

His advocacy of land-nationalization was a stirring reply to landlordism, the sensational bone of contention in the Irish rent-war. But the land-question at that time was a world-question as well, and Henry George soon had followers in every country. His agitation accelerated the general movement for a better social system, attained by whatever theory and whatever means. For he wrote with imagination and with passionate feeling, grieving over the human suffering and the tragic waste of human powers that were caused in part by unjust institutions.

In his theory, Henry George no doubt oversimplified human motives. But with Tolstoy, Edward Bellamy and others, he crystallized in the eighteen-eighties a widespread popular feeling for social reform, a feeling reflected in Howells' novels and in Mark Twain's *The American Claimant*.

*Henry George tried to put his theory* to a test in a "Western Plan," while the Massachusetts plan sprang from Edward Bellamy's *Looking Backward*.

Both Mark Twain and Howells favoured the movement and acclaimed this book. Howells wrote a preface for Bellamy's *The Blindman's World,* and he and this country editor had much in common; for, while Bellamy was a villager, — he lived at Chicopee Falls, — he had seen enough of the world to horrify him. He was convinced that America was going the way of the old world and losing its democratic hope and basis. He saw the future steadily growing darker. Within a few years, he had written *Looking Backward,* with his plan for a better system of human relations. A new political party sprang from his teachings.

Bellamy had a fresher mind than even this book suggested. He liked to play with stories about homeless ghosts and queer old doctors and young men who fall in love with portraits. The atmosphere of all these tales reflected the Yankee village life that Bellamy knew so well in the seventies and eighties. This was a world of lonely people who had lost their vital interests and were bored and ailing; and Bellamy's tales mirrored this boredom, as they also

Edward Bellamy
outlined in
Looking Backward
*a plan for better
human relations.*

mirrored the shifts by which the villagers tried to escape it.

In the small towns of which he wrote, with all their interest in pseudo-science, there was an interest in actual science also. Science stood for rest and comfort, anodynes for aching bones, peace for the heavy-laden, hope for all.

Bellamy's stories reflected this interest in science, and the vistas of the worlds of speculation to which it led, in astronomy, psychology, mechanics and physics. The dreamer in *The Cold Snap* enters interstellar space and experiences the ineffable cold that prevails there. The astronomer in *The Blindman's World* passes into a state of mind in which he is independent of his body. His consciousness visits Mars and finds that the Martians have developed beyond the earth-people. The physician in *Dr. Heidenhoff's Process* invents a galvanic-mesmeric device that extirpates unhappy recollections.

Ten years after Bellamy, H. G. Wells began to write similar stories. Wells, a student of science in London, was full of the same ideas. He imagined time-machines and visits to Mars and trances from which the sleeper wakes in a world that has changed beyond all recognition. With Wells, as with Bellamy earlier, these fantasies led to Utopia-building. For both were obsessed with the miseries of the social system, and for both science seemed to point the way to a just and more sensible order of things.

# The Problem of Europe in American Breasts

*artists and writers leave America, where "the sky is of brass and iron." Others meet the native challenge.*

*The Utopian novel indicated* disapproval of present-day America, and there were other voices and acts of protest. The atmosphere of the new generation, the rush for money, the corruption repelled the imaginative mind. The great hegira had begun that was to take so many abroad, — Bret Harte, Whistler, Henry James, and others. Charles Godfrey Leland expressed the feeling of frustration behind this exodus when he wrote: "I have nothing to keep me here. There is nothing to engage my ambition." He went to Europe, to return only for visits.

The old culture had broken down, the old causes were dead and forgotten, and no new ideal had arisen to rally the minds of the younger men; and, while many turned westward, almost as many turned towards Europe, in despair of the civilization they saw before them. Of these, the younger

Henry James was the great exemplar in years to come; but there were numbers of others, from New England and elsewhere, who also sought for haunts of ancient peace.

For most writers, the question of facing the new America, with its worship of "bigness" and numbers, seemed overwhelming. The national mind was dispersed, clearly focussed only on the things of Mammon. How could a novelist handle this chaos? How could a philosopher synthesize it? Incapable of creating new esthetic patterns out of this native chaos, many American writers closed their minds to America and its problems. They agreed with Matthew Arnold that for the artist there was no room in a country where "the sky was of brass and iron." Henry James' yearning for Europe had the same motive; to forget America, — hard, crude, vacant, with its terrible glare. For him, as for many other sentient artists and writers, the drama of Europe in American breasts remained a central problem.

Naturally, the artists themselves, the painters, sculptors and architects, were those who felt most powerfully the attraction of Europe. The element of "native character" that had given strength to the

*Albert Ryder and Winslow Homer accepted local conditions, and so founded a new American art.*

### THE STAY AT HOMES

*Those whose local attachments were deep chose America. They remained in the frying pan and paid the full price of their courage. They felt that whatever artists gained in Europe was less than what they lost by living there.*

earlier artists and that strengthened the home-grown artists of the age to come had little weight for Whistler, for instance, and Sargent, predestined cosmopolitans, like Henry James. Whistler and Sargent, like Henry James, achieved pre-eminence even in Europe as masters of technical processes. The brilliance of these artists no one questioned, and for many this virtuosity was all-sufficient. For others, it was insufficient, either then or later; they saw that both Whistler and Sargent were light-armed soldiers of art. Since they did not have their "native character" to deal with, they could turn their whole attention to technical questions. It was natural that Whistler, Sargent and James should have excelled in technique all but the greatest of the Frenchmen.

Many of the young writers returned from Europe after a stay of a few months or even some years, prompted by their essential Americanism, with all that this implied in regard to the old world. It implied a divided life for them, and deeper than all this was the general feeling that America, at its lowest reach, was better than Europe. Howells and Mark Twain, the Western writers, were those who took this feeling most for granted; but even Henry James confusedly shared it. Sargent shared it also, and so did Whistler, who remained, with all his blague, a "West Point man."

### THE EXPATRIATES
*There were many artists and writers who were repelled by the tumultuous air of the new America. They hankered for the repose of England. Many Americans, once they had arrived there, felt their hearts tremble over the question of what the English thought of them and whether they would be accepted as social equals.*

*Sargent, in London not over-burdened with "native character," achieved technical mastery.*

*Whistler, with all his Franco-English swagger, remained at bottom a West Point man.*

*James, who had chosen Europe, could not, in the end, come to grips with Europe.*

# Henry James

Henry James, Senior
and Junior, 1854.

*after giving this country a good*

*trial, he looked for*

*Europe as his home.*

*Henry James, Sr., an amateur reformer* and subsoil plower (as his friend Emerson called him), was drawn to Europe, but he always returned to America. He lived at times in New York, but latterly in Boston, where he enjoyed the meetings of the Radical Club and where he abounded in his own humour.

Generally speaking, he adored his country; and although, in America, he often longed for Europe, he longed much more for America as soon as he got there. When William James was born, — his eldest son, — Emerson bent over the cradle and gave him a blessing. This was in a New York hotel, the infant philosopher's birthplace, for hotels were a constant element in the life of the Jameses. The family had large means, and the elder Henry James preferred a detached existence on behalf of his children. He was vaguely opposed to their going to college, opposed to their forming any attachments that might perhaps lead to their undoing; for so many of his brothers and cousins had come to grief that he was afraid of America, or afraid of New York, as a nursery for the younger generation.

The elder James brooded over his children's problems, for, more than anything else, he was a parent. He was one of those uncrystallized geniuses who are often the parents of real geniuses with a largeness and power of nature that everyone felt; and if, in the autumn of his days, he had come to Boston, it was mainly for the welfare of his offspring.

His sons William and Henry were "hotel children," floating vaguely about the world. They knew nothing of politics or business, the primary occupations of their sex. The historical instinct of the country was scarcely in them, though the elder James was American through and through. In later years, William James adjusted himself to this condition; he over-adjusted himself, in fact, a little. For was not his "plunge into the muddy stream of things" a more or less conscious reaction against this detachment? He might have been described as more American than the Americans, as Henry James was less, or rather different, — he became more English than the English. Both had to fight for a local foothold, and both were constrained to overdo it. Meanwhile, Henry was "at sea" about his "native land" and all it represented for a storyteller.

When he arrived in Cambridge, therefore, the younger Henry James' mind was torn already by a problem that he never really solved. He was bent on becoming a novelist, but novelists always had "native lands." Yet as he looked at his "huge, queer country" he felt he could scarcely endure an American existence. He had been struck too deeply by the "outland dart," he had absorbed the "European virus." The English writers had filled his mind, and he knew the names of the London streets as he never knew the streets of New York. America, for him, afforded no objects of interest to compare with this European "fantastication."

The problem remained on James' hands unsolved during all the years that he was to spend in Cambridge. That he tried hard to solve it one saw in his earlier stories, in which he showed with what determination he strove to meet the exactions of the "native soil," to become an American novelist, a successor to Hawthorne. For, as to his being a novelist, this question was settled, whatever the

166

Ambrotype taken in Boston
at age of about 16.

At Newport, aged 20, when he
was a student at Harvard.

At the time of his temporary
return to America, 1882.

With his brother William James,
at the turn of the century.

In 1912, taken
in London by
E. O. Hoppe.

conditions might be. No one had ever possessed a clearer vocation, and his mind was an inexhaustible well of stories.

To test his feeling Henry James had crossed and recrossed the Atlantic trying to solve his great dilemma, whether to live at home or to live in Europe. In 1875 he settled in Paris, and it seemed at first that he meant to remain there, partly because Paris was the best of meeting-places in which to view his countrymen abroad. He had concluded that the "international novel" was the type that he was qualified to write; and where were the auspices happier for a writer of novels?

So, for a twelvemonth, Henry James lived in Paris, in constant association with La Farge's friends and the novelists whom he had studied with rapture at home. Art, he had always felt, lives on discussion, the interchange of views, the comparison of standpoints; and in Paris, the Goncourts, Flaubert, Turgenev and Zola, gave him a place in their circle. James had never dreamed of such conversation, such confidences about plans and ambitions, such counsels of perfection that spoke of an intense artistic life. The intelligence of these writers was truly infernal.

All this confirmed James' resolution to carry his art of the novel to a pitch of perfection. How deep this resolution was one saw in his work and his prefaces later, but the themes of many of his stories also showed it. In the continual recurrence of this motive one saw how much his own development occupied James' mind; and there were other motives that drove him forward. He had to justify his expatriation; and he had to counterbalance his Amer-

*Daisy Miller, the rich girl from Schenectady, an "inscrutable combination of audacity and innocence," was misprized in Europe and died. Innocence wronged and at the mercy of the dark old world was the theme of most of the works of James. That he himself had failed to take root in England was evident as time went on.*

ican birth. For James believed that art was a European secret. An American, to excel, had just ten times as much to learn as a European.

At the end of a year, however, James moved to London. He had wearied of the company of the French writers. He felt that he could not establish relations in France; and to know the great world of Europe, to penetrate its secrets,— this had been James' object in coming abroad. "I feel forever how Europe keeps holding one at arm's length," he wrote in one of his letters, "and condemning one to a meagre scraping of the surface."

*James had been drawn to London as* one of the "American claimants" for whom it was a paradise as well as a world.

He was soon in the centre of the picture. He shared the prerogatives of travelling Americans in realms that native writers seldom entered. James submitted himself to the "Londonizing process." He dined out almost every evening; by day and by night he roamed the streets. He went everywhere, shy, sedate, grave and watchful, with his guarded, formal manner and his dark brown beard.

Meanwhile, in a rapid succession of novels and

stories, James pictured the world of wanderers that he knew so well, the Americans in Europe whom he had watched as a child and whom he was encountering in his peregrinations. Who were these Americans, and what were the motives that drew them abroad? Most of them were products of the post-war years. The drop of the national thermometer had alienated many, who had lost interest in their country. The men existed to make money, and the women were bored by business and knew nothing about it. With leisure on their hands, in a world that made no provision for leisure, they were drawn to Europe, where leisure was an art.

What happened to the migrant Americans in the novels of James? There were prettily innocent Daisy Millers who lived in a round of dressing and dancing. They had found, at Vevey, a better Saratoga, and they flitted hither and thither in their muslin flounces. Sometimes they nursed a secret dream of marrying a son of the Crusaders.

They drifted about in isolated groups, satisfied merely to bask in the sunlight of Europe. They floated on the edges and surfaces of things. They

*Scene from* Washington Square.

*James walking with J. M. Barrie in London. England was a paradise to James, and he submitted himself readily to the "Londonizing process."*

were charmed and then they were beguiled; for they were usually innocent creatures, virginal, upright, and open-hearted, and in almost every case they came to grief. Daisy Miller was misprized and died. Isabel Archer was led astray, like Roderick Hudson and so many others, — for innocence wronged was the theme of James' work. And this innocence was American innocence at the mercy of the dark old world that so charmed it, deceived it, destroyed it and cast it away.

James seemed to feel, from first to last, that the world into which they were drawn, the great world of Europe, and especially England, was arrogant, base, corrupt, insolent and greedy; and that he himself had failed to take root in England was more and more evident every day in his work.

This was the outstanding fact that explained the events of his middle years, the vague anxieties that weighed upon him, the nature of his later work and the strange hiatus in his career in which he abandoned the novel and turned to the theatre with results that were calamitous and futile.

Charmed as he was with England, he had too little in common with it. He was lost, as he said, in the "fathomless depths of English equivocation." Hovering about the English mind, circling round and round it, hankering for some deeper initiation, he was perpetually baffled, like the people in his later novels who hovered about one another with the same effect of strained curiosity. At the same time, in this alien world, with which his relations were so tenuous, he drifted further and further from life itself. He lost his feeling for the "vital facts of human nature," as his brother William said.

*It was obvious in these later years* of Henry James that the living sense of objective reality had slipped from his grasp, and that he often was reduced to the "grain of suggestion." What concerned him now was form, almost regardless of content, the problems of calculation and construction. His characters were to grow dimmer and dimmer, like flames of an exhausted lamp, while his technical virtuosity worked its wonders.

It was in this period that he developed the method which remained as a model for novelists in days to come. He had emerged as a passionate mathematician of art. Wonderful metaphors blossomed in his pages, like airplants from the tropics. All the devices of James, in which he rejoiced as a craftsman, served him as a smoke-screen behind which to vanish; for had he not always been fleeing from something, the American self that he deprecated and that he longed to lose in the European?

The world of the later James was a subjective world, peopled by dim projections of the author's fancy. Its figures drifted about in a curious limbo as insubstantial as ghosts. But James could turn everything into art. His own perplexities served him well; and, if his people were ghosts, he could make ghosts people. Playing his labyrinthine games, James remained a happy man, with a sense that, if he was a mystagogue, he was a master. He knew he was teaching novelists in times to come to look for the half-resolutions, the nuances of motive, the velleities, disinclinations, misgivings, obsessions that also govern the mind. For them he extended the sphere of human consciousness, even as he added greatly to the novelist's craft.

But James somehow felt that he had been deluded, like the American characters in so many of his stories. Innocence and good will exploited and abused remained James' theme to the end of the chapter. Was it not the story of the scrupulous child in himself who had toiled up the slope of the British Olympus and found that the gods had turned into "cats and monkeys"?

Sensitive as his later novels were, impressive as technical achievements, James' great tales had dealt with Americans at a time when he had understood them. He had then been at home with himself in his own domain, alert, witty, tender, benevolent, freely at play with a world that he saw from above and behind, from without and within. That had been his major phase, although he remained to the end an artist of extraordinary power and a lover of perfection, with an inexhaustible fund of ideas and subjects and a style that was often magnificent; and those for whom his later novels were grey webs of speculation, peopled with phantoms in a fog, could always rejoice in his shorter tales. There, in *The Pupil* and *Brooksmith*, in *The Author of Beltraffio* and *The Beast in the Jungle*, in *The Turn of the Screw*, flawless and full in their tone and structure, with their softly flowing outlines, one saw him in his clearest autumnal beauty.

*The Garden Room, Lamb House, Rye, the study of James.*

# *Emily Dickinson*

*withdrawn from the world, she wrote her fairylike*

*poems that "moved like bees upon a raft of air."*

*The Dickinsons lived in the* principal house in Amherst. A large square red-brick mansion that stood behind a hemlock hedge, with three gates accurately closed, it was a symbol of rural propriety and all the substantialities of western New England. Edward Dickinson, the lawyer, had always had his office in the village, and four times a day, in his broadcloth coat and beaver hat, with a gold-headed cane in his hand, he had passed through one of the gates, going or coming. He was said to have laughed on one occasion, but usually he was as cold and still as the white marble mantel in his parlour.

While the Dickinson mansion was somewhat forbidding, with the stamp of the Squire's grim ways and his invalid wife, his son Austin's villa next door was a centre of hospitality with its rolling lawns and charming garden. But the eldest daughter Emily did not share in this hospitality.

Emily usually "elfed it" when visitors came. She was always in the act of disappearing. Through the blinds of her western windows, overlooking the garden, she observed the hospitalities of the villa, and snatches of whatever was current in the books and talk of a college town, in the politics and thought of the moment, reached her when the guests had gone away. But even her friends seldom saw her. While sometimes, in the evening, she flitted across the garden, she never left the place by day or night. To have caught a fleeting glimpse of her was something to boast of.

While her friends seldom saw Emily, they were used to receiving little letters from her. The letters

*The Dickinson house at Amherst.*

*Emily Dickinson's father.*

themselves were brief and cryptic, usually only a line or two: "Do you look out tonight?" "The moon rides like a girl through a topaz town." Now and again, some fine phrase emerged from the silvery spray of words. But her messages often contained no words at all. She would lower baskets of goodies out of the window to children waiting below. It was evident that Miss Dickinson had lost the art of communication, as the circle of her school-friends understood it. She vibrated towards them, she put forth shy impalpable tentacles. But she did not speak the language of the world outside her. She had been a recluse since the early sixties, and her family surmised the reason. She had fallen in love with a married man, a Philadelphia clergyman, and had buried herself at home by way of refuge.

Her inner life took a definite turn when Thomas Wentworth Higginson entered the picture. Higginson had written an appeal in *The Atlantic,* addressed to the rising generation. He said that to find a "new genius" was an editor's greatest privilege. If any such existed who read *The Atlantic,* let him court the editor, — "draw near him with soft approaches and mild persuasions." Higginson added a number of admonitions: "Charge your style with life . . . Tolerate no superfluities . . . There may be years of crowded passion in a word, and half a life in a sentence."

Presently Colonel Higginson, who was living in Worcester, received an odd little letter. The letter was unsigned, but the writer sent four poems, and she placed in a separate envelope the signature

"Emily Dickinson." She begged this distant friend to be her "master."

She continued to send him poems at intervals, signing her notes "your gnome" and "your scholar." In one note she said, "If I read a book and it makes my whole body so cold no fire can ever warm me, I know that is poetry. If I feel physically as if the top of my head were taken off, I know that is poetry. These are the only ways I know it. Is there any other way?"

At last Higginson visited Emily in Amherst in 1870. In her enigmatic remarks, during the visit, she seemed to the amiable Higginson as unique and remote as Undine or Mignon or Thekla. There was something abnormal about her, he felt. He had never met anyone before who drained his nerve-power so much.

At that time, Miss Dickinson was forty years old and had long since withdrawn from the world; and the friends who came to see her sister were used to the "hurrying whiteness" that was always just going through a door.

That Miss Dickinson in her solitude had been writing poems, very few of her friends knew. They all knew the little rhymes she sent them with arbutus buds, but they did not know how seriously she pursued her writing, at night, beside the Franklin stove, in the upstairs corner bedroom, by the light that often glimmered over the snow. From her window she had caught suggestions that gave her a picture, a fancy, an image. A dead fly on the windowpane stirred her imagination. She saw the bluebirds darting round and these observations went into her verses. She wrote on sheets of note-paper, which she sewed together, rolling and tying the bundles with a thread or a ribbon and tucking them away in the drawers of her bureau; sometimes the back of an envelope served her as well. But, casual in this, she was anything but casual, — she was a cunning workman, — in her composition. Poetry was her solitaire; she watched the motions of her mind, recording its ebbs and flows and the gleams that shot through it.

The visible setting of these poems was the New England countryside, the village, the garden, the household that she knew so well, a scene, the only scene she knew, that she invested with magic, so that the familiar objects became portents and symbols.

Her whimsies sometimes turned into bold ideas. She domesticated the universe and read her own experience into the motions of nature and the world she observed. The wind had fingers and combed the sky, and March walked boldly up and knocked like a neighbour. The moon slid down the stairs for her "to see who's there," and the grave for her was a little cottage where she could "lay the marble tea." She saw hope, fear, time, future and past as persons to rally, welcome, play with, or tease.

The turns of fancy that marked these poems were sharp and unpredictable, and yet they were singularly natural, — nothing was forced. Miss Dickinson lived in a world of paradox, for, while her eye was microscopic, her imagination dwelt with mysteries and grandeurs. To juxtapose the great and the small, in unexpected ways, had been one of her prime amusements as the wit of her circle, and this, like the laconic speech that also marked the Yankee, had remained an essential note of her style as a poet.

The poems were fairylike in their shimmer and lightness, they moved like bees upon a raft of air; and yet one felt behind them an energy of mind and spirit that only the rarest poets have possessed. Where others merely glowed, she was incandescent.

Emily Dickinson died in 1886 at Amherst in the red-brick house where she was born. Fifty-six years old, she had been for a while an invalid and more invisible than ever. She had left word to have her poems burned. She had kept them in envelopes and

boxes in her desk and her bureau, rolled like parchment in bundles bound with ribbons. Her sister destroyed her papers; then, struck by the poems, she saved them in a fever of excitement. She turned them over to Higginson, and four years later they began to appear in the series of volumes that announced a unique and original American poet.

The Dickinson children,
Emily, Austin and Lavinia.

A typical note from Emily.

*The new novel. Water colour by Winslow Homer, 1877.*

*"Reading harness, a boon to housewives," lampoons women's interest in literature.*

*One of the great changes in literary* taste after the war followed the ascendency of women as both writers and readers. There were fifty thousand "extra" women in Massachusetts alone, women who were widowed by the war, or whose lovers had died in the war, or who had been left behind in the movement of the young men westward.

In New Haven the story was told that a student threw a stone at a dog and, missing him, hit seven old maids. The "glorious phalanx of old maids" that rejoiced the heart of Theodore Parker was to dominate New England for an age to come, the age of the "strong-minded women" that might have been called the age of the weak-minded men. Hawthorne had complained, years before, of the "damned mob of scribbling women" who were swarming all over America; and the clan of women writers grew apace. They won their influence by default. In the new frenzy of speculation, the excitement over oil and railroads, the absorption of young men in business, literary and ethical interests and those involving human rights were taken over by women.

Helen Hunt Jackson, the author of *Ramona,* which appeared in 1884, was an impulsive, attractive, clever woman who called herself "H. H." Emily Dickinson's early friend, she had long been a popular author when she wrote this book, her only work that later times remembered. Her prose and her verse were alike undistinguished till she happened on a theme that stirred her to the depths and electrified her talent for a moment.

"H. H." had gone to Colorado in search of health, and the state of the Indians there excited her pity. As she studied their history, the conquest of the Indians by the whites, the old crusading zeal of the Yankee abolitionists awoke in this mind of a later indifferent New England. She thereupon determined to write the romance that paralleled *Uncle*

*Tom's Cabin,* the book that roused the popular mind to the sorry state of the conquered race and led to a change of policy in dealing with it. *Ramona* thus became a part of American history. With all its faults, this novel remained, with its high vitality, a popular classic.

*H. H. Jackson aroused with* Ramona *the public's feeling for the suffering of the Indians.*

# Gain in Influence

*with men immersed in business, women take*

*over literary and ethical interests.*

*Miss Jewett in her South Berwick home. Her stories pictured the town with sympathetic insight.*

*Sarah Orne Jewett spoke for a New England* that seemed to be fading and dying. But her people were genuine Yankees and stood for the rest. They all reflected her own transcendent self-respect.

Miss Jewett lived at South Berwick in Maine, twelve miles from Portsmouth. She was "one of the doctor's girls," as people called her. Born in 1849, the daughter of Dr. Jewett, who had once been a professor at Bowdoin College, she had grown up in a world of square white houses, picket fences, some of them ornamental, with high posts and urns. As the port declined, one felt as if the clocks in the town had stopped, and as if the population had stopped with them. The gravestones outnumbered the people.

As a girl Miss Jewett was often with her father, who liked to take her with him on his rounds. As they drove along, they discussed the household of some patient, or the doctor described some incident in the family's life. The doctor was a local historian, although he never recorded these stories, but they helped Miss Jewett to understand her people, and to understand her people was all she wished. For Miss Jewett was a natural story-teller. She saw stories on every side, — in a funny old man in a linen duster, in an old countrywoman on the train, in a poor old soul who had run away from an almshouse.

*The Atlantic* accepted one of her sketches when she was not yet twenty, and eight years later, in 1877, she published her first little volume. This book, called *Deephaven,* was the story of two Boston girls who came to spend the summer in a town like Berwick. They opened the long-closed Brandon House and rediscovered their family past in the relics and bundles of letters in the drawers of the desks. Miss Jewett found her own world in the persons of these Boston girls, and Howells caught, in the delicate fancy that marked this youthful book, the note of a rare new talent.

Sometimes she went to Tenant's Harbour, where, in the summer, she hired the schoolhouse for fifty cents a week and strolled to her morning's work through a bayberry pasture. In this "country of the pointed firs," with its long frost-whitened ledges and its barren slopes where flocks of sheep moved slowly, she found the Dunnet shepherdess and Mrs. Todd, the herbalist, and many of the scenes and persons of her finest stories, — stories, or sketches, rather, light as smoke or wisps of sea-fog, charged with the odours of mint, wild roses and balsam.

Most of the people she described were like the trees that grew in the cracks of the rocks and kept their tops green in the driest summer. Miss Jewett knew where to find their living springs. No one since Hawthorne had pictured this New England world with such exquisite freshness of feeling.

# The Poet
## "Silenced by Science"

*Thomas Bailey Aldrich wore a waxed moustache, the symbol of his mundane taste.*

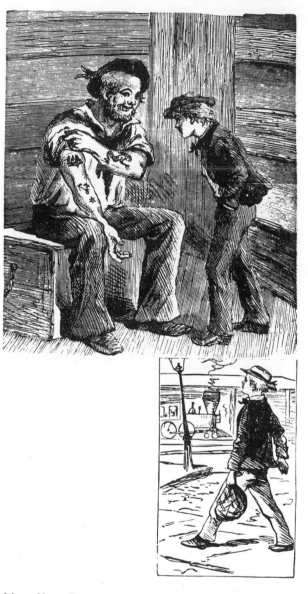

*With Howells and James, Miss Jewett* and others, the interest in fiction steadily grew in the eighties. Meanwhile, the interest in poetry lapsed, perhaps because, as Godkin said, the spread of science "killed the imagination." The poets seemed to be disappearing in the regions where they had thriven of old. They seemed to have retired before civilization. No new poets of equal scope had appeared in the train of the older poets, who were gradually falling silent, one by one. It was true that Emily Dickinson, in her hermitage at Amherst, excelled in her special intensity all but the greatest; but Miss Dickinson throve in conditions that throttled the rest. The great social causes and the spiritual causes that had stirred the romantic poets of the earlier time, the faiths and the adorations all were gone; and poetry was left high and dry in a world that had ceased to nourish poets, who remained as idle singers of empty days.

The best of all these idle singers was Thomas Bailey Aldrich. This alert little man, blond, erect, ruddy and jaunty, had arrived in Boston as recently as Howells. Born in Portsmouth, he described himself as Boston-plated because he had lived in New York in his formative years. He wore a waxed moustache, the symbol of his mundane tastes, in the style of Napoleon III, the Paris-plated. His magazine, *Every Saturday,* reprinted selections from foreign papers, reflecting the new cosmopol-

The Story of a Bad Boy — *a picture of Aldrich's childhood in Portsmouth, New Hampshire.*

*Marjorie Daw, lovely beyond compare. The novelist's dream of the perfect reader.*

itan interests of Boston. It was "eclectic," to use a word that was much in vogue, and Aldrich's own mind was eclectic also, — it borrowed freely from every source that appealed to a roving fancy. He was a lesser Lowell, a "household poet" already in 1866.

By 1881, when Aldrich took Howells' place on *The Atlantic,* his own best-known work had already appeared. He was popularly respected as a poet and a story-teller whose writing was always accomplished and sometimes brilliant. In his cool and polished prose and verse, he revealed himself as a notable craftsman. His writing was undoubtedly distinguished. It was lucid, skilful, crisp and fresh; and the neat-handed Aldrich always knew when to stop, an unusual virtue. The fluent elder poets had not possessed it. Aldrich's care was not to say too much, and these literary virtues marked his stories.

Their touch was almost invariably expert and clever. *Marjorie Daw,* the cleverest, was the novelist's dream of the perfect reader, in a day when the novelist's readers were mostly young ladies. For Marjorie was lovely beyond compare; and what was she doing under the trees, lying in her hammock, swaying like a pond-lily? Reading, — and what but a novel? — and a novel by whom? Would not Howells and Henry James have liked to know?

Aldrich's most original invention, *The Story of a Bad Boy,* was destined, on all accounts, for the longest life. This picture of Aldrich's childhood at Portsmouth was the first of the series of books about boys that his friends of Mark Twain's circle were soon to write. In this somewhat inglorious post-war epoch, boyhood seemed better than manhood. At least, the leading authors wrote about it with a relish they seldom brought to the rest of life.

Round Aldrich, as an editor, clustered most of the other poets who spoke for this twilit world of the later New England. The characteristic note of the earlier poets, through whom the American scene had found expression, was lost in its general reversion to English models. These poets, — imitators of Tennyson all, — were the "caged warblers" whom Amy Lowell silenced in her effort to revivify poetry thirty years later; and indeed their weary verse, as Miss Lowell called it, devitalized, nebulous, dim, slipping along the path of least resistance, invited, and even demanded, a bold reaction.

# Epilogue ~

*With the advance of the nineties,* the New England mind was steeped in disappointment and chagrin. The impulse that had characterized it seemed to be exhausted, and its mood was sad, relaxed and reminiscent. "We are vanishing into provincial obscurity," wrote Barrett Wendell, the Harvard professor, in 1893. "America has swept from our grasp. The future is beyond us."

But the older were the bolder in Boston, as elsewhere; and the older and bolder, the less inclined they were to think the world was going to the dogs. They were tough enough to know that the good was tough; and, like all true aristocrats, they believed in their country, if only because their country included themselves. The patriarchs and matriarchs such as Edward Everett Hale, who looked like an untidy pilgrim father, and Julia Ward Howe, the romantic old sibyl, were prepared to take the long view. These magnanimous worthies, for whom nothing had ever existed that was common or mean, were destined to see mankind as forever triumph-

ant. They ignored the signs of the times and lived above them, as Emerson had lived all his life.

But the Yankee stock which had leavened the nation was somehow wearing thin. The stories of many writers were preoccupied with the ends of things, families running out, forlorn old women, ramshackle dwellings, lone eccentrics. The almshouse and the village pensioner figured largely in these stories. All the authors took fag-ends for granted. Their theme was desolation doing its best, or so at least it seemed to Boston readers; and up and down the scale, from roots to flowers, the New England mind repeated its tale of exhaustion.

Had Hawthorne perhaps been right when he said to Howells that the apparent coldness of the Yankees was real, that the suppression of emotion for long generations would extinguish emotion at last in the soul of New England?

Literature seemed indeed to have vanished from Boston. The Bostonians felt so. The bells tolled every year for a great man gone: Lowell in 1891,

*FROM FARM TO FACTORY*

178

Whittier in 1892, in 1893 Francis Parkman. Holmes, who died in 1894, had lived to "sing the swan-song for the choir." These were "pitch-pine" Yankees of the stoutest timber. They had withstood the storms that battered down the lesser men, and the second growth had yielded few equals or rivals.

Holmes' verse had had its day, but his "high-bred amicability," — Goethe's word for Molière, — was a lasting possession. He had permanently enriched the Yankee scene with his genius of good sense and his gaiety and vigour. Green was the golden bough of life for him.

Whittier, too, stood lastingly for the gods of New England, the passion for goodness and justice and the household lares; and Parkman, who never drew morals, lived the moral that all his books conveyed. These men had fought good fights in one way or another, and all of them had won the Promethean prize. They had carried their lamps unextinguished to the end of the race.

Literature proper seemed to be evaporating. In Gautier's verses, the bust outlived the city, but in Boston the bust had also outlived the poem. Literature became merely literary, — to use the phrase of the hour, — because it had lost its native impulse. It was driven to follow models more abjectly than ever, and models that were also arbitrary, unlike the coördinated models of the earlier writers, who had borne an organic relation to the men they followed. Learning took the place that poetry had held in a day when men shared heroic passions; and no one better than Bostonians knew what this implied, however their prosperity had grown.

Boston was left to gather up its relics, with a feeling that its forbears had had "all the fun." The New Yorkers laughed when Oliver Herford characterized New England as "the abandoned farm of literature." The Bostonians did not laugh, — the barb struck home. *The North American Review* had gone to New York, and *The Atlantic Monthly* was doing its best to forget that it represented Boston.

There brooded over the town, as a stranger noted, "an immense effect of finality," as if all intellectual movement had ceased there, and a dreadful sense of conviction overcame this stranger at a certain club of Boston bibliophiles. The mind of the world was dead, he said to himself; and this was a distribution of souvenirs. "I felt," H. G. Wells recalled, "that all the books had been written, all the pictures painted, all the thoughts said." Wells, dismayed, rushed from the room and roamed through the streets in the moonlight, till he caught the glimpse of a ray in a bookseller's window; and there, in fresh covers, lay books that had just come out. The mind of the world was still alive! — in spite of the bibliophiles and in spite of Boston.

*FROM COVERED WAGON TO RAILROAD*

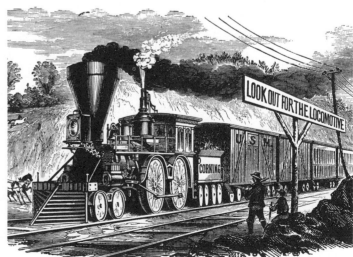

# Book Five

# The Confident Years:

# 1885 — 1915

*In the decade preceding 1890* the growth of the great American cities had gradually changed the character of the country and the people, and the tone of the rising civilization was less and less rural and agricultural and more and more industrial and urban. New York had become a world-metropolis and Chicago, with almost a million inhabitants, had become the second city of the nation, with Detroit, Milwaukee, Columbus and Cleveland expanding in the Middle West, where the centre of population had come to lie.

On every hand one heard the phrase "the lure of the great cities," and the comic press and the stage abounded in jokes about "hayseeds" and "rubes" and the old American life of the village and the farm. Many novelists pointed out that the farm and the village were moribund while their characters dwelt on the curse of existence in the country, where life was sad and sterile with its unrelieved physical strain and its sternly narrowed groove of toil and thought. Since the writers could no longer live in communion with nature, they turned to the city.

To many of the new novelists, the city was enchanting, compact of marvels or horrors but magical in charm, and they saw it with some of the excitement of Balzac in the Paris of sixty years before and the special wonder of American country boys. Theodore Dreiser and "O. Henry" Porter were only two of a score of young men who were soon to evoke this magic of the modern great city, where at every corner, as one of them said, fingers beckoned or eyes besieged and the perilous clues of adventure were slipped into one's hands.

From the breadline and the morgue to the glow of the crowds at night, the newcomers were spellbound with sensations in this whirlpool of life; and while there was much of the provincial still in the literary tone of New York, the world-influences that emanated from Howells, who had come here from Boston in 1890, flowed through many others. Well before the turn of the century the town was becoming the "new cosmopolis" in literature as in every other sphere.

The great theme of debate in the nineties, in literary circles, was the battle between realism and romanticism, especially in the novel, a subject which *The Atlantic Monthly* had been airing in the seventies and eighties, or ever since the advent of Howells and Henry James. While realism generally won the day, with democracy and science, — which, in a fashion, it expressed through the art of fiction, — the romantic mind had its revenge in popular novels.

The popularity of the historical romances that appeared round the turn of the century, with their aristocratic feeling for the poetry of the past, concurred with the vogue of Henry Sienkiewicz. The vogue of Robert Louis Stevenson favoured it also. Besides, these romances fell in with the rule of the time that novels must deal with agreeable and palatable subjects, that they must end happily, that the leading characters must be beautiful and good and that even the base must have some redeeming virtue.

In time this convention of the fiction of the moment was to breed a reaction in the American mind and produce during two generations a variety of novel that reversed these more or less arbitrary laws of the nineties, which had required a note of "courage," a "measure of lawful and pure love" and "a happy marriage to come out of it all." The type of the American young-girl reader whom the novelist H. H. Boyesen described as the "Iron Madonna" was to disappear, — or at least she ceased to count as the arbiter of fiction, — she who, as Boyesen put it, "strangled the novelist in her embrace" and to whom he sacrificed all his "chances of greatness."

It was the plight of the novelist in this paradise of women to repress the best that was in him, Boyesen continued; but even in the nineties, with Stephen Crane and several other rising writers, the potent stream of realism made steady progress. It was more and more the settled tendency with Harold Frederic and Hamlin Garland, Frank Norris and Robert Herrick, — disciples of Howells, — who expressed the maturing of the national mind that followed the passing of the frontier, the new immigration and the sobering growth of the cities. In their fears for the way the country was going and their grave regrets for its broken promise, — regrets and fears that were shared by Mark Twain and Howells, by Henry Adams and so many others in the nineties, — they anticipated the feeling of countless Americans later; and this was a feeling that realism alone could convey.

# The Ghetto ~ A School for Writers

*their imagination was stirred by the colour and variety of the foreign types in the slums.*

*A ghetto newspaper.*
*Sketches by Jacob Epstein for* The Spirit of
the Ghetto, *by Hutchins Hapgood.*
*Sweatshop romance.*

*The old Rabbi.*

*Some of the writers and reporters* who came to New York were drawn to the fashionable up-town circles. Others discovered a new world in the down-town slums. The police reporters, Lincoln Steffens and Jacob A. Riis, were stirred by the misery and depravity they found in these sections. Jacob A. Riis in 1890 wrote *How the Other Half Lives* to describe the life of the poor, — the slum-dwellers, — in New York. Stirred in part by Riis' realistic tone, dozens of writers of the nineties were drawn to the slums, perhaps as readers of Tolstoy or Zola or seekers of Gorky's "creatures that once were men."

Other writers, drawn less by charity than for aesthetic reasons, turned to the slums in search of strong sensations. They were

182

interested in the types there also. They found the stir of the streets exciting after the dullness of village life, and the colour and variety of the crowds of Italians, Poles, Chinese and Russian Jews a relief from the ordinary drabness of an Anglo-Saxon world. Even the squalor possessed its attraction for minds that were tired of the unreality of so much contemporary American literature and art, minds for which all variations from the normal and the usual, however unlovely or sordid, had their charm. Here the writers and poets found fresh impressions and local colour.

Henry C. Bunner, the editor of *Puck,* was an ardent collector of slums, who wished, he said, not to miss any of them. His fellow-journalist, Lincoln Steffens, roamed the East Side and observed that in those days he was "almost a Jew." Steffens, a Californian, loved the ghetto, touched by its heart-breaking tragedies and the conflicts between the old and the new, the medieval parents and the children of the New York streets. In this exile-world of old-country merchants, artisans, teachers, rabbis and beggars, whatever one had known at home was turned upside down, and well-known grammarians sold papers for a living, poets became real-estate brokers and great Talmudic scholars pressed pants and coats.

Meanwhile, the ghetto had its own theatre and its poetry and press. One of its indigenous authors was Abraham Cahan, the novelist, who wrote in English. The editor of a great Yiddish paper, he had come to America in 1882, retaining the traits of many a Russian writer, admiring Tolstoy, Turgenev and Howells, who was also a Tolstoyan and who spread Cahan's reputation among American readers. His novel *The Rise of David Levinsky* was a typical story of the place and the times, the ascent of a millionaire cloak-manufacturer who had been a push-cart pedlar and who never outgrew his original love of learning.

No one knew this area better than Hutchins Hapgood, who described it a few years later in *The Spirit of the Ghetto.* This book was illustrated by a young sculptor, the Sir Jacob Epstein of later days, who was living in a Hester Street garret, entirely unknown. Epstein had observed from his window there many of the types which Hapgood described. Hapgood, though not an important writer, was a type of the new intellectual who was soon to abound in Greenwich Village. He was attracted not merely to the Jewish "intellectual debauchees" but almost equally to the down-and-outs on the benches of Washington Square, to tramps, pickpockets, shop-lifters and Chinatown misfits. He liked to associate with toughs whose speech was direct and picturesque, a language that was naturally literature, although nobody knew it, and who were the real thing in character for him, living and acting a drama for all to see.

Another explorer of the East Side and the Bowery was Josiah Flynt, who passed as a genuine bum, for he was an actor as well who could change his whole manner, his vocabulary and his accent in a moment. In time, as the writer of *Tramping with Tramps,* Flynt became the prime authority in the somewhat unsavoury field he had taken for his own, as much a master of the tramp world as Audubon had been of the world of birds.

*Abraham Cahan, ghetto novelist.*

*Josiah Flynt, student of tramps.*

*A clothes carrier.*

*He seemed equally hard-bitten and sensitive, lighthearted and cynical.*

# Stephen Crane

*one of the most puzzling and powerful American*

*authors, he wrote his masterwork at the age of 24.*

*Stephen Crane once told a friend:* "It was on the Bowery that I got my artistic education." This was the first phase of one whom the novelist Wells described as "beyond dispute, the best writer of our generation."

Just out of college in 1891, Stephen Crane had come to New York as a newspaperman. Bent on getting at the core of life, to observe it in the raw, he once slept in a Bowery shelter to watch the men there. He studied the bums and outcasts in City Hall Park, standing in the rain like chickens in a storm, and he haunted the doorways and lodging-houses round about Chatham Square that later appeared in some of his *Midnight Sketches*. Crane hoped to be able to picture these scenes with some of the intensity of Tolstoy.

These explorations of the New York slums resulted in 1893 in Crane's first novel, *Maggie, a Girl of the Streets*. It consisted of verbal impressions mainly, pictures of tenement scenes, the chaos of the back-yards, the side-doors of corner saloons whence children constantly emerged with pails of beer. A tragedy of a deserted girl of the East Side world, the book was remarkable for its visual power, as well as for its art of reporting conversation and the freshness that characterized Crane's later work.

But it was *The Red Badge of Courage* that made Crane famous overnight, the white-headed boy of the nineties in a dozen circles, the hero of editors, hostesses, reviewers, old soldiers and the men in the printing-shop who set the book up in type and read the proofs. What gave the book its immediate vogue? Its handling of one of the greatest themes, the novelty of its treatment of war as the private sees it, the "little man" who had always been the pet of the American imagination as the officer and the gentleman appealed to the imagination of Europe. Henry Fleming, the farmer's boy, the focus of interest in the tale, was "just one little feller" among a lot of others, and war as it impinged on him had a kind of actuality that readers had seldom found in a book before. They felt they were shuffling in the mud in Henry's shoes.

Yet Crane himself had known nothing of war in 1895, when *The Red Badge of Courage* appeared, outside of books, old magazines and old illustrations. Before writing the story, at the age of twenty-nine, in ten days and nights, Crane had pored over the drawings of Winslow Homer, those campaign sketches of the Civil War that corresponded in black and white to Whitman's notes on the soldiers

*Crane as a war correspondent on horseback. He took delight in danger and described with insight a man's sensation in the presence of death.*

184

in *Specimen Days*. Henry might have been one of Homer's figures, as he might easily have been one of the hardy intuitive quiet young men whom Whitman nursed in the hospitals in Washington in war-time.

Crane's men ran "with starting eyes and sweating faces," and they fell "like bundles" when they were shot, while the officers neglected to stand in the picturesque attitudes of the usual historical novels and battle-paintings. One saw, through constantly excited eyes, "each blade of the green grass . . . bold and clear" and one heard the woods crackle like burning straw and the "cat-spit" sound of the bullets that "kept pecking" at the men. These fresh new-minted images of life on the battle-field recurred in Crane's later books that dealt with war, — his leading theme as a writer of stories.

Crane's ruling passion was curiosity. He once remarked, "It must be interesting to be shot." He was drawn to war because it occasioned a sense of life at its highest pitch and challenged his own skill in conveying sensations precisely. No painter was ever more intent on stating what he saw, — leaving the deductions and the inferences to be drawn by the reader.

One could scarcely imagine anything less contrived than his *Whilomville Stories,* which had all the spontaneity and the naturalness of *Huckleberry Finn.* Indeed Crane was a bridge between Mark Twain and the writers who followed him later, as he was a bridge in poetry between Emily Dickinson and the "free-verse" poets.

Howells had read Emily Dickinson's poems to him and he had written *The Black Riders,* suggested by them. The frequent ellipses and the economy of style of these bitter little verses were to leave their mark on the poetry of the future.

In their generally bleak negativity these poems were emblematic of one of the most puzzling of American literary minds, a writer who seemed equally hard-bitten and sensitive, high-hearted and a cynic for whom war and life were meaningless and even absurd. He was interested in the types that fascinated Hemingway later in Key West and Cuba, while he prefigured the writers to come who liked to flaunt their pretended ignorance of "Balzac and Dostoy-what's-his-name." For his own "fast sharp seeing," he was un-rivalled. Eager for sensations, he was always ready to risk his own existence in order to know "how it felt," and he was so sensitive that neither the tremor of a butterfly's wing nor the quivering of a leaf ever escaped him. Crane's touch, moreover, was invariably light and swift. To use one of his own phrases, he wrote with the "pace of youth."

*The chaos of back-yards filled with slum children was the scene of Crane's first novel: "Maggie, A Girl of the Streets" (1893).*

*Winslow Homer's sketches were one of Crane's sources of inspiration for "The Red Badge of Courage."*

*Crane conveyed the terrible realities of battle with freshly minted images.*

185

*Emma Goldman: Her mind was filled with visions of a better world.*

*In cafés the intelligentsia met ... refugees from Russia, serving a cause, asserting the rights of man.*

*More and more after 1900, as* Hamlin Garland noted, the literary life of America centred in New York, where as many races were represented as there were in the crew of the "Pequod" in *Moby-Dick.* "Of all the ambitions of the great unpublished," said Frank Norris in *Blix,* "the one that is strongest, the most abiding is the ambition to get to New York." The young writers on their first dazzled approach to the wonderful and awesome town could scarcely contain their excitement. Many of the newcomers haunted the cafés in the Village or East Houston Street where Yiddish poets, cartoonists, playwrights and actors met around marble-topped tables.

It was in one of these cafés that Emma Goldman spent her first evening in New York, — the young corset-maker whose mind was filled with the glorious vision of a better world. These visionary ideas later found a focus in her magazine "Mother Earth," whose office, like Alfred Stieglitz's "291," became one of the liveliest centres of thinking in New York. The intelligentsia were joined here by political refugees from Russia, pale students with prison consumption, who mirrored every shade of revolutionary feeling. Most of them were devoted to movements "serving the cause," — asserting the brotherhood or the rights of man.

These thoughts soon reached the main stream of American literature. Emma Goldman discovered the new dramatists who were making literary history in Europe and awakening a social consciousness in people who might not have been reached in any other fashion. Strindberg had said that the modern artist was a "lay preacher popularizing the pressing questions of the time." Hauptmann described in *The Weavers* the age-long misery of labour, Bernard Shaw was discussing prostitution, Ibsen exposed the crimes committed against the unborn. Emma Goldman felt that these writers were destroying ignorance and fear and paving the way for the birth of a new free race. Literature for the rising generation ceased to be merely literary. It was regarded as a form of social dynamics, in the phrase of Floyd Dell. These ideas of reform and social consciousness focussed the minds of the writers as the cause of abolition had focussed them fifty years earlier.

*The muckrakers — Lincoln Steffens, Ida Tarbell and others — wrote stories of "frenzied finance," insurance, railroads, Pullman strike.*

186

*the muckrakers fought squalor, injustice and*

*corruption by means of the exposé, the drama, the novel.*

Upton Sinclair used the novel as a vehicle to spread his ideas of humanitarian reform. This young Baltimorean was one of those hyper-compassionate men who cannot sleep at night when they think of children working in mills. Convinced that society is ruled by organized greed, he felt that the burden of changing it rested upon him. He was a born promoter of isms, a teetotaller whose father had drunk too much and who ate raw food himself or none at all, a pacifist, a non-smoker, a physical-culture enthusiast and a "conscientious objector to capitalism." He always felt that by starting a magazine, writing a novel or winning a strike he might change the world into what it ought to be.

The main object of his scorn was the invisible government of business that created the system. He saw the resources and the wealth of the country thrown into an arena to be scrambled for and carried off by the greediest and strongest, and the world for him was a "slaughter-house where the many were ground up into sausages,"— as he presently wrote, — "for the breakfast of the few."

It was in 1906 that Upton Sinclair published *The Jungle,* the novel that Jack London described as the *Uncle Tom's Cabin* of wage-slavery and that was almost as important in its practical effects. This story of the stockyards affected legislation, but rather because the public was shocked by its revelations of the food-supply than because of the author's disclosure of social conditions.

The story was a nightmare and all quite true, — it was never disproved in any part, — and the book worked mightily for the physical welfare of the nation. Besides, it had a kind of vitality that appeared in Sinclair's later work and that sprang from his passionate feeling for outraged justice.

Personally a lover of all genuine goodness, Sinclair was weak as a novelist. His characters were too often puppets, and this remained true, in the future, in the *World's End* series that might have been one of the first great planetary novels. Still, Sinclair was never a writer to be taken lightly. As

an able and voluminous pamphleteer, he was a power in his time, one who stood consistently for the "deepest instinct of the human heart, the longing," as he put it, "for justice between man and man."

*Illustration from the Argentine edition of* The Jungle.

*Upton Sinclair at the time he wrote* The Jungle — *the Uncle Tom's Cabin of wage-slavery.*

# O. Henry

*hobnobbing with bums on park benches, he pictured*

*well the New York of the four million.*

*At about this time the publisher,* S. S. McClure, initiated a new dynamic form of journalism. The exposé articles he commissioned appealed to a large group of readers, — a huge new public with unexacting tastes. In turn, these new readers called into existence an expanding class of writers whose work was more or less comparable to the product of machines. Frank Norris and Theodore Dreiser were connected with these cheaper magazines, which produced an author of their own, the genius of the Sunday supplements, a North Carolinian who called himself "O. Henry."

This writer pictured the glittering city as he knew the provinces wished to see it, "inhabited by four million mysterious strangers" to whom almost anything might happen between sunrise and sunrise. These people had come from Topeka or Nome, from Jackson, Topaz or Cactus City, drawn by the love of money, by ambition or the stage. O. Henry, — William Sidney Porter, — wrote for the "folks back home" who liked to share vicariously in their imagined adventures.

O. Henry was the typical New Yorker of the popular saying, — the man who has come from somewhere else. Leaving North Carolina as a boy,

he had lived in Texas and in Central America, as well as in prison for three years, and all these settings he used in stories, forty of them dealing with Texas alone, where he had punched cattle, dipped sheep and worked in a bank.

In San Antonio, Porter, accused of embezzling, absconded to Honduras. In all probability he was innocent enough; his mistake was rather in running away, which made his case much worse when he was caught; and he was to live like a man condemned, under a veil, behind a mask, anonymous, pseudonymous, humbled for the rest of his existence. In the penitentiary he picked up stories on his night rounds from cell to cell, administering medicines, for he had been a druggist's assistant, stories that appeared in *The Gentle Grafter.* His first collection, *Cabbages and Kings,* consisted of tales of the Central American republics, where adventurers still thronged the cabinets of the rulers with proposals for railroads and concessions.

A handful of O. Henry's stories dealing with Latin America and Texas, where he had encountered desperadoes and witnessed a belated war with cattle-thieves, were among the best he was to write and by no means all trick stories of the artificial

*The City, inhabited by four million mysterious strangers to whom almost anything might happen between sundown and sunrise.*

*O. Henry's Coney Island.*

*From* The Gentle Grafter.

variety he produced so often. But, good as a few of these tales were, New York was really O. Henry's own, — it seemed to belong to him by right. He had come there in a sense to hide, to merge his identity in the crowd, after the profound humiliation of his experience in prison. O. Henry, who was forty when he arrived, was drawn to the "Four Million" as naturally as Edgar Saltus was drawn to the "Four Hundred," and he lived a solitary secret life, avoiding even literary friends or all but a handful of editors and newspaper men. Putting up in furnished rooms or in shabby hotels near Madison Square, where he hobnobbed with bums on the park benches, he cultivated the "little" people of Mr. Dooley and Stephen Crane, shop-girls and casual acquaintances picked up in bars. Humbled himself, with still humbler souls he could play the caliph in disguise.

He never ceased to be surprised by the wonders of a city where something was always happening round the corner. A piano-player in a cheap café might have shot lions in Africa, a bell-boy might have fought with the British against the Zulus, and O. Henry knew of an expressman who had been rescued from a cannibal feast when his arm was crushed for the stew-pot like the claw of a lobster. For the rest, in O. Henry's vision, the city was a quicksand. It shifted its particles constantly; it had no foundation. Its upper granules of today were buried tomorrow in ooze and slime, and mysteries followed one another closely in a town where men vanished like the flame of a candle that has been blown out.

O. Henry had a special feeling, even at times an incomparable feeling, for the sad millieu that he pictured in *The Furnished Room*. With what skill

*Humbled himself, with still humbler souls he could play the caliph in disguise.*

*O. Henry told stories of shop-girls who remained inviolate, mistress of themselves.*

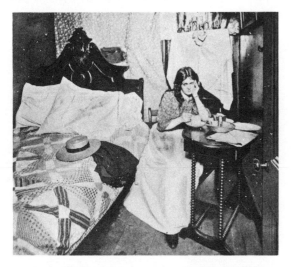

he described the ragged brocade of the chipped bruised chairs and the broken couch, distorted by bursting springs, the shredded matting that bulged in the rank sunless air. Over and over he told the stories of the girls whose parlour was the street-corner and whose garden-walk was the park. They dreamed of a bungalow on the shores of Long Island, or a home in Flatbush. Whatever their fate, they remained inviolate and mistress of themselves.

With his brisk and often too obvious stories, O. Henry was occasionally an artist who escaped from the mechanical formulas of the cheap magazines, the last to vindicate Howells' belief that the "more smiling aspects of life" were the most characteristic of America, as no doubt they had been.

189

# New York High Society

*old New York and the fatuities of the fashionable world found a penetrating chronicler in Edith Wharton.*

*Davis, the society man, sketched by Gibson.*

*Richard Harding Davis, the war correspondent, by Frederic Remington.*

*One of those dynamic types, often otherwise second-rate.*

*There were other writers in New York* whose milieu was Fifth Avenue. If these writers lacked the depth of Stephen Crane, they had a dash and daring that fired the imagination.

These were the times of Richard Harding Davis, a young man who was so dramatic in such a special way that he became the symbol of a "young man's epoch." Davis was one of those magnetic types, often otherwise second-rate, who establish patterns of living for others of their kind, and the notion of the novelist as war-correspondent which prevailed so long in American writing began in the early nineties undoubtedly with him. His legend was part of the atmosphere in which John Reed grew up, like Vincent Sheean, like Ernest Hemingway. He struck the note of a long generation in which the "kingly state of youth," — a phrase of Henry Harland, — ruled in letters.

Davis had arrived in New York in 1889, and he had written the Van Bibber stories about a young man of the "Four Hundred" that struck another note of the eighteen-nineties. Courtlandt Van Bibber, the perpetual bachelor who was everyone else's best man, was one of the characters of Davis that was drawn by Gibson, the American disciple of the English Du Maurier who had soon established a style of his own. Famous like Davis, the originator of the Gibson girl, whom countless young American women adopted as their model, satirized in his drawings in *Life* the fatuities of the fashionable world of New York and the "gold rush" of the Western millionaires.

A few years later, Edith Wharton was to picture this New York world of fashion "in all its flatness and futility," to quote her own phrase, and she was to show how "a frivolous society can acquire dramatic significance" and where its "tragic implication" lies.

Edith Wharton had grown up in the world she pictured in *Old New York,* in the "age of innocence," in the region of Washington Square, a time and place of which Henry James, her own predestined master, had caught the note he had known a generation before her. The circumstances that shaped her mind were much like those of Henry James, for, however much she was in America, she was of it only in a sense. The frontier did not exist for her, the Western world that was coming to the fore, nor the melting-pot that seethed in her native city. Europe was a large fact in her imagination. On the other hand, when she referred to the West, her tone assumed a marked hostility. She complained of its "soul-deadening ugliness."

Perhaps this conflict was only important in marking the limits of her world, the somewhat narrow field in which her talent blossomed. Certain it was that, as a writer, she was not at ease with American life when she left the small magic circle of her old New York. As a rule she could not yield herself to her native world as it actually was, she felt obliged to see it in terms of England, so that she constantly suffered lapses in which her people and her scenes no longer corresponded with the reality they assumed to represent. But Edith Wharton had a gift of creating atmospheres that extended to a score of scenes, from the Berkshires to North Africa, Italy, France and England. This power was marked in Edith Wharton, — it was perhaps the greatest of her gifts. It was one secret of the lasting charm of her tales of old New York, *False Dawn, The Age of Innocence, New Year's Day,* and it produced astonishing effects in some of the ghost and horror stories in *Here and Beyond* and *Certain*

*Edith Wharton as a debutante and in her later years, which she spent mostly in France.*

*People.* In its power of transporting the imagination, planting it elsewhere in space and time, few novels could have greatly surpassed *The Valley of Decision.*

Edith Wharton could always count on her magic carpet, — she had only to think of a scene to whisk one there. Her unusual gift of the pictorial phrase matched her gift of the atmospheric, for who else could evoke in two pages a livelier image than Edith Wharton evoked in half a dozen words? As marked as Edith Wharton's knowledge, her cleverness often sustained her even in the somewhat commonplace novels that she turned out year after year towards the end of her life, stories of Americans abroad or stories of the exile's return, noting the contrasts and the changes in their native New York. She only came into her own, at last, when she relived her old New York, when she gave up trying to defend it.

Was this not the secret of the beauty and the charm, the poetry of *The Age of Innocence, False Dawn, The Old Maid, The Spark, New Year's Day,* in which she reëntered the world of her childhood, almost with the vision of a child, a world that could not be defended but could surely be loved? In this world she ceased to be on her guard; she knew no strains or tensions there; nothing existed in the scene to provoke her abhorrence; and its "pathetic picturesqueness," stirring her affection when the first world war destroyed all vestiges of it, fused her imagination, her mind and her heart.

*Drawing-room of the house on West 25th Street where Edith Wharton grew up. She pictured this milieu in her stories of Old New York.*

191

*With the World's Columbian Exposition of 1893, the old frontier village of Chicago had become a metropolis.*

*Along the Chicago River ... puffing tugs ... grain elevators ... a scene that appealed to the pictorial imagination.*

# Dynamic Chicago

*a "dashing flashing crashing" metropolis ... electrifying ...*

*teeming with types and stories for novelists.*

*With the World's Fair of 1893,* the old frontier village of Chicago had become a metropolis, a cosmopolis, as it were, overnight, and there were not wanting those who said it was the heart of the nation already and would soon be the national centre of letters and art. The aspiring writers of the Middle West thought little of the East. Chicago was the goal of literary youth in the corn-belt, in the prairie states, in the flat and comparatively waterless, treeless towns there.

The Chicago Art Institute swarmed with students from Indiana, Ohio, Nebraska, Illinois, Texas, New Mexico. There was the Auditorium, which shocked Frank Harris to "speechless wonder" and which he regarded as one of the great buildings of the world. There was Jane Addams' Hull House, a centre for artists and writers, where they saw the new races that were meeting to create a new nation, with names that Dreiser's novels were soon to reflect.

Chicago, the most radical of American cities, had become a laboratory for the study of social movements and the new ideas which the recent immigrant strains had served to introduce, ideas that Jane Addams tried to relate to the older Amer-

ican traditions. The city teemed with types and stories for the novelists who were soon to come or who had arrived and were writing their books already. Its spirit was best expressed by a novel written later by Frank Harris and dealing with the trial of the "Chicago anarchists,"— the Sacco and Vanzetti case of the eighties. *The Bomb* gave the most graphic picture perhaps of the radical immigrant mind of the new Middle West.

However, at the moment, the best-known living Chicago writer, Eugene Field, had little use for such explosive thought. The fanciful whimsical Field preferred fairy godmothers and valiant knights whom he depicted with sympathy and charm. A newspaper paragrapher, sometimes called the original "columnist," he had spent most of his childhood in Emily Dickinson's Amherst and retained the distinctly bookish taste that throve there. Sketchy and thin as his tales were, his humour was sometimes robust and his satire pointed.

Eugene Field ironically referred to the "tremendous spring rush of local literature." One of its pioneers was Henry B. Fuller, who loved his native town, though he was distressed by the spec-

Eugene Field wrote whimsically about Chicago, the new metropolis.

Eugene Field lampooned himself as "the Chicago Dante" with a laurel wreath of frankfurters.

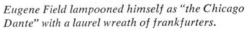

"A mighty good sausage stuffer was lost when this man became a poet." From Field's Tribune Primer.

tacle of its present turmoil. *The Cliff-Dwellers* was one of his novels, presently followed by *With the Procession*. Both books presented the town and its people at home with an intimate native knowledge of the scene, a style that was nimble and witty and an amplitude that no one at the moment could rival.

How the sensitive New England mind reacted to the Chicago milieu was clearly shown by Robert Herrick. Arriving from Cambridge in 1893, Herrick detested the lust for money that he saw in Chicago all about him, the note of the great untidy city with its hoarse cry "Success!" He admired the older business types, the pioneers of trade who had kept their faith in the goodness of American life. Somewhat cold and hard in his manner and approach, he was a conscientious man who was troubled about many things, the miseries of the poor, injustice, the cruelties of the sexes, about

which he wrote with a kind of humourless truthfulness. He brought all his anxiety to the study of Chicago, surveying the history of the city, in *One Woman's Life,* the story of a successful adventuress, Milly Ridge, who rises in the world as a society reporter and ends as the wife of a ranchman further west. In the *Memoirs of an American Citizen,* he followed the life of a great meat-packer. He was notably good in his treatment of the daughters of the rich, the restless readers of Ibsen and Shaw, childless, bored by the business of their husbands, neurotic and constantly moving hither and thither.

It was symptomatic of the next generation that, reviving an interest in Henry B. Fuller, it continued to ignore Robert Herrick, for Herrick was the kind of moralist whose work bored readers in the world-war years while Fuller's aesthetic qualities were in the mood of the time.

*Henry B. Fuller's* Cliff Dwellers *dealt with the lives of the people in a Chicago office-building.*

*Robert Herrick measured Chicago by the standards of his Puritan conscience.*

196

# The West's New Voices

*Chicago had become a laboratory of fresh ideas,*

*a centre for satirists and avant-garde poets.*

*George Ade used the Western vernacular, deriding the "conversational parsley of the culture-seeker."*

*The census of 1900 showed that* the centre of population had shifted from the East to the Mississippi valley, the land beyond the Alleghenies where Europe ended, as Emerson had said, and a world both American and polyglot as surely began. Chicago was the focus of this "valley of democracy." It was there that the "American language" took shape. This was a new linguistic form, the result of a common American life that was only in part Anglo-Saxon and that found its first effective expression in George Ade's *Fables in Slang* and the work of Carl Sandburg and other novelists and poets.

George Ade was able to rejoice without constraint in the "sweet vernacular," as he called it, of his native region, privileged to use words, he said, that were "years ahead of the dictionaries." He was all in the mood of his place and time in avoiding "long Boston words."

A native of Indiana, Ade knew the rural and small-town types from all the region round about who swarmed in the city streets and lodging-houses and whom he observed in police-courts and shops, in theatres, parks and poolrooms, for by 1892 he was a star reporter. He conducted a column with sketches of street-car conductors, working girls and "actorines." His shop-girls were like O. Henry's in New York and many of his young men foreshadowed James T. Farrell's drugstore cowboys. George Ade had something in common even with Sherwood Anderson, and his world occasionally reminded one of *Winesburg, Ohio*. The novelty of the *Fables in Slang* consisted in their juxtaposition of the imagery of the farm with the metropolitan point of view, the sharp confrontation of city and country.

In another vein Finley Peter Dunne's dialect sketches marked the shift from the country to the city. "Mr. Dooley" appeared as an urban sage. In

*A cartoon sequence from George Ade's*
Breaking Into Society.

him the sagacity of the saloon, the poor man's club, supplanted the crackerbox wisdom of the village store, where one had met the corresponding types. He looked at the nation from a Chicago window. He criticized with scorn the Eastern Anglomania, the "diluted Englishmen, the dudes around New York," as he called them, "the enfeebled literary men around Cambridge and New Haven."

Dunne had grown up in his native Chicago in an Irish world that he re-created in Mr. Dooley's saloon in Archey Road. In his conversations Mr. Dooley always stood for the "little man" in the presence of big abuses, bombast and bluff. He satirized the "big business" which he said was "so hard to tell from murder" when it got above selling nails in a brown paper bag.

It was the Western homeland that nourished the imagination of three poets who came to stand as symbols of this region. Edgar Lee Masters, Vachel Lindsay and Carl Sandburg were regional poets, steeped in the life of the old frontier, its legendary lore and prairie landscape, its memories of log-cabin days, the wolf-hunt, the fiddler, the buffalo-grass and the sons of thunder preaching in the forest. The Middle West came into its own with these three folk-poets who shared so fully its language, tastes and interests, and who replaced with heroes of its own like Johnny Appleseed and Daniel Boone the Eastern Paul Reveres and Commodore Perrys.

Masters, the Chicago lawyer, Vachel Lindsay, who lived in Springfield, and the newspaperman Carl Sandburg, all of whom were to find themselves famous in the days of the "Poets' Renascence," had already appeared as poets in these earlier years.

*Peter Finley Dunne, creator of Mr. Dooley.*

*Mr. Dooley always stood for the little man in the presence of big abuses.*

Masters had conceived the *Spoon River Anthology* in 1906, while Lindsay, who wrote in 1909 *I Heard Emmanuel Singing,* had long since attempted to "trade rhymes for bread." He came up to Chicago now and then and gave his friends odd little books which he had privately printed with his own decorations, drawings of comets, moons and ships. In the minds of all these poets, the hero of the Great Valley, Lincoln, the "prairie-lawyer, master of us all," — as Vachel Lindsay called him, — loomed mountain-high, towering over the town of Galesburg, where Sandburg had lived as a boy and where Lincoln had carried on one of his debates with Douglas.

There was much emotional warmth as well in the work of Masters in poetry and prose, with a feeling for Western tradition that allied him to Lindsay and a feeling for Chicago that related him to Sandburg.

The child of Swedish immigrants, Sandburg had grown up in a prairie town and wandered all over the West with a guitar or a banjo. He had served, like Sherwood Anderson, as a soldier in the Spanish-American war; he had ridden the rails

*Vachel Lindsay and Edgar Lee Masters were steeped in the life of the old West. The region found its own voice in the balladry of these folk poets.*

like Jack London. During hobo-adventures through cotton-fields and on freight-trains and river-boats, through most of the Mississippi valley towns, he had written down on scraps of paper, storing the melodies in his mind, the ballads that he was to publish in *The American Songbag.*

In one way or another, first or last, the whole life of the Middle West appeared in Carl Sandburg's free-verse poems. One found there the wheat and red clover of the prairie and the padding musk-rats with their fans of ripples. These poems were full of the roar and whirl of street-crowds and work-gangs, coal-boats ploughing the river and the flame-sprockets of steel-mills. Over all rang the confident laughter of a spirit for whom life was hale and full and the world was born again every morning.

For a long generation to come Carl Sandburg was to live and write, the poet who reminded one of the skalds of old, the singers of the deeds of heroes in the days of the Vikings, — another Walt Whitman of the new Western frontier.

*Carl Sandburg, a Walt Whitman of the new frontier. Photograph by Edward Steichen.*

*Hamlin Garland's dark mood deepened to bitterness when he observed his family marooned on the treeless plain.*

*Observing in the early* nineteen-hundreds that "the literary supremacy of the East" was passing, Hamlin Garland said this must fall to Chicago and the Mississippi valley. Here was an America that was no longer basically English but a new composition altogether. Boston, Philadelphia and New York were of small account here, for the people of Wisconsin, Minnesota, Iowa, the Dakotas and other Western states were largely of Scandinavian and German extraction. The traditions of England for them were unimportant and weak, and they were already articulate and prepared for their writers.

Garland, a Wisconsin man, had spent several studious years in Boston before his first stories appeared at the end of the eighties, stories of farm-life on the prairie that were new in their candour and tragic feeling. After a renewed stay in his native West, he set to work on a series of tales that he presently collected in a book, *Main-Travelled Roads*. On his Western visit he had reabsorbed his native atmosphere like a sponge. He had seen the note of the tragic everywhere in what had once seemed to him dull and petty, and his dark mood deepened to bitterness when he found that his

*Illustration from Garland's "Son of the Middle Border."*

mother was marooned in a dismal cabin on the vast treeless plain.

When Garland began to write, he followed the realism of Eggleston and Howells, though his touch was rather more drastic than theirs had been; and he liked to describe his own method as "veritism," or work that could always be verified in comparison with facts.

In all this Garland was preparing the way for the darker school of realism that was more and more dominant in time throughout the West. There at present, especially in Indiana, the home of the poet Riley, the "more smiling aspects of life" occupied the writers.

# Theodore Dreiser

*the note of reality and compassion was*

*so strong in his stories that one*

*forgot their artless journalistic style.*

*As a barefoot boy at Terre Haute,* Indiana, young Theodore Dreiser had sat astride a high board fence at dawn. He had wished, as he said, for so many things, watching the long trains go through, wondering when he would be able to go out into the world. Picking up coal between the tracks or stealing it from the standing cars, he lived in awe-

*Dreiser's New York with the Butterick Building, where he worked as an editor. Lithograph by Max Polak.*

*Theodore Dreiser's mind never forgot the squalid frontier conditions, with which his mother had to battle.*

some fear of the winter cold. While his dreamy, poetic mother did all she could as captain of the family ship, he saw nothing in his immediate surroundings but poverty, defeat and failure. One of his first childhood memories was creeping around the floor observing his mother's worn-out shoes. There was always want in the Dreiser household. Dreiser's mind was governed to the end by the tragic image of his mother, and the heavy plodding German note of his childhood home was never to leave him.

By contrast, the rural world outside imprinted in his mind many pleasant scenes reminiscent of the genial pictures that James W. Riley conjured up in his Hoosier poems. There was more of the Hoosier in Dreiser than many readers were to realize.

Years later, Dreiser, looking back at the old American rural world, said that he could no longer share its idealism and faith, the dreams, the courage of the American tradition, for the tragic features of frontier living were deeply imbedded in his mind. And the new industrial America had also repelled him. He had lost faith in it because, as he explained it, "I had seen Pittsburgh." He saw this city as the dividing point between the humane old

America and the industrialized nation that had sacrificed harmony to noise, beauty to bulk.

Still, it was in his wanderings through this new America that the genius of Theodore Dreiser came to fruition.

As a journalist, Theodore Dreiser had drifted from city to city, — Chicago, St. Louis, Toledo, Cleveland, Pittsburgh, — before he settled in New York in 1895 as a free-lance writer and editor of magazines. He turned out "life stories of successful men" about Philip Armour, Marshall Field, and other financial magnates and popular artists, haunting the lobbies of the great hotels that appeared in so many of his novels later, allured by the luxurious crowds of well-dressed people. He saw himself in Lucien de Rubempré, Balzac's young provincial, the journalist who longed to be a novelist, when he went to Paris, where he was dazzled by the beautiful women and struck by the contrast of poverty and wealth that appealed with even greater force to Dreiser.

*In 1900 Dreiser had published a novel, Sister Carrie,* which Frank Norris, the publisher's reader, acclaimed as a "wonder" although it was virtually stillborn and withdrawn from circulation on the ground that it was too sordid or pornographic. This event was all but disastrous for Dreiser; it drove him into neurasthenia; for nearly three years he was confused and lost, drifting for a while to Philadelphia, sweeping out carpenter shops, working on a railroad. Reëstablished in the end, he became a conspicuous editor before *Sister Carrie,* reissued in 1907, was taken up by college students who saw in Dreiser an American author of the calibre of the great new Europeans.

How could he have been surprised by the failure of *Sister Carrie* to achieve recognition? He knew the *Century, Scribner's, Harper's.* In their pages prevailed an atmosphere of unruffled peace and charm in which there was never a hint of the cruel, the vulgar, or the base, that every journalist saw as the substance of life. In the city news-room where Dreiser was at home the mask was always off and life was handled without gloves in a rough and ready fashion.

If what one desired was the "real life" that every novelist professed to give, one found it in *Sister Carrie,* and even with a vengeance, as one found it later in *Jennie Gerhardt,* a story that was better

still and equally abounding in the reality of flesh, blood and heart. For one felt in both the "uncritical upwelling of grief for the weak and the helpless" that Dreiser imputed to the heroine of his first novel, the pity with which he himself had regarded his German-American parents and the sisters who appeared in disguise in both these books. His throat tightened and his heart ached over the miseries of these wistful, affectionate creatures. Dreiser had

*Roberta and Clyde at the lake.*

seen too much of the sadder sides of life to accept conventional American standards in fiction, and, besides, one felt in his reports the authoritative note of Whitman's phrase, "I was the man, I suffered, I was there."

It was the note of actuality that won the day for *Sister Carrie,* for all the banalities and stylistic defects of the novel, — the sense it conveyed of the breathing presence of this "lone figure in a tossing sea." *Jennie Gerhardt* was still more appealing, though scarcely more living than Carrie, because of the tragic depth of this girl's devotion to the poor German parents who were so like Dreiser's, to the child whom her first lover left as well as to the man who abandoned her and claimed her again at the end. These books gave vivid pictures of the chaos of much of American life, the ambitions and interests of the men who swarmed in the hotels, the commercial travellers whom one saw "flashing a roll of greenbacks," the proprietors of "polished resorts" and "swell saloons." Both these novels brimmed over with a sense of the wonder, the colour and the variety of life, and its cruelty, rank favouritism, uncertainty, indifference and sorrow.

All this triumphed in Dreiser's work over the journalistic style, flat-footed, unleavened at best, inept, elephantine, the occasional bad grammar, the grotesque misuse of words.

*Roberta's body found.*

*Clyde in prison.*

*Scenes from* An American Tragedy, *illustrated by Reginald Marsh, © Limited Editions Club.*

It was Dreiser's deep perception of the tragedy of life,—and of American life especially,—that had made reporting too shallow an occupation for him. Even in his early days as a reporter in St. Louis he was obsessed with the "lightning of chance" that was always striking blindly, leaving in its wake good fortune for some, for others destruction and death. This obsession led him to say later, "I acknowledge the Furies. I believe in them. I have heard the disastrous beating of their wings." Society, as Dreiser came to see it, was a counterpart of nature, a chaos of inscrutable forces, a "chemic drift," in which wealth and poverty were inevitable facts and a man was an atom in the whirl to be blamed for nothing he did or failed to do. He was so struck by the cruelty of what he saw, haphazard and casual as it seemed, that he felt he was obliged to explore the mystery of it. He felt he could no longer remain on the surface reporting events, that somehow he must interpret his observations, get to the bottom of social injustice and squalor.

But, filled as Dreiser always was with a genuine passion for the woes of the weak and a sense of the "blundering inept cruelty of life," he was equally drawn to the forceful, to powerful men. If Dreiser was to be remembered later as the best painter in American fiction of the great type of the capitalist in the age of exploitation, — the Cowperwood of *The Financier, The Titan* and *The Stoic,* — it was partly because he sympathized with it through another line of feeling that also had its origin in the conditions of his childhood. Who could forget, in *An American Tragedy,* the craving of the young bell-boy Clyde for the luxury, wealth, beauty and show that he observed in the hotel, his envy of the rich well-dressed people whom his eyes followed in the lobby, starved as he was for want of any pleasure. When Clyde longed to escape from the squalor of his childhood, when he dreamed of the high world in his uncle's home town and pined for money and fine clothes, was he not the image of the Dreiser of *A Book about Myself?* Dreiser, the cash-boy in a dry-goods store, the newsboy, the driver of a laundry wagon, had shared Clyde's hunger for a beauty he connected with wealth. "Luxury is a dream of delight . . . to those who have come out of poverty," he remarked, referring to the artist in *The Genius,* — in great part, Dreiser's self-portrait. He understood the robber barons who ruled the great world of finance, in which he, like Eugene, "had vaguely hoped to shine."

Thus Dreiser sympathized in his way with the "swift" and the "strong," the victors of life, in the sense of sharing their dreams and aspirations, almost as much as he sympathized with the weak, the victims; and if the novels he wrote about them were scarcely less close to the bone it was because he had lived their life as well.

It was Dreiser's own masculine love of life, the strength of his desire that enabled him to recreate this American type, as it enabled him to traverse, — "wide-eyed, with an open heart," — a great range of experience. He never lost the sense of wonder, the wonder that characterized Balzac and Tolstoy. It gave him the perpetual feeling of a "guest at a feast," and he for whom in early life the newspaper-office was a "wonderland" found wonderlands on all sides in after life, in smoky groups of factory buildings, in theatre-going crowds at night, in shop-girls brushing their hair by open windows. Some of Dreiser's prose vignettes in *The Colour of a Great City* paralleled the pushcart-men of the "ash-can" school, their bread-lines, beaches, morgues and slaughter-houses. They sometimes suggested John Sloan or Stieglitz's early photographs of battered old street-cars with teams of unkempt horses struggling through swirling winds and flying snow.

Dreiser, always a religious man with a tragic sense of the mystery of life, was drawn more and more to Elias Hicks' teachings, which had something in common with the faith of his Mennonite mother. His religion finally began to appear in his novels. In *The Stoic,* the novel he was finishing at the moment of his death, Berenice, Cowperwood's mistress, who had studied Yoga, became a nurse and built a hospital in order to express her new-found belief in "something beyond human passion." This was Dreiser's own final note when, joining the Communist party, he also received communion in a Protestant church, on the Good Friday of the year in which he died, attempting thus to reconcile the contradictions in a mind that felt life more deeply perhaps than any other in his time.

*Dreiser was filled with a sense of the blundering inept cruelty of life. He both felt the woes of the weak and admired the prowess of the swift and strong.*

# Small Town

*Sherwood Anderson's world was made up of the little*

*people, the obscure, the starved, the searching.*

*Sherwood Anderson said he followed* in the steps of the heavy feet of Dreiser . . . "the heavy brutal feet . . . tramping through the wilderness of lies . . . making a path."

*Sister Carrie* and *Jennie Gerhardt* "jolted" Sherwood Anderson's mind and turned him away from books to the life about him. With his deep feeling for the natural and the human, he was to become the perpetual student of life. No one avoided more than he any suggestion of the artificial. He rejected O. Henry as a model because he had "learned too many tricks." He shrank from everything that was meretricious. If he was drawn to Gertrude Stein, it was mainly because she reminded him of a countrywoman baking her own bread, and he was determined not to write stories of the factory-made kind with sawdust inside, in standard-sized shapes. His were rather to be stories that "began nowhere and ended nowhere," as life itself seemed to begin and end.

As for "good old human nature," this storyteller born had been absorbing it ever since he was a boy,

sitting on the curb of the main street of a small Ohio town, listening to people, watching, wondering about them. As a house-painter, a salesman, a soldier, an assembler in a bicycle factory, a worker in a Chicago warehouse rolling kegs, and especially as a stable-boy following race-horses from town to town, he had been all eyes and ears for "horses and men."

While Sherwood Anderson himself had broken with this small-town life, he was always returning to it both in fact and in fancy, in search of the little people he liked to write about, the "obscure" people who, as he put it, had given him life. Years later he would disappear at times and stop for weeks in one of these towns in some dingy hotel room, walking the deserted streets at night with a heart that went out, as he later said, to all the defeated people in the little wooden houses. He had wished to escape from them at first, hoping as a boy to get up in the world and even to be one of the Western captains of finance, for the story of *Windy McPherson's Son* was largely his own story.

Anderson's father appeared in many of his books. He was, in a way, the son's greatest creation, side by side with the mother of the family who saved the household by desperate ruses like those to which Dreiser's mother had also been driven. Anderson's own chosen world was mostly made up of the obscure, or what he called the "starved side of small-town life." He was drawn to the misfits, the half-wits, the sex-mad. What was new in Anderson's tales of solitary souls and village grotesques was the sense of a buried life they gave the reader, the hidden depths that lay behind the mechanical gestures and banal remarks that expressed the surface-existence of all these people, "twisted little apples that grow in the orchards of Winesburg." His inarticulate people with their strange turns of mind seemed curiously emblematic of American life. They were types of a post-pioneer world in which countless individuals felt they were astray or somehow lost, while their lives went on like the prairie, an infinity of flat lands.

*Booth Tarkington took for his subjects the folksy*

*prosperous souls who formed one big jolly family.*

*The small-town America of* the Middle West was the setting of Booth Tarkington's novels as it was that of Sherwood Anderson. These writers, however, looked at their towns from different sides of the railroad track.

Many of Tarkington's characters suggested the normal kindly folksy souls of whom William Dean Howells had written with such affection, the "really happy people." In the Plattsville of *The Gentleman from Indiana,* he described a small-town world whose members belonged to "one big jolly family."

All his more sensitive characters disliked the growth of their Midland city, the noise, the dirt, the rush of machinery, the "mere shapelessness on the run." But, as Tarkington himself observed, his people had always longed for "size," though they sometimes disliked the consequences when they achieved it.

Thus, while Tarkington found much to condemn in the genial Western scene, he was far removed from the writers whose heroes disgustedly left the town or saw only its drabness and dullness, its errors and frustrations. How fiercely in *The Plutocrat* he turned on the three young highbrow snobs who sneered at his "middle-class Middle Western" hero, Tinker.

This portrait of Tinker, the "plutocrat," was one of Booth Tarkington's triumphs, which was only equalled by Sinclair Lewis' *Dodsworth,* though the story was not quite subtle enough and the humour was laid on too thick for the book to be an authentic masterpiece. *The Magnificent Ambersons,* perhaps his best novel, a typical story of an American town, presented the great family that locally ruled the roost and vanished virtually in a day as the town spread and darkened into a city.

But there was an obvious weakness in Tarkington's novels. They did not follow their logical course but were modified to conform to Hoosier folk-ways. The arrogant George Amberson, suddenly poor, becomes a considerate, hard-working young man, already on the way to retrieve the family fortunes. Just so old Sheridan, the tyrant in

*The Turmoil,* bull-headed, stubborn and hard, becomes, in the end, imaginative, kind and gentle. These swift regenerations and lightning-like changes of character destroyed the coherence and integrity of Tarkington's novels. It was notable that in his failure to conduct his stories to their logical end, he always wound up in a fashion that pleased his neighbours.

. So Tarkington, the prince of popular novelists, was never taken seriously, — in critical circles he sat below the salt. The fallacy of the "happy ending" in stories that call for something else destroyed thousands of novels in Tarkington's time, among them Tarkington's own.

# Willa Cather

*the Nebraska plains filled her memory and her gift*

*of evocation had a certain buoyancy and freedom.*

Scenes from My Ántonia. *Its people were "mines of life, like the founders of early races."*

*Meanwhile, further West, a new* wave of emigration was pouring over the prairies, infusing fresh life into the region. The farmers who were pouring out from Nebraska and Kansas were of half a dozen European races. Some were Swiss; others were Norwegians, like Per Hansa's people in South Dakota to the north, the heroes of Rölvaag's *Giants in the Earth,* or the Czechs who were to appear in Willa Cather's novels.

This Virginia girl who had come to live on the windy Nebraska table-land in the year of Jules Sandoz's arrival, further northwest, had grown up on a ranch there and largely out of doors, because there was no school for her to go to. Early she drank in the sights and sounds of the plains, the song of the meadowlark, the drumming of the quail, the burr of the locust over the tremendous silence. Her novels were to overflow with memories of these early years, which also filled her poems of dawn and the spring, the fragrance of ripe wheat, the pale yellow corn-fields, the roads that were mere faint traces in the buffalo-grass. Then she remembered the wind in winter singing over hundreds of miles of the snow through which Ántonia drove the cattle home. Many of the settlers, overborne, returned to Iowa and Illinois, where they had previously known a more habitable country, but there were others like Ántonia and Alexandra Bergson for whom this new land seemed beautiful, rich and strong. They were "mines of life" for Willa Cather, "like the founders of early races," and they prompted her observation later that "the history of every country begins in the heart of a man or a woman."

Willa Cather was always to look back with wonder to the scenes of her Nebraska youth, — they fed her poetic imagination and formed her point of view. She disliked the industrialized present and the murky modern cities as she loved the "irregular and intimate quality of things made," as she said, "entirely by the human hand." The only present that appealed to her was the foreground of the world of art, especially the musical world of New York and Chicago, and at the same time she was drawn to French Quebec and Santa Fé, the remains of venerable civilizations that had strayed across the ocean. It was in Santa Fé that Willa Cather was to write her *Death Comes to the Archbishop*.

Along with her sensuous imagination, her feeling for colours, tastes, odours and sounds, for the flavour of fresh lettuce and good wine, a note of composure characterized Willa Cather, all but uniquely at a time when the brilliantly rapid report was the mark of so many other novelists. She had discovered this same repose in Sarah Orne Jewett, whose stories were so light and so tightly built that to read them, Willa Cather said, was like watching the movement of a yacht. Miss Jewett expressed her own taste for presenting scenes by suggestion rather than enumeration. It was Willa Cather's own special quality, in a day of reporting, to recollect in tranquillity whatever had impressed her, and she had seen Nebraska in the light of Miss Jewett's Maine before she wrote of Quebec and Santa Fé. Her Alexandra and Ántonia, so "tireless in serving generous emotions," stood for the "unalterable realities at the bottom of things."

She was too full of the exhilaration, the excitement of youth and discovery to dwell on the cracks in the mirrors and the gauntness of the houses, while she was constantly on the alert, in her studies of the Western scene, for every trace of distinction, vitality or talent. On all sides Willa Cather found striking and singular people who knew "how to live," as she put it, humble Jewish store-keepers who read philosophy and French, Bohemian peasants who had brought their fiddles with them. There was Thea Kronborg, finally, "like a flower full of sun," who became the great opera singer in *The Song of the Lark*.

Until Willa Cather wrote her stories, no one had ever conveyed a sense of the teeming aesthetic resources of the multi-racial West, the dawning talents of the new immigrant strains that were beginning to find expression and that contributed so largely to the renascence of the moment. She knew, for the rest, the tragedies that characterized the frontier life and the pathos of old souls like "Aunt Georgiana," who had taught music once at the Boston Conservatory and had been exiled for years to the Nebraska plains. How finely Willa Cather evoked the tall, grim, naked prairie house to which Aunt Georgiana didn't "want to go back." Her gift of evocation and what Vachel Lindsay called her "passion for the skyline" had something soft, wild and free about it. Sometimes her note was elegiac, sometimes idyllic, while her style, so luminous, buoyant and fresh, recalled the fragrance of sage-brush and clover, the wind and the snowy peaks flashing against the sky.

*Willa Cather at the age of 28 in 1902.*

*Managing editor of McClure's Magazine.*

*At her height as a novelist in the twenties.*

# Saving the Cowboy From Oblivion

*Owen Wister recalls the days of the ranchman's glory, and tries to save him from oblivion.*

*As the emigrant farmers of* Willa Cather's novels swarmed over the open ranges, the cowboy was vanishing with the Indian and the buffalo. No one felt this more keenly than Owen Wister, a Philadelphia lawyer who spent his summers in Wyoming. He had kept a careful diary of the still typical plains life that was gradually coming to an end. He had recorded innumerable details about cow-punchers, pack-horses, round-ups, about barbecues, camping in the mountains or hunting with Indians. Frederic Remington was making pictures of this, but fiction, he felt, was doing nothing about it.

Wister's freshly written stories of the West were beginning to appear at the turn of the century. They had an elegiac tone, like the Mississippi tales of Mark Twain. Many of the songs of the cowboys revealed that they felt their day was over, though cowboys of a kind were to last as long as there were cows. No doubt the classical type of the cowboy that Owen Wister pictured had passed his prime when he began to write, the type of the wide-eyed Lin McLean and, still more, the "Virginian," who became the model of a thousand horse-operas and stories. The Virginian had wandered over Arkansas, Texas, Arizona, New Mexico, Oregon, Idaho, Wyoming and Montana, — "the world's greatest

*"When you call me that, smile," — an often-quoted phrase from Wister's* The Virginian.

playground for young men." Some of the towns were graveyards mainly, with rotting head-boards of murdered men; others swarmed with cowboys leaning over bars or strolling across to the trader's to buy presents for their sweethearts. It was a hopeful and full-blooded epoch, as it seemed to many in retrospect, that Wister treated with a touch of both poetry and truth. The "Virginian" was a sort of cross between Melville's "welkin-eyed" Billy Budd, the "handsome sailor" of English legend, and the lonely figure of Natty Bumppo, whom he also resembled in his humble birth, his reverent nature and his shy respect for women. "Never speak ill of any man to any woman," the "Virginian" says. "Whatever you undertake you must do well. In the East you can be middling and get along, but in the West if you claim to be quick with a gun you must be quick."

Within a few years Hollywood stereotyped the plains life, which the cheap periodical press had already taken over, so that writers could no longer see it innocently and freshly, as, within his limits, Wister had seen it.

*Owen Wister had kept a diary with details of the plains life that was gradually coming to an end.*

*Theodore Roosevelt with John Muir, the naturalist, on Glacier Point above Yosemite Valley, California.*

The West found perhaps its most forceful spokesman in Theodore Roosevelt. He knew this region from the plains to the Western mountains, and retold its history in his fine scholarly narrative. *The Winning of the West*. A literary statesman, Roosevelt saw so much of so many writers that a list of his friends would virtually amount to a literary history of the epoch.

# San Francisco in the Nineties

*writers emerge from this "story city," "where things can happen" as Frank Norris said.*

*No doubt Bierce's irony was a protective mask for a sensitive man.*

*In San Francisco, in the eighteen-nineties,* Ambrose Bierce was the cock of the walk, a military martinet in literary matters, a cold, ironical, arrogant man and a great reader of Voltaire and Swift who had written *The Devil's Dictionary,* a "cynic's word-book." In this he described himself as one who preferred dry wines to sweet, as he preferred sense to sentiment, defining, at the same time, patience as "a form of despair, disguised as a virtue." But, forty-six years old in 1888, when he began to publish his Civil War stories, he had become a sort of oracle in literary circles on the Western coast.

It was true that in the early nineties he had no rivals in San Francisco. He also wrote with a certain elegance of which he was highly conscious and extremely proud. He had had little education, his early work was rough and coarse, and his tardy discovery of good English rather went to his head, as one could see by the manner in which, as an unofficial teacher, he later gave his little Senate laws. No doubt his irony had been at first a protective mask for a sensitive man. It had been established in him during the Civil War and after because of the romantic idealism with which he had fought. His stories revealed the horrors he witnessed and much of his feeling about them, and only an idealist could have been so disillusioned by the fraud and corruption of the regime that followed the war. Bierce's *Tales of Soldiers and Civilians* resembled and rivalled the stories of Stephen Crane.

His earlier whimsical sketches of miners had been influenced by Bret Harte, but Poe was the master of his imagination. He shared the "fantastic realism" that Dostoievsky had found in Poe and that no one in America had exemplified since as well. For nothing could have been more realistic than some of Bierce's battlepieces, in spite of their occasional touches of melodrama. Bierce followed Poe in a dozen ways or shared his tastes and tendencies, his obsession with graveyards, coffins and mortuary chapels, men who are buried alive, hallucinations and murderers who quote antique treatises on the marvels of science. As in the Western tall tales with which Poe, too, had something in common, the incongruities were emphasized by the matter-of-factness. Perhaps *An Occurrence at Owl Creek Bridge* was the finest of all Bierce's tales, the story of the Confederate planter who is hanged from the bridge in Alabama and lives through a whole dream-existence in the moment of death.

Never obliged to match his wits with first-rate minds, Bierce rode his hobbies freely and indulged his whims. He dogmatized at his ease with a too facile cynicism that over-expressed his somewhat acrid spirit. But his singular force of imagination gave permanent value to a dozen or a score of his tales. In addition to these, he poured out a mass of uncensored writings, epigrams, essays and stories, that filled twelve tasteless volumes at the end of his life.

For Frank Norris, San Francisco was one of the American "story cities," a "place where things can happen." He had been brought there in 1885 as a boy of fifteen, the son of a Chicago business man whom he was supposed to have pictured in the broker Curtis Jadwin, the hero of *The Pit*. It was the influence of Zola that had turned the young Norris to novel-writing when he was already inoculated with the "Kipling virus." Norris' own high vitality drew him to Kipling, and he found himself dancing, as he said, to the pipe of the "little bespectacled colonial." The transition to Zola that followed was natural enough.

Frank Norris' humanitarianism was a late growth in his brief life, for he was a worshipper of force in his early stories, one who shared "the gladiatorial theory of existence." Celebrating the "man with his shirt off . . . fighting for his life," Norris became the founder of the "red-blood" school, the school of the "primordial," the "primeval," that ended in the pulp-magazines and the Tarzan books. This was the beginning of the "cave-man" tendency in American writing that reappeared in Hemingway and John Steinbeck a generation later.

Frank Norris' thirty-two years of life, like Stephen Crane's twenty-nine, which covered more or less the same three decades, were packed with adventure, both outward and inward. Norris, preparing for his *McTeague,* studied low life in San Francisco not long after Crane had studied the Bowery in New York, and the two were to meet in the Spanish-American war.

The "story-city" itself was the enchantment of his boyhood. He absorbed its waterfront and riverboat life with all of Zola's thirst for documentation. Later he talked with drunkards and prostitutes in saloons and brothels of the Barbary Coast and learned the mean streets by heart, as one saw in *McTeague*. Before he wrote *The Pit,* he went back for a while to Chicago to make a study there of the wheat-exchange.

Norris despised what he called the "literature of chambermaids," the historical romance that was popular in the later nineties, with the sickly pallor of the genteel and all that was thin and insipid in the work of American novelists and story-tellers. Why, for the rest, should Western writers look eastward any longer or look to the legends of Europe? Was not the prairie schooner as large a figure as the ship of Ulysses? Norris was to satirize in several stories what he regarded as the insipid culture of New England. When he began to write novels, in

*McTeague* and *Vandover and the Brute,* he went to the other end of the human scale.

In *The Octopus* Norris offered a vast panorama of California, with its ranch-life, barbecues, feuds and Homeric feasts and the dying Mexican world that lay behind them. His careful eye for detail gave a massive reality to the Zolaesque *McTeague,* to the portrait of the ponderous dentist, the ox-like giant with the salient jaw and the vast red hands that were covered with stiff yellow hair. Norris' portraiture was one of the merits that Howells pointed out when he reviewed *McTeague* in 1899, denouncing the hypocrisies of the old-fashioned novel and praising a novel that was fit for the experienced and mature.

*Frank Norris: his thirty years of life were packed with adventure both outward and inward.*

# Jack London

*veritable waves of force seemed to rush out of his stories. Yet his will to power destroyed his will to live.*

*In the year in which Frank Norris* published *A Man's Woman,* — 1900, — appeared the first book of a younger San Francisco writer, a collection of tales of the Yukon country, *The Son of the Wolf,* that had more than a little in common with the work of Norris. This was a coincidence, for the two writers had never met and in all probability Jack London knew nothing of Norris, but Kipling was

*On his return from Alaska, he was hailed as the Kipling of the Klondike.*

also his "British idol" whose stories he had copied out by hand at a time when he was too poor to buy a book. London had all of Norris' relish in presenting the survival of the fittest in conditions that recalled the primordial scenes of the Stone Age, in which men fight for the privilege of eating the carcass of a dog and subdue by force their "mate-women," as Jack London called them.

London had grown up as a water-front hoodlum. The natural son of a wandering astrologer, a clever quack whom he never saw, and a spiritualist mother who gave piano lessons, he had sold newspapers, worked in a cannery, stolen boats and inherited a girl with the sloop in which he raided the oyster-beds. He had travelled as a hobo to Washington, riding the rails and sleeping in boxcars and jungles. At twenty-one he set out for the Klondike where, in 1897, the gold-rush recalled the days of the forty-niners.

On his return voyage Jack London began to plan the stories that presently made him famous as the "Kipling of the Klondike," though he wrote later of other scenes and many other types, Mexican prize-fighters, Chinese, Hawaiians, and what not. In his Alaskan stories he sounded the note of the "strenuous life" that Roosevelt had struck in a speech one year before him, the theme that life is a struggle for survival in a world that is cruel and grim but in which the fighting will has a chance to triumph. In the title story of *The Son of the Wolf* the daughter of an Indian chief in the North is captured, in the teeth of her suitors, by a white lover, and most of the stories, with their Kiplingesque swagger, abounded in scenes of violent death and the conflict of man with the "white silence" and the savagery of nature. This second, wilder Bret Harte world of miners' cabins, bars and flats, of Russian fur-traders, Eskimos, half-breeds and

214

*He had worked in a cannery, stolen boats and raided the oyster-beds.*

*In* The Call of the Wild *London implied that fastidious ways would not do in a world of club and fang.*

squawmen, was the last corner of the Western frontier that bordered on a wilderness where only the caribou and the wolf were able to survive. One felt that Jack London's stories had been somehow lived, — that the author was not telling tales but telling his life.

In later stories, long or short, *The Call of the Wild, The Faith of Men, A Daughter of the Snows, Children of the Frost,* Jack London continued to recreate this world of the long arctic night in which men fought with men and with hunger and cold.

Jack London seemed as electrically alive as the prophet of the strenuous life himself. Like Frank Norris, he broke the spell of what came to be called, —*ad nauseam,* — the genteel tradition. With what contempt he presented the two young tenderfeet, those "two effete scions of civilization," in *The Son of the Wolf,* the "clubman" and the "society boy . . . shirkers and grumblers . . . the sort that talk big and cry over a toothache." One could understand why Lenin, as he lay dying, rejoiced in Jack London, as hundreds of thousands of Americans had rejoiced before him.

Alive, imaginative, alert, Jack London became within four or five years the best-known younger writer in the country, not only with readers of popular books but among the intelligentsia, who were struck by his dramatization of serious ideas. For his stories had a philosophical bearing, — they were illustrations of the theories of Darwin, or of Karl Marx, Nietzsche or Herbert Spencer, — and they made battles of the mind as actual and thrilling as prize-fights, adventures in the gold-fields or scenes of war.

Jack London was a success until his own thirst for money and power destroyed the artist in him and he wrote what he called the "pap of pretty lies." His will to power destroyed his will to live. Beginning in illegitimacy, he ended in suicide. Jack London had within him the "delicate sensitive spirit" that he imputed to his Everhard, the labour-leader, the "ingenuous boy" with the bulging muscles and the prize-fighter's throat that were like Jack's own, together with the "smashing sledge-hammer manner of attack." The sensitive spirit existed in London or he would never have been a writer; and he was, after all, a writer with an unconscious *to write out of,* — which could not have been said for his followers in the pulp-magazines. But he had repressed this spirit too effectively, too long. Was not this the reason for the "long sickness" that killed him at last?

215

# Ellen Glasgow

*in revolt against the mournful nostalgia of former writers,*

*her novels championed the resurgent South.*

*In the opening decade* of the twentieth century the light and air of a larger world were filtering through the once closed shutters of the old solid South, and within a generation the time was coming when William Faulkner and various others were to make this in a way the most luminous of American regions. The day had not come for *Tobacco Road,* for *God's Little Acre* and *Strange Fruit,* for those numberless novels and stories in which Southerners in time were to sweep the dust of their skeletons out of the closet.

But already, in Asheville, Thomas Wolfe, ten years old at the end of this decade, was aware of the less pleasing realities of the world he saw. A child of the mountain stock, remote from the amenities of life in the South, Wolfe had known from the cradle that mountain life was really, as he said, "terrible" and "sordid." He was to turn bitterly away from the standardized fictional patterns, the polished bits of whimsy that Southern writers created about their region.

In a similar vein Ellen Glasgow had turned away from the romanticized view of her own Virginia. The whole state, Ellen Glasgow felt, was blind and nourished by illusions, groping through a memorable epoch in history, unaware of the changing world, passionately clinging to the "ceremonial power of tradition." She was only the first of a number of writers, soon to appear, who were very sure that life was "not like this" and that, after the unreality and evasiveness of the older writers, the South needed "blood and irony."

Miss Glasgow's first novel, *The Descendant,* had appeared in 1897, and she had already begun the series that was to record the social history of Virginia through three generations. Of the same racial intermixture that had made Thomas Jefferson the type of the Virginian a century before her, she had an inherited knowledge of the countless phases of Virginia life that appeared in the panorama of her twenty novels. In these she pictured sympathetically the social and industrial revolution that was transforming the old romantic South.

It was often said later that with Ellen Glasgow a whole new literature began in the South, where a mournful nostalgia had governed the minds of writers. She felt the charm of the old South and even conveyed it herself with far more actuality than earlier writers, passionately in revolt as she was against its stranglehold over the mind as against the pretentious and the stereotyped in Southern writing. It was not therefore against the past that Ellen Glasgow was in revolt, — it was only against the elegiac tradition in letters. The "new" South, the changing South, was passing through phase after phase that offered great opportunities, as she saw, for writers, and she observed, with a devouring curiosity, the developing scene.

Temperamentally, as she said, on the side of the disinherited, she was also on the side of energy, on the side of life, when energy and life were in conflict with the moribund and the static, and in two novels, *The Voice of the People* and the *Romance of a Plain Man,* she followed the upward course of two leaders from the ranks. One was the story of a bright farm-boy who becomes a great governor of the state, — a theme that recurred in another novel, *One Man in His Time*. In her own feeling for public life, Ellen Glasgow was a reincarnation of the famous political women of the older South. For her the statesman was still the great type of the hero.

In one fashion or another, the conflict of two regimes was the general theme of Ellen Glasgow's novels, — the agrarian regime in its twilight hour and the rising industrial system that was largely in the hands of the despised and rejected of the past. Always on the side of life, she sided with the new life only when it was more generous, more abundant than the old, for she had small use for the new regime when the sordid or the narrow spoke for it. Her old families again and again showed themselves in their brightest light as admirers, supporters or lovers of the rising and the risen.

She revered the firm fighting strength that formed the core of the characters whom she loved and admired, men like the "white trash" Governor Vetch who had been born in a circus tent, women like her Roy Timberlake or Gabriella. It was an inborn strength that supported Gabriella in her struggle for survival, — the "primordial instinct" that prompted her "not to yield."

For the rest, in her reaffirmation of reality and life against what used to be called the dead hand of tradition, Ellen Glasgow was a part of the world movement of her time. While anchored in her native South, the people in her novels belonged to the all-American scene. Thus Ellen Glasgow, the first novelist to picture the true Southern life, was also the first to take the South out of the South. She gave it in fiction a touch of the universal.

*As a young novelist.*

*The garden at One West Main Street, Richmond, Va.*

*With Joseph Conrad in England.*

*The living room.*

# The Southwest

*writers find a new creative impulse inspired by*

*the simplicity and depth of Indian life.*

In 1903 appeared *The Land of Little Rain,* a collection of sketches and stories of unusual distinction in which a new writer, Mary Austin, related her impressions of a California desert region near the Sierras. There she had observed the Mission Indians, the Spanish-speaking cowboys and the radiance of spring breaking over the desert. The desert was the only world in which Mary Austin felt at home. There, walking or on horseback every day, she picked up stories of the wilderness people and made friends with lonely shepherds guarding their flocks.

In the hills near by there were still Bret Harte mining-towns with stage-coaches of the old lumbering kind in use. Mary Austin learned to drive them, as she studied the traces of animals and the resorts of the birds. She saw young eagles taught to fly, bobcats training their kittens to hunt. Pink soft clouds floated past in the clear smooth paths of the middle sky.

This was the country, enchanted for her, that appeared in Mary Austin's books, *The Land of Little Rain, Lost Borders* and *The Flock,* three singularly happy books, both deeply felt and picturesque, though perhaps a little too cunningly, or too consciously, wrought. They were full of the strange characters whom she had met in her desert life. There were the shy hairy shepherds, taciturn, giving to seeing visions, who might have been David's brethren on the ancient plains. Mary Austin knew them well, she had shared haunches of venison with them, stuck full of garlic corns and roasted in the coals. She had boiled her own kettle

in the brush, under the large palpitant desert stars wheeling to their stations in the sky.

This was in tune with the state of mind that certain types acquired in the solitude and silence of the desert, under the stars, the result of a kind of concentration that narcotized the outer man and evoked both hallucinations and genuine powers. The religion of the Indians made much of this, and Mary Austin saw much of the Indians. She sometimes felt that she was one of them. She absorbed their medical lore, their ritual, their dances, a knowledge that appeared in her writing. She could never establish a real relation with the world beyond the desert and her writing was always abortive when she left this world.

Mary Austin was not alone in her adoration of the Indians. Another apostle of their ways was the nature-writer Ernest Thompson Seton. Like most Americans with imagination, Thoreau and Whitman among them, Seton admired the manly qualities of the red men. Later, in New Mexico, he established a school of Indian wisdom. There were many who felt this was just what the sick world needed, for they believed that the Indians had a gift for living which more civilized people had lost.

This movement of feeling was infused with vitality when Mabel Dodge founded her colony at Taos. A "femme fatale," as Berenson called her, who had grown up in Buffalo with what she described as a marvelous flow of life, she had longed for a head-hunter's career in her rich, safe existence. After she had lived for a time in Florence she tired of its human collection that rivalled the Uffizi and went to New York to dynamite the town. There she established her little court at 23 Fifth Avenue. A twentieth-century Margaret Fuller with no hampering distaste for publicity, she became the symbol of the experimental impulse of the moment. Her rooms were a focus of the new illuminati, the writers, artists, agitators, movers and shakers who expressed the insurgent spirit of pre-world war New York.

Disillusioned in the early nineteen-twenties, she moved to Taos and married the Pueblo Indian Antonio Luhan, at a time when many imaginative minds for whom civilization was played out found something "like the dawn of the world" in Indian life. Mabel Dodge, who had lived two lives, first in Italy, then in New York, called D. H. Lawrence

*In this region she and others felt they were witnessing "the dawn of a new world." Mabel Dodge became the centre of a writers' group at Taos, New Mexico.*

*D. H. Lawrence was called to Taos by Mabel Dodge to see the true primordial America.*

to Taos too, "from across the world," as she remarked. Along with her desire for domination, she wished to give Lawrence "the truth about America: the false new America in the East, the true primordial undiscovered America that was preserved, living, in the Indian bloodstream."

More and more people, as the years went on, were drawn to this region where time had stood still, where the first wagon had left its track in all the territory of the United States in the year in which Shakespeare wrote *The Merchant of Venice*. For many who had tasted life too much, who were bored or disillusioned, or weary of the burden of their own individual existence, the life of the Taos community was a kind of nirvana, like the Buddhism that Henry Adams had sought in Japan. But perhaps it required a world war to provide the occasion for this coming-to-rest on the bosom of the Indian faith.

*During her New York* days, Mabel Dodge had preached the gospel of Gertrude Stein and spread the fame of her new style. Like Miss Stein, Mabel Dodge had long planned to "upset America . . . with fatal disaster to the old order of things."

Gertrude Stein, who looked and walked like a corpulent monk, had no interest in anything that was not aggressively modern. She had conceived it as part of her mission to "kill" the nineteenth century "dead," and she was convinced that her work was "really the beginning of modern writing." Her story *Melanctha* in *Three Lives,* privately printed in 1907, was the "first definite step," as she wrote later, "into the twentieth century." There was at least a grain of truth in this.

Just then the movement of "modern art," so called for many years, was also beginning in Paris with Matisse and Picasso, and Gertrude Stein and her brother Leo were friends of these protagonists. The Steins had the means to buy their pictures. Gertrude shared, moreover, the point of view of these avant-garde artists, and she endeavored to parallel in words their effects in paint.

Gertrude Stein wrote her *Melanctha* while posing for Picasso's portrait of herself. Picasso had just discovered African sculpture, previously interesting only to curio-hunters, and this may have set her mind running on the Negro girl Melanctha, whose story was the longest and most moving of her *Three Lives.* It was not difficult to find in these a trace of the influence of African art, with the influence alike of Matisse and Picasso.

In *Melanctha* the feeling for Negro life was so deep and so fresh in every way that the story became a landmark in American letters. That Gertrude Stein was a true creator, one of the rare minds who originate styles, could never have been questioned by a reader of her first stories, entirely new as they were in the vision as well as the manner that was to mark her work for forty years.

Only when she was possessed by a subject that stirred her emotionally first of all were her faculties clearly brought into focus. This was the case in her *Autobiography of Alice B. Toklas,* actually the story of the modern art movement, and *Wars I Have Seen,* the story of the "coming of the Americans" in 1944.

For the rest, there were bits in all her work that one happened upon with pleasure, sudden shrewd perceptions, buffooneries and what not, but when she began to "write cubistically," as her brother Leo called it, she dispensed with the subject that had stirred her and focussed her mind. So her writing became a chaos of words and rhythms. At the moment when Picasso was painting her portrait, he was entering his own cubist phase, — he was turning away from representational painting, — and Gertrude Stein followed him again in *The Making of Americans, Tender Buttons* and the portraits that seemed to parallel his work in paint. She too, in her literary still-lifes, disintegrated objects, apparently aiming at an incoherence that was later supposed to express the distortions and disruptions and discords of a world in collapse, and various young writers were influenced by her powerful individuality, her original simplifications and the movement of her style. Hemingway's prose was to bear the stamp of *The Making of Americans,* of which he had copied the manuscript and read the proofs, and Sherwood Anderson was moved by Gertrude Stein's experiments in what he described as "separating words from sense."

Many of her writings, including *The Making of Americans,* were records of a kind of self-hypnotization. At Radcliffe, as a pupil of William James, she had worked out experiments in automatic writing, and the incantatory style she developed in her books was the fruit of a similar kind of auto-suggestion. She had found a way of tapping her unconscious freely, and, opening *The Making of Americans* with one of her old college themes, she conjured up whatever floated there. All manner of other flotsam and jetsam rose from the psychic under-world that came to light in these novel com-

*a true creator of style. Her sibylline gift, accounted*

*for the power she exercised over her circle.*

positions, along with the advertising slogans, the riddles and tags of childish games that were verbal equivalents of objects on a montage.

Writing in Paris, seeing her language without hearing it spoken, Miss Stein could see it divested of association, while she herself soliloquized like a solitary child. Relishing nursery jingles, she made up jingles of her own, "A rose is a rose is a rose" and "Honey is funny," "Pigeons on the grass, alas," — like Edward Lear's, a new variety of nonsense. "The Germans cut down trees to bar the roads that lead to the mills that grind the corn" was suggested by the House that Jack Built. The monotone and the repetitions that marked her work were infantile; and was this not largely true of the mind they expressed? — in a style that abolished all distinctions between the less and the more important and reduced great things and small to a common level. This is the way that children write because these distinctions mean nothing to them, — they do not know the difference between the great and the small.

But who could have been more independent or freer from the clichés of the past, — the "conventional secondary appreciations" that destroyed the authentic and primary, as Leo Stein was always pointing out? Gertrude Stein was not mistaken when she said she was clairvoyant. Her intuitive sibylline gift accounted for the power that she exercised over the young. She had, moreover, a flair for talent and a spirit of eager helpfulness where young American writers were concerned. Her positive note was reassuring at a time when all values seemed insecure, when old standards and habits of thought had apparently vanished. What did her egomania matter or even the megalomania that no one challenged in this circle of youthful adorers, the hunger for adulation, the yearning for fame and the arrogance that was only equalled by her kindness?

*In her Paris apartment with Picasso's portrait (at right), Gertrude Stein tried to translate Picasso's cubistic style into literary terms and so turned to subjectless writing.*

*Gertrude Stein and Alice Toklas touring the French countryside.*

*Leo Stein, a critic born, quite as remarkable in his way as his peremptory sister.*

# Mencken of Baltimore

*a pungent humorist, he stabbed a flabby, fatuously*

*optimistic America wide awake.*

*Huneker, a real enlivener for Mencken, made art seem a magnificent adventure.*

*While in 1915 the first shoots* of a more vigorous epoch were appearing on every side, the prevailing tone of the moment was complacent and dull, and a few critics were lamenting already the sterility of the literary scene and the general flatness and tameness of American writers. At the head of this group stood James Huneker, the all-curious lover of half a dozen arts. His work was a running indictment of what he described as the "mean narrow spirit in our arts and letters." As Henry L. Mencken said, Huneker made art seem a "magnificent adventure" and brought this spirit into American criticism.

Mencken, an offshoot of Huneker's circle with his own "assertive clang," had inherited, as he remarked, a "bias against the rabble." He had gone to a German school in Baltimore where the "pure American children" were regarded as "dunces." If Mencken was later inclined to regard most grown-up Americans as dunces too, it was partly because of these impressions that he gathered as a boy. En-

tering a newspaper office, he became, at eighteen, a police-reporter and was soon reviewing the theatre and music as well. He picked up the jargon and ways of thought of the city-room. When he came to compile his great work *The American Language,* Mencken was to know whereof he spoke.

The satirical humorist in him had led him to devote his first book, — the first of all books on the subject, — to Bernard Shaw, though he had no sympathy with Shaw's socialistic doctrines; and meanwhile his discovery of *Huckleberry Finn,* which he reread every year, was the "most stupendous event," as he said, of his life. But most of his intellectual gods, as he admitted, were German, and Nietzsche formed his mind more than anyone else. That Mencken should have been drawn to Nietzsche and his notion of the slave-proletariat was in a sense preordained.

At the outset of his career, he said, an ancient had advised him to make his criticism telling at any cost, to "knock somebody on the head every day" with a "meat-axe." For the way to get rid of obstructive ideas was "not to walk softly before them but to attack them vigorously with clubs." So Mencken laid about him in a slashing style that was full of Nietzschean mannerisms.

Thus, with all the brasses sounding, the great Menckenian campaign began, like the coming of

*Son of a German cigar manufacturer.*

*Newspaper reporter and art reviewer at 18.*

the circus in the springtime, with showers of epithets, attacks on democracy, and shouts of defiance hurled at the "shamans." In Mencken's America the general average of intelligence, integrity and competence was so low that a man who knew his trade stood out as boldly as ever a wart stood out on a bald head, and the scene was a welter of knavery and swinishness, the operations of master rogues, the combats of demagogues, the pursuit of heretics and witches. American literature was colourless and inconsequential, timorously flaccid and amiably hollow, falteringly feeble and wanting in genuine gusto. Mencken attacked the "crêpe-clad pundits, the bombastic word-mongers of the *Nation* school."

Now there never could have been any doubt that Mencken played a decisive part in stabbing a flabby society wide awake, in shaking up the American spirit and rousing it out of its lethargy of optimistic fatuity and dull conventions. By this he harrowed the ground for the literature and art of the future. Still, Mencken was hardly a literary critic, for his mind was devoid of the feminine traits this type must have in order to be effective. He was a social critic and a literary showman who had taken lessons from Macaulay, as well as from Nietzsche, Huneker and Bierce, and he fought with all his masculine force against the elements in American society that impeded the creative life and stifled its growth. A transatlantic Attila, with his own Teutonic fury, a coarse mind that had undertaken a literary spade-work, he accomplished a task that only a coarse mind could do.

Later, after the jazz age passed, when he had become an institution, Mencken's limitations and faults were more generally apparent. It was evident that he had the vaguest of literary standards or he could scarcely have spoken of the "harsh Calvinistic fables of Hawthorne" or of Emerson as "an importer of stale German elixirs." Mencken remained a child in this region of feeling.

Mencken's realistic note was admirable and useful, as one saw in his book, for instance, *In Defence of Women*. He was as shrewd as Benjamin Franklin, but elsewhere his arid rationalism blended with a hedonism that was quite without spirituality and completely fatalistic. It was this tendency of his that blossomed in the jazz age in which so many writers were influenced by him.

With all his reactionary cynicism, Mencken was a liberator who opened paths for writers and made straight their way by turning many of their obstacles into laughing-stocks, but his campaign against democracy lost any glamour it might have had when Hitler murdered seven million Poles and Jews. When virtually every thinking German was only too happy to escape to America, Mencken's assaults on the country lost much of their force, and he ceased to be a spokesman for the "mongrel and inferior" Yankees. It was almost forgotten that he had performed a major work of criticism in giving the *coup de grace* to the colonial tradition. By fully recognizing the new interracial point of view, he contributed to the nationalizing of American letters. More than anyone else perhaps, Mencken broke the way for writers who were descended from "foreign" stocks and who were not yet assured of their place in the sun. It was he who signalized Chicago as a literary centre and praised the new writers who used his "American language."

*George Nathan and Mencken, "bent on destroying tradition."*

*Author of* The American Language — *a genuine artist in words.*

# Sinclair Lewis

*a typical reformer at heart, he devoted his satirical*

*gift to the purging of what was evil in America.*

*Mencken, with Shaw and Wells,* exerted a marked influence on a writer whose work was to open up new vistas of a native America. It had often been said that American writers lacked an enamoured localism, an affection for the land they reproved and chastised.

Not till Sinclair Lewis wrote *Cass Timberlane* could readers have realized fully how much of the poet lay under the dry surface of this writer's mind. Lewis was a satirist and critic. But he had always shared Cass Timberlane's vision of the "fabulous great land of the year 2000 A.D.," a new Athens, stark and clean, a new land for a new kind of people. A typical American reformer at heart, Lewis was to expose in his novels various facets of American life that were less luminous than they should be. But at bottom he had the warmth of affection for the people and the country that Booth Tarkington had for Indiana. The difference was that Tarkington measured this life by the Hoosier scale while Lewis was able to see it in the scale of mankind.

As early as 1905, on one of his college vacations, returning from Yale to his native Minnesota, he had begun to write a novel called *The Village Virus,* which placed him already as a rebel. This book, which Lewis never finished, was a prophecy of *Main Street,* and so, in its way, was the setting of *The Trail of the Hawk,* the densely provincial small-town Plato College. There the Bible was still "good enough for us" and socialism and evolution were equally "un-Christian." Lewis' hero rebelled against the "virus" when the brilliant Professor Fraser was forced to resign.

This novel foreshadowed in certain ways Sinclair Lewis' later work, for one saw in it the kind of world that he was to measure society by and the kind of man that he was to choose for a hero. His model

*In France, when he wrote* Arrowsmith.

*The house at Sauk Center where he was born.*

*Sauk Center, Minnesota, scene of Sinclair Lewis' Main Street (1920).*

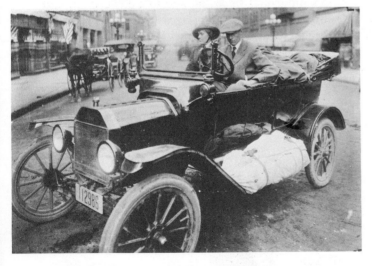

*At Duluth, Minnesota, ready for a cross-country trip with his wife, Grace Hegger Lewis.*

*Sinclair Lewis in the early thirties, when he worked on* It Can't Happen Here.

world was the Utopia of Wells and many of his heroes were devoted to the building of a world of the future. Typical of these was Gottlieb, the hero of *Arrowsmith,* the lonely seeker of truth, a hater of all forms of greed and fraud, the type for which Lewis cared most. All his heroes were working in some fashion or other for the kind of enlightened society that Shaw, Wells, Rolland and Veblen variously dreamed of.

Behind the novels that Lewis was to write, most of them after the first world war, one felt the hovering presence of this image of a world with which the author was always comparing the visible world as it was, with even perhaps too much of its imperfection.

At a moment of national self-scrutiny, it was almost the mission of Lewis to devote his great gifts as a satirist to the scourging of this world, to the scarification of American society and the purging of all that was evil in it, whether merely complacent or unlovely or definitely base. With his fierce desire for a good society and his furious passion for justice, he made war upon these evils, great and small.

It was "Revolution in terms of Rotary" that won the day in *It Can't Happen Here,* — the Berzelius Windrips, in short, sprang out of the Babbitts, the "Christian business men" who made "Patrick Henry orations about windshield-wipers," the boosters with pep and business-punch who respected only bigness, in mountains, jewels, muscles, wealth or words. In a town that led the world in the making of loud-speakers, Lowell T. Schmaltz was also a conspicuous success.

Such was the business civilization that appeared in Sinclair Lewis' books, a world that was mainly interested in size and numbers, a world in which Lincoln would have been the president of the Wrigley Gum concern and Hawthorne would have written ads for the new Hupmobile. But Lewis also found admirable types in these settings, — lawyers and business men, Samuel Dodsworth, the captain of industry who was not a Babbitt, and the honest and courageous judge, Cass Timberlane. Lewis' chosen heroes were realistic, magnanimous, frank, lovers of gallantry, haters of fencing and posing, tenacious, laughers at shams and loyal in a fashion that was too casual and natural to seem heroic.

In his temperamental zeal for reform, Lewis suggested Dickens, while he resembled Mark Twain in his high animal spirits, his pity for the under-dog, his hot head and his warm heart, his passionate, impulsive, mercurial quixotism. There was a touch of the philistine too in Lewis' relative disregard of the treatment and style of his novels as compared with the subject. For Lewis, indeed, the treatment was secondary, while he devoted all his care to the documentation of the all-important subject. Each of his novels had a major theme, a type and phase of American life, the theatre, editing, evangelism, manufacturing, science, hotel-keeping, prison-routine, the law or marriage, so that, while some of them were weak, their total effect was a panorama of twentieth-century American civilization. That his influential fables altered this civilization, and, by making his readers aware of it, often for the better, was a proof of the vitality of Sinclair Lewis, the irrepressible human force that might have been described as the conscience of the country.

*Sinclair Lewis and his second wife Dorothy Thompson.*

# The Imagists

*aiming for preciseness and technical perfection,*

*they attempted to "take the cold fat out of poetry."*

*While Eugene O'Neill and* the Provincetown Players were opening an era of the American stage, poetry was undergoing a "renascence." This was the title of Edna St. Vincent Millay's first long poem, published in 1912. The field of painting had been stirred by the first Armory Show. In the same vein, critics urged the American poets and novelists to give up their faded anaemic writing and recapture their "own essential madness." Soon the new poetry movement got under way with Ezra Pound as its master mind. Largely from the London of the circle of Pound, an art had begun to emanate that was to govern the poetry of the coming generation.

As the European editor of *Poetry,* Pound had fanatical convictions, he said, regarding the art of verbal expression, together with a singular gift of "orchestra directing." His learning, occasionally inaccurate, followed new paths with adventurous vigour.

Pound's attitude was reminiscent of the swagger of Whistler. He challenged one poet to a duel because he was "stupid," as he attacked the "elderly muttonheads" and the Victorian "doddards" much

in the manner of Mencken, his friend, at home. With an element of the gangster in him, a lover of sensations and violence, he also responded to Marinetti, whom he found, as he remarked, "thoroughly simpatico," as he was to find Mussolini, who was Marinetti's pupil.

What was the secret of his influence in London? In large degree the seriousness with which he affirmed the importance of poetry as an art. With his fresh learning and his feeling for the European tradition as a whole, he introduced new cadences and metres. He urged young minds to break away from the flaccid poetry of the past which he described as a "system of echoes," — "glutinous imitations of Keats, diaphanous dilutations of Shelley, woolly Wordsworthian paraphrases or swishful Swinburniana."

Pound had joined forces, for the rest, with the young Englishman T. E. Hulme, who shared his own ideas on poetry and art. Poetic merit, in Hulme's view, depended on precision, not on the importance of the subject; it was not to display emotion; it was to express the "temporary moods of cultivated, artificial people." Hulme added, "Personally I am of course in favour of the complete destruction of all verse more than twenty years old."

Pound, meanwhile, with his blasts in prose, and with poems to illustrate them, undertook to "desuet-ize" the work of the poets, — to "take the cold fat," as he said, out of current poetry, while incidentally "de-lousing" sculpture and music. As a literary soldier of fortune who was a schoolmaster born, he set out to change the tone of writing in English. For he was interested also in prose, in "exact presentation," in the clearness and hardness, the precision one found, for instance, in Stendhal and Flaubert. He called Milton "donkey-eared," "asinine," "disgusting." He also called Wordsworth a "silly old sheep." Pound agreed with Mallarmé who said, "All art hates the vague," and Verlaine who said, "Take eloquence and wring its neck," and he fought against "rhetorical din," "drivel," "gas," "mush" and "upholstered" words.

In a letter of 1908 Pound had listed the great subjects about which nine million poets had "spieled," spring, love, war, voyages, a young man's fancy, asking why he should write what he could translate out of Renaissance Latin or crib from the sainted dead.

He was all for concentration as opposed to diffuseness, and he looked for a twentieth-century poetry that would be "saner and harder . . . as much like granite as it can be." For Pound was possessed with a genuine passion for keeping the language "efficient," and, more than any other writer, he contributed to bring about the technical virtuosity of the poetry of the post-war years.

*Ezra Pound, a literary soldier of fortune, a village cracker-barrel crank with a touch of genius.*

*In the garden of his Paris studio.*

*Shortly before World War II.*

*In Paris before World War I.*

*Milton: "donkey-eared, asinine."*

*Wordsworth: a "silly old sheep."*

*Verlaine: "take eloquence and wring its neck."*

## AMY LOWELL

*In the early years of the poetry* movement, Pound was only one, however, of a chorus of new voices, and Amy Lowell was a rival of Pound as a leader of the Imagists, with whom she too forgathered for a while in London. Rebellion was the essence of her Yankee tradition and Amy Lowell's rebellious force of will was the secret alike of her success and failure. She was a born promoter. Seeing that America was giving birth to a first-rate product, she put her shoulder to the wheel and pushed it on the market. The product was American poetry, which was plainly on the rise again and which she handled like any other big business. It was another form of Standard Oil; and Miss Lowell set out to put it on the map. What scorn she felt for the "caged warblers" and "phonograph" poets who thought they still lived in Victorian times.

Like Eliot's Cousin Nancy, she "strode across the hills and broke them"; and if she was not bearded she was full of oaths. Her bed had eighteen pillows, and she had ten thousand black cigars and seven megatherian sheep-dogs that mauled and all but murdered her visitors.

For literary soldiership, or literary statesmanship, America had never seen Miss Lowell's equal. The poets had reason to thank their stars that they had a Lowell behind them, for whom editors and publishers were factory-hands and office-boys. Her voice over the telephone had the force of a gun, and one almost heard this going off at the other end of Texas.

Miss Lowell was a pyrotechnist, but some of her scenic effects were permanent; and when she was not permanent she was salutary. At a time when the *fond* of poetry was so weak, the way to sting it into life was to assert that nothing was important but the *forme;* and all the new poets made much of technique, — they sometimes talked as if nothing else mattered. For this was a time for tuning instruments. And how good was the new audacity after so much futile indirectness. The new poets reacted against bad technique by making technique an end in itself. What of it! The poets of the future would redress the balance.

The inner life of Miss Lowell knew no repose. She had solved none of her vital problems. Indeed, she was never a poet, properly speaking, — the poet in her never struggled through, — so she seized upon the outsides of things as her only chance of

effectuality, and her dramatic instinct achieved the rest.

Well, was it all for show? Was it merely a night of the Fourth of July? Was it only a parade and swagger of Boston fashion? There was surely enough of the material in Miss Lowell's talent, too much noise, too much excitement; and yet much remained that was new and crisp, vividness of colour, joy of action.

*Amy Lowell felt scorn for the "phonograph poets, the caged warblers" of the Tennysonian tradition.*

*Her house at Severels, headquarters for her campaign to "put poetry on the map."*

# Eugene O'Neill

*his imaginative grasp of contemporary life made him*

*a major spokesman of twentieth-century America.*

*Young O'Neill with sketch-book.*

*As early as 1910, perhaps, in* Sinclair Lewis' *Main Street,* Carol Kennicutt, surveying Gopher Prairie, dreamed of a little theatre there that would stage the kind of plays she associated with Paris and Moscow, London and Dublin. In the end, wishing to produce Bernard Shaw's *Androcles and the Lion* she was obliged to compromise on *The Girl from Kankakee,* and this was emblematic of the first tentative phase of the little theatre movement that soon swept the country. Within ten years, following the lead of the Provincetown Players, who brought out the work of American writers alone, scores and hundreds of little theatres were producing Shaw, Maeterlinck, Wedekind and Schnitzler, together with Ibsen and Strindberg, the precursors of them all.

The first American writer of plays to rival these eminent Europeans, — for the theatre in America lagged behind the novel, — Eugene O'Neill, the chief insurgent against the romantically banal, had become the unquestioned master of the drama of the country. He was the symbol of a renascence that paralleled on the stage the so-called renascence of poetry and other arts.

O'Neill had been writing since 1909, — poetry in the manner of Kipling at first, — and by 1914 he had written some one-act plays, among them the ever-memorable *Bound East for Cardiff*. It was the little theatre that enabled him to show these one-act plays, which sometimes served as sketches for long plays that followed, as it also enabled O'Neill to develop the experimental methods and the technical innovations in which he excelled. It was evident from the first that O'Neill belonged to a family of American minds that included Frank Norris and Jack London, while he was influenced by Freud as well, by Conrad, the novelist of the sea, and what he called the "behind life" plays of Strindberg. Like Stephen Crane, he was drawn to the underworld, and his first little play *The Web* concerned a prostitute and her protector in a squalid rooming-house on the lower East Side. O'Neill himself had wished to be a "two-fisted Jack London he-man sailor," and, as one might have guessed from this, he was actually in delicate health. He was the son of a well-known actor with whom he toured the United States and who felt that romantic acting had ruined his career. Distrusting what he had grown up to regard as the false dreams of romantic art, O'Neill shared the anti-romantic "homesickness for the gutter" that so many other young writers felt at the moment and, between terms at Princeton and Harvard, he had bummed with outcasts on the docks and lived in waterfront dives in New York and Buenos Aires.

In the forecastle O'Neill had known the sailors, their superstitions and their pipe-dreams, their touching credulity concerning "tomorrows." Were they not perfect illustrations of the perils of the romantic mood that had wrecked so much in his own childhood and his father's career? From first to last this was a theme that possessed O'Neill's imagination from his early story *Tomorrow* to *The Iceman Cometh.* He shared the feeling for the saloon that filled, in the American imagination, the place which the drawing-room had filled in the traditional novel, and he shared as well the feeling for the primitive types that appealed to writers from Norris and London to Hemingway, Steinbeck and Faulkner.

It is true, O'Neill wrote other plays that sprang from his perception of other types and other walks of life, plays about mentally developed people and about the New England country scene that he had observed as a reporter on a New London paper. He also discovered a great range of Negro life in plays like *The Dreamy Kid* and *The Emperor Jones.*

No one ever questioned the range of Eugene O'Neill's imaginative grasp of contemporary life. He touched in his plays at so many points the twentieth-century American scene that he seemed for two decades a major spokesman of it, a compeer of all the exposers of "suppressed desires." *The Dynamo* was a dramatization of a cult of Henry Adams. There was the hatred of family life that ran through *The First Man,* an obsession of so many novels, tales and poems. In *Desire Under the Elms,* in *The Robe,* above all in *Mourning Becomes Electra,* he dramatized "what's warped and twists and eats into itself and dies for a lifetime in shadow." There was an emotional intensity in him that reminded one of Dreiser, a passionate desire to discover the meaning of life. There were elements of greatness in him that established a number of his plays as landmarks of their time, while as a literary personality he left in the mind a chaotic impression as if he had not quite crystallized and found himself. Perhaps he seemed all the more the American of this latter end of the confident years because he was uncertain, tentative, puzzled and groping.

*O'Neill at Provincetown, when his plays were first staged by the Provincetown Players.*

The Long Voyage Home. *O'Neill shared with many writers from Norris to Hemingway the feeling for primitive types.*

*Edwin Arlington Robinson: his austere integrity revived a vital strain of the New England tradition.*

*After the trumpet calls of* Pound and Amy Lowell, — noisy at times, but tonic, — American poetry seemed destined for a liberation. When poets talked of this renascence, Edwin Arlington Robinson appeared to their mind among the prime precursors of the new art. At a time when American poetry had reached its lowest ebb, he in his obscurity had remained real and vibrant. His probing, questioning, doubting mind was the mind of the new generation. His austere integrity revived a vital strain of the New England tradition and his style cleared the ground for other growths.

Robinson's view of life was formed in "Tilbury Town." This stood for Gardiner, Maine, a moribund port on the Kennebec River where Robinson had spent his youth. Robinson, whose father had been a prosperous timber-merchant, had witnessed in his own household the decay of the region. The men of the once prosperous town, left with the "dusty ruins of their fathers' dreams," had lost their confidence, as the years went by, and they crept away into their houses and grew queerer and queerer. Eccentricities multiplied and misery walked patch-clad through the streets.

Abandoning New England, Robinson had carried to New York an aura of blight, desolation, decay and defeat. His view of the world was wintry, — so was his life, — and his style and his personality were bleak and bare. In the down-east phrase, Robinson was "master chilly." There was something starved and cold about him, as if his clothes were too scanty and his blood was too thin, as if the Maine wind had invaded his marrow. Taciturn, shy as an owl, diffident, lonely, he could only establish relations with others by drinking.

Unable to sustain himself by his writings, he had worked on the construction of the New York underground railroad and became vaguely known as the "poet in the subway." There, all day, in his long black coat and broad-brimmed hat, he paced the damp dark tunnel, with its odour of gases. If he saw a light at the end of the tunnel, it was usually choked with mephitic mist: it was not so much a light as a murky glimmer. And this was like the light in Robinson's poems. His faith was only a dim conjecture. More often he looked out upon "dark tideless floods of nothingness," where men escaped from their dungeons only to drown.

Most of Robinson's "lost" souls possessed some spirituality, and it was just for this reason that they were "lost." The people who were queer were the people who were real. Such was Robinson's message for an age of rebels.

When in the years before the first world war the literary arts were stirring anew in New England, Robinson returned to his native region. At the MacDowell Colony at Peterborough, a haven for writers, Edwin Arlington Robinson came into his own; and there, as time went on, his life achieved the rhythm that had once been broken and sporadic. The "misfit" became the master-poet in the cabin in the woods that faced Monadnock. The wintry mind of Robinson burst into summer in a passionate glorification of love and joy. He had his first popular success in *The Man Against the Sky,* which appeared as a part of the general chorus of new poets.

The Yankees were writing again with talent and vigour, and the new writers, appearances notwithstanding, remained in the New England tradition which they seemed to flout. They sometimes thought they were outside it, they sometimes wished

*At the MacDowell Colony at Peterborough, the misfit became the master-poet and the wintry mind of Robinson burst into summer.*

# Poetic Renaissance in New England

*the Yankees were writing again with talent and vigour.*

to be outside it, but unconsciously they were within it, which was more important; and was it not part of their tradition that they should flout tradition, even as the greatest of the Yankees had flouted it before them? That one should flout tradition was the first of laws for Emerson's heirs.

*This was distinctly the case* with E. E. Cummings and Edna Millay. Both delighted in turning topsy-turvy the house of the mind they had grown in, as in decking their "amorous themes with the honester stenches," and both had accepted the word of Blake, in face of their Yankee inheritance, "The road of excess leads to the palace of wisdom."

It sometimes seemed as if Cummings' governing motive was to thumb his nose at Cambridge and all it stood for, propriety, regularity, the neat and the tidy; but what, at bottom, was this motive if it was not the love of freedom that had always marked the Yankee mind? This passion filled *The Enormous Room* and constituted, in *Eimi,* the protest against the compulsions of Soviet Russia, a "joyless experiment," as he saw it, "in force and fear." With what gallantry and tenderness he painted, in *The*

*In* The Enormous Room *he expressed his love for men who could not be pigeon-holed.*

*Enormous Room,* the portraits of Jean le Nègre, Mexique, the Zulu, magnificent representations in the Rabelaisian vein that expressed his high animal spirits and his love for men who could not be pigeon-holed. With his burlesque-loving spirit, he saw the world through a child's eyes. He liked, as he said, "shining things," he liked barber-poles and hurdy-gurdies; and he liked to play the clown in the universal circus and knock over ministers, veterans, policemen and bankers. He was an enemy of clichés, pomposity and cant, and he played havoc with the English language as a way of protesting against them. Behind his mockery lay a sense of the infinite worth of the individual, coerced and constrained and menaced by a standardized world; and he showed that the Yankee mind, the more it changed, remained the more irrepressible and the more the same.

Much of Cummings' symbolism suggested his New England inheritance. His play *Tom* was based upon *Uncle Tom's Cabin,* and *The Enormous Room* abounded in symbols from *The Pilgrim's Progress.*

*E. E. Cummings, an enemy of clichés, pomposity and cant. Behind his mockery lay a sense of the infinite worth of the individual.*

*In Edna Millay's high lyrical* talent, the Yankee note, which one felt from the first, increased in depth and clarity as time went on, as the flippancy of her earlier verse, — its conscious naiveté mingled with wonder, — yielded to profundity of feeling. She had begun with fairy-tale fancies and travesties of nursery-rhymes, in which she turned the moral inside out; but this mood of an infantile mischief-maker had always been half-rapturous, and the rapture grew along with her force of passion. An accomplished and disciplined craftsman, Miss Millay was a learned poet, with the Yankee love of Virgil, Catullus, Chaucer and especially the Elizabethans whose vein she recaptured in her tragic sense of youth and the brevity of life. She was direct and lucid because her feeling was intense, like that of the ballad-makers whose forms she so generally followed. Her gift of music was like theirs, so was her physical perception, her sense of the miracle of consciousness and the things of earth. Her poems were full of the odours and flavours of New England, bayberry, hay, clover, seaweed and sorrel, and the salt smell of the ocean in them, of weedy mussels on rotting hulls, mingled with the rustle of eel-grass in the cove and the tinkling of cowbells in stony pastures.

*Edna St. Vincent Millay, an intense and learned poet.*

*Her poems were full of the odours and flavours of New England.*

234

*Robert Frost after his return from England in 1915.*

tree, the barn and the orchard; and through his gnarled poems, twisted and tough, a still music ran, like the music Thoreau heard in the poles by the railroad. Sometimes this was like the music of a hidden brook, lost in the grasses of a pasture, or the whisper of the scythe, or the whir of the grindstone; and it spoke of a tranquil happiness, drawn from fathomless wells of living, more often tragic than otherwise, but jubilant and hardy. A boy and a sage at once, Frost carried with him an aura as of infinite space and time. Yet so paternal was he, and so human, that many a younger writer felt about him as Gorky felt about Tolstoy, "I am not an orphan on the earth as long as this man lives on it."

*It was Robert Frost's function* to mediate between New England and the mind of the rest of the nation. In him the region was born again, — it seemed never to have lost its morning vigour and freshness; and one felt behind his local scene the wide horizons of a man whose sympathies and experience were continental. He had discovered New England after a boyhood in California, and he had tramped through the Carolinas and wandered over the West. He had made shoes and taught school between intervals at Dartmouth and Harvard. Two decades were to pass before the public heard of Frost. He stayed for a while with his family in England, and, returning home in 1915, lived the obscure existence of an upland farmer.

A true folk-mind, Frost was a mystical democrat, compassionately filled with a deep regard for the dignity of ordinary living; and he was an artist as well as a poet, a lover of goodness and wisdom, who found them, not by seeking them, but rather along the path of gaiety. At home, like Hawthorne's snow-image, in the frosty air of polar nights, he felt the wild and the strange in the low and familiar, and the stones in his walls were meteors, and the tamarack-swamps were playgrounds for his boreal fancy.

Frost invested with his white magic the woodpile, the log-road, the blueberry-patch, the birch

*In the twenties, in front of his study at South Shaftesbury, Vermont.*

235

# Epilogue

*mainspring of American literature: the faith of its writers in a better tomorrow.*

*In the dark epoch that followed* the first world war, disappointment beclouded the minds of many writers, especially the minds of those who had "believed in tomorrow."

To those who had shared the secular hopes not of the nineteenth century only but of the European world since the French Revolution, — the hopes that had filled Americans from still earlier times, — the change was like a backward leap from springtime into winter, one that was symbolized in literature in all manner of ways.

When Scott Fitzgerald said, "We are tired of great causes," he expressed the dominant mood of this epoch. Despair and a cynical aloofness seemed to prevail in all the centres of writing, — New York, Paris, London. In Paris, Marcel Proust had exiled himself in another way by sealing himself up from the world in a cork-lined bedroom to express his hatred of action and his contempt for men, while Ezra Pound, escaping there from a "mouldy" England, "as dead as mutton," escaped still further from his own "half savage country." In Paris too, long since, Gertrude Stein had withdrawn within the magic circle that excluded the "imbecilities of the multitude," while T. S. Eliot appeared in Paris, now and then, from London where he cut the cord that bound him to his American past.

In America, Henry Adams' pessimism dominated many of the young. Moreover, the great myth of *Moby-Dick* rose in the American imagination, and Melville's overpowering sense of the omnipotence of evil blacked out the sunniness and whiteness of Emerson and Whitman. The poet Robinson came into his own, and his feeling of the spiritual frustrations of men paralleled the fatalism of Eugene O'Neill and Dreiser, and Robinson Jeffers, in his "perishing republic," described humanity as "the wound that festers." The burden of the new generation of novelists was a sort of preordained despair, a note of defeat or failure, regression or decay that seemed to express the bewilderment of depolarized spirits.

T. S. Eliot exercised a singular power over the minds of writers in his time, — the poet of the "Waste Land," the "immense panorama of futility and anarchy which is contemporary history," as he once put it. That Eliot felt he was "living in a dying civilization," as a certain Bengali poet said, was enough in itself to explain his vogue when so many had thrown up the sponge and surrendered all faith in humanity and all hope of the future.

Still, Eliot had a distinct position and a positive personality in a day of confusion, hesitation, evasion and doubt, while he had the cosmopolitan tone that a deprovincialized world required, with its anthropological interest and its love of erudition. He restored the respect for learning in the minds of writers who had gone in for a shallow "self-expression." When all values, finally, were at risk in a world of idol-smashers, when many of the young were deliberately striving to turn themselves into barbarians, he reaffirmed the transcendent importance of tradition.

It was only logical that Eliot should have ignored the tradition of the country in which he had grown up. To this, in fact, he seemed to be actively hostile. He spoke of his aversion to Whitman's form and much of his matter, and he called Emerson's essays "an encumbrance," although Emerson and Whitman spoke for the only American tradition that had ever affected the outer world. Bound up with the tradition of the Revolution, of Jefferson, Paine and Crèvecoeur, this tradition gave Matthew Arnold his hopes for the United States along with thousands of intelligent Europeans from Goethe onward. The belief in the goodness of man was the core of America, in fact, — to the world America meant this or nothing, — it was what the "Latin genius" was to France.

Yet this was more or less forgotten in the season of earthquake weather between two wars, although, even if the exuberant hopes of Whitman had been dampened, it was virtually certain to recur. The future of democracy obviously hung on a faith in *some* goodness in human nature, some inborn moral feeling and capacity for freedom; and, inasmuch as the American tradition meant this or nothing to the world, one continued to look for its traces in American letters. Were the authors of the twenties really as nihilistic, as life-denying, as they seemed to be, or was there something else beneath their surface? Observing of Whitman that "his bequest is still to be realized in all its implications," Hart Crane, like Vachel Lindsay in his very different way, perpetuated the American Utopian train of thinking.

This was the traditional American feeling, and did not the writers continue to share it behind the masks they were generally apt to wear, underneath the cynicism that covered them like a film of steel, hiding their actual sympathies, concerns and wishes? Behind virtually all the "pitiful creatures that people contemporary fiction,"— a phrase of Krutch that remained appropriate for years,—one discerned an indictment of the world that had made them, on the part of their creators, that was bound up with a desire for their welfare and growth. As Thomas Wolfe said, "The essence of all faith for people of my belief is that man's life can be, and will be, bet-

ter," and this was as true of Dos Passos and Steinbeck, of Hemingway and Farrell, as it was of Carl Sandburg or Lindsay or Sinclair Lewis. All were concerned in some fashion, as Faulkner was also concerned, with the fate of the "little man" for whom Jefferson and Lincoln had shared an affection with so many American writers. He was the hero of Cummings' *The Enormous Room* as much as of Stephen Crane's *The Red Badge of Courage,* and as much in the case of *The Grapes of Wrath,* which asserted his dignity and rightful claims as Hemingway asserted the claims of the Spanish peasants. Behind all the negations of the novelists there still loomed the expectant mood of the pre-war time when "poet" and "radical" were almost interchangeable terms. Neither Sandburg nor Lewis Mumford nor Archibald MacLeish was more clearly in this line than Hemingway when he first acquired in Spain a respect for human nature.

Thus, behind whatever masks, all these typical American writers continued to express the traditional American faith; and was it not, in fact, because they cared for the fate of men on earth that they seemed so chagrined and disenchanted? Were they not denunciatory in proportion as they cared for this, in proportion as America had fallen short of its promise, as the gap had widened between reality and the idea of the country that Americans had always had in mind? This was the idea of *what ought to be,* and the promise of America was that *what ought to be, will be.*

It was in the name of these Utopian insights that the American novelists condemned their world. They were the "eternal necessary human values" to which Scott Fitzgerald paid tribute in a passage of *The Crack-Up,* "the old verities and truths of the heart, lacking which any story is ephemeral and doomed" to which William Faulkner referred in his speech at Stockholm. That progress exists even Mencken, the professional pessimist, came to believe.

True or not, this belief was so deeply ingrained in the American mind that it seemed to be ineradicably connected with it, along with Thomas Wolfe's belief that "the true fulfillment of our spirit, of our people, of our . . . land, is yet to come." This was the general American belief, and it was bound up with another belief, that men could be trusted to set things right in time, the basis of what Thomas Jefferson called "the unquestionable republicanism of the American mind."

# Acknowledgments

The authors express their thanks to the following individuals for their generous help in the assembling of the picture material for this volume.

Mrs. Sherwood Anderson
Lincoln Wade Barnes
J. Terry Bender
Francis L. Berkeley, Jr.
Carey S. Bliss
James Branch Cabell
Dr. Harold Dean Cater
Mrs. Ralph Caterall
Josephine Cobb
William Cole
Mrs. E. E. Cummings
George Cushing, Jr.
Mrs. Hildreth Daniel
Thomas De Valcourt
A. C. Edwards
Kimball C. Elkins
Albert Erskine
Charles M. Fleischner
Edward W. Forbes
James W. Foster
Donald C. Gallup
Dr. John Gordan
Charles R. Green
Wilhelmina S. Harris
William Henri Harrison
Robert Hill
Adeleide Howe
James P. Howe
Professor William W. Howells
William Jackson

John Melville Jennings
Mrs. Hannah Josephson
Dorothy Hale Litchfield
Augustus P. Loring
George Macy
Keith Martin
Helen C. McCormack
Ken McCormick
Patricia McManus
Addison M. Metcalf
Norma Millais
Clifford P. Monahan
Robert G. Newman
Georgia O'Keeffe
J. Gilman D'Arcy Paul
Virginia H. Patterson
Irene M. Poirier
Max Pollack
C. Park Pressey
John Richards
Stephen T. Riley
Elizabeth Roth
Carl Sandburg
Upton Sinclair
Carl Stange
Louis Stark
Vincent Starrett
Frieda C. Thies
Mrs. Irita Van Doren
Edward Weeks

Isabelle Wilder

# Source of Illustrations

All illustrations, unless otherwise credited, are from the Bettmann Archive, New York.

The following organizations have kindly permitted the use of their material:

American Academy of Arts and Letters: p. 191 top left; p. 207; p. 232 bottom; p. 235 bottom r.
American Museum of Natural History: p. 23 bottom r.
Amherst College: p. 5
Appleton-Century-Crofts: p. 137
Berg Collection, New York Public Library: p. 121 top r.
Berkshire Atheneum: p. 110
Boston Museum of Fine Arts: p. 42-43; p. 73 bottom l; p. 93 top; p. 113 top
Boston Public Library: p. 48 r.
Brown Brothers: p. 225 bottom
Brown University Library: p. 32 top l.
Doubleday & Company: p. 188 bottom l.
Essex Institute: p. 78 r; p. 101
European Picture Service: p. 235 top
Fogg Museum of Art: p. 45 center; p. 99 top
Frick Art Reference Library: p. 29 bottom; p. 36 center
Harcourt Brace & Company: p. 219 top r; center l.
Harvard University: p. 65 bottom r; p. 152 top r; p. 167 top l and center; p. 175; p. 229
Harvard University Press: p. 64 bottom l.
Haverhill Public Library: p. 87 top and center r.
Houghton Mifflin: p. 59 top r; center; p. 208
Indiana University Press: p. 200 center
International News: p. 224; p. 228 bottom l.
Johns Hopkins University: p. 135
Jones Library: p. 172-173
Keystone: p. 187 bottom r.
Alfred A. Knopf: p. 184; p. 209 bottom l; p. 222-223

Little Brown: p. 93 bottom
Augustus P. Loring: p. 111 center; p. 113 bottom l.
Macmillan Company: p. 200 bottom; p. 210; p. 214; p. 215
Massachusetts Historical Society: p. 53 bottom; p. 89 center; p. 99 bottom; p. 154 top and center l; p. 155 top
Norma Millais: p. 234
Nickolas Muray: p. 209 bottom r; p. 219 bottom; p. 231 top
National Archives: p. 52 top l; p. 115
New York Historical Society: p. 16 top l.
New York Public Library: p. 38; p. 104-105
New York State Historical Society: p. 16 bottom l; p. 18 center
Orchard House: p. 76 bottom l.
Peabody Museum: p. 46 center
Picture Post: p. 169 bottom l.
Rand McNally: p. 82 bottom r.
Charles Scribner's Sons: p. 190
Stanford University Library: p. 212 top r.
Sunnyside Restoration Project: p. 15
U. S. Department of the Interior: p. 68
University of California: p. 213
University of Virginia: p. 21 7
Valentine Museum: p. 31 bottom c., r.; p. 32 bottom; p. 216
Vassar College Library: p. 234 top l.
Worcester Art Museum: p. 50 l.
Yale Collections of American Literature: p. 125 center; p. 220-221; p. 226 bottom; p. 231

# Index

Adams, Brooks, 153
Adams, Charles, 156
Adams, Charles Francis, 6, 150, 152, 153
Adams, Henry, viii, 6, 150, 151, 152-56, 181, 219, 231, 236
Adams, John, 48, 85
Adams, John Quincy, 152
Addams, Jane, 194
Ade, George, 197
Addison, Joseph, 8
Aeschylus, 49
Aesop, 4
Agassiz, Alexander, 153
Agassiz, Louis, 98, 99
Alcott, Bronson, 68, 72, 74-76, 83, 93, 94, 100, 133
Alcott, Louisa May, 75
Aldrich, Thomas Bailey, 176-77
Alger, Horatio, jr., 157
Allan, John, 30, 31
Allston, Washington, 58, 93
Ames, Fisher, 6
Anderson, Sherwood, 131, 146, 197, 206, 221
Armour, Philip D., 202
Arnold, Matthew, 164, 237
Asbury, Francis, 25
Astor, John Jacob, 20
Audubon, John James, 23, 39, 40, 183
Austin, Mary, 218

Balzac, Honoré de, 158, 180, 185, 204
Bancroft, George, 3, 50-51, 79, 109
Barlow, Joel, 6, 7
Barnum, Phineas T., 102, 105, 106, 107, 131, 157
Barrie, James M., 169
Bartram, William, 5
Beadle, Erastus, 129
Beard, Charles A., ix
Beecher, Henry Ward, 3, 89, 102, 107
Beecher, Lyman, 88
Beerbohm, Max, 121
Beethoven, Ludwig van, 4
Bellamy, Edward, 163

Bennett, Arnold, 147
Berenson, Bernard, 218
Bettman, Otto L., vii
Bierce, Ambrose, 212, 223
Billings, Josh, (H. W. Shaw), 133
Billy the Kid, (William H. Bonney), 128, 129
Blake, William, 233
Blaxton, 44
Boker, 3
Boone, Daniel, 22
Bowditch, Nathaniel, 46
Boyeson, H. H., 181
Brady, Mathew, 82, 105
Bras-Coupé, 140
Breughel, ix
Brevoort, Henry, 12
Bridger, Jim, 22, 128
Brown, Charles Brockden, 5
Browne, 112
Browne, Charles Farrar, (see also Ward, Artemus), 131
Browne, Ross, 129
Brownson, Orestes, 73
Bryant, William Cullen, 2, 21, 36-39, 40, 103, 109
Buckminster, 44
Buddha, 63, 154
Buffalo Bill, (William F. Cody), 128
Bunner, Henry C., 183
Burke, Edmund, 60
Burns, Robert, 100
Burritt, Elihu, 60
Burroughs, John, 119
Butler, Benjamin F., 151
Byron, George Gordon, Lord, 12, 47, 88

Cable, George W., 140-41
Cahan, Abraham, 183
Calamity Jane, (Mary Jane Canary), 128
Calderon de la Barca, Pedro, 49
Campbell, Thomas, 62
Capers, Uncle Bob, 136
Carey, Mathew, 4
Carlyle, Thomas, 61, 63, 75

# Index

Carson, Kit, 128
Cary, Alice, 3
Cartwright, Peter, 25
Cather, Willa, 208-209, 210
Catlin, George, 24, 40
Catullus, 234
Cervantes Saavedra, Miguelde, 49, 128
Champlain, Samuel de, 53
Channing, Edward Tyrrel, 44, 45
Channing, Ellery, 68, 70
Channing, William Ellery, 3, 47, 52, 62, 75
Channing, William Henry, 73
Charlemagne, 53
Chateaubriand, François René, 49
Chaucer, 234
Chivers, Holley, 32
Christy, 131
Clemens, Samuel, (see also Twain, Mark), 109, 142
Clemm, Virginia, 33
Cole, Thomas, 39
Coleridge, William, 5, 12, 61
Conrad, Joseph, 217, 230
Constant, Benjamin, 49
Cooke, P. Pendleton, 3
Cooper, James Fenimore, 3, 16-20, 21, 39, 40, 89, 102, 103, 107, 138
Cortez, Hernando, 51
Cozzens, 3
"Craddock, Charles Edward," (see Murfree, Mary)
Cranch, Christopher, 64, 73
Crandall, Dr., 86
Crane, Hart, 237
Crane, Stephen, 181, 184-85, 189, 213, 230
"Crayon, Goeffrey," (see also Irving, Washington), 12
Crèvecoeur, Michel, 237
Crockett, David, ("Davy"), 22, 118, 144
Cromwell, Oliver, 84
Cummings, E. E., 233, 237
Curtis, George William, 3, 73, 107

Dana, Charles A., 72, 73
Dana, Richard Henry, 2, 45, 58-60, 85, 157
Dante, 49, 56, 75
Davis, Richard Harding, 190
Darwin, Charles, 96, 157, 215
Dell, Floyd, 186

Dennie, Joseph, 103
de Staël, Madame, 49
Dickens, Charles, 89, 116, 125, 131, 132, 133, 226
Dickinson, Austin, 171, 173
Dickinson, Edward, 171, 172
Dickinson, Emily, 100, 157, 171-73, 176, 185, 194
Dickinson, Lavinia, 173
Disson, 49
Dodge, Mabel, 219
Dos Passos, John, 237
Dostoievsky, Feodor M., 89, 185
Douglas, Stephen A., 199
Dow, Lorenzo, 25
Dreiser, Theodore, viii, 180, 188, 194, 201-205, 231, 236
Du Maurier, George, 190
Dunne, Finley Peter, 197-98
Durand, Asher B., 38, 39, 40
Dwight, John Sullivan, 73
Dwight, Timothy, 6, 7
Dymock, Atkinson, ix

Earp, Wyatt, 128
Eddy, Mary Baker, 160
Edwards, Jonathan, 6
Eggleston, Edward, 132, 200
Eichorn, 49
Eliot, Charles William, 156, 157
Eliot, T. S., 229, 236, 237
Emerson, Ralph Waldo, 3, 23, 26, 45, 62-66, 70, 75, 92, 93, 98, 99, 102, 103, 107, 110, 114, 134, 157, 166, 178, 197, 223, 233, 236, 237
Emerson, William, 62
Emmett, Dan, 131
Endicott, John, 77
Epstein, Jacob, 182
Everett, Edward, 48, 50, 54, 85

Farrell, James T., 197, 237
Faulkner, William, 216, 230, 231, 237
Fichte, Johann Gottlieb, 61
Field, Eugene, 194, 195
Field, Marshall, 202
Fields, James T., 93
Fink, Mike, 22, 118
Fiske, John, 157
Fitzgerald, F. Scott, 21, 236, 237
Flaubert, Gustave, 167, 227
Flaxman, 79

# Index

Flynt, Josiah, 183
Foster, Stephen, 103, 133
Fox, George, 116
Franklin, Benjamin, 4, 6, 63, 223
Frederic, Harold, 181
Frederick the Great, 49
Freiligrath, 57
Frémont, John Charles, 103, 118
French, Daniel Chester, 62
Freud, Sigmund, 96
Froissart, Jean, 49, 51, 134
Frost, Robert, 235
Fuller, Henry B., 194, 196
Fuller, Margaret, 3, 71, 72, 74, 90, 219
Furness, Horace Howard, 120

Garland, Hamlin, 181, 200
Garrison, William Lloyd, 84, 85
Gautier, Théophile, 179
George, Henry, 162-63
Gibson, Charles Dana, 190
Gilchrist, Herbert, 121
Glasgow, Ellen, 216-17
Godkin, E. L., 176
Godwin, 3
Goethe, Johann Wolfgang von, 63, 75, 99, 179, 237
Goldman, Emma, 186
Goncourt Brothers, 167
Gorky, Maxim, 182, 235
Grady, Henry, 137
Grant, Ulysses S., 153
Gray, Asa, 98
Greeley, Horace, 102, 106, 107, 108, 144
Greenough, Horatio, 58
Gluck, Christopher von, 83
Griswold, Rufus, 33
Gibbon, Edward, 52

Hale, Edward Everett, 45, 92, 178
Halleck, Fitz-Greene, 2, 20, 21
Hampden, John, 84
Hansa, Per, 208
Hapgood, Hutchins, 182, 183
Harland, Henry, 190
Harper, James, 28
Harris, Frank, 128, 194
Harris, Joel Chandler, 134, 136-37

Harris, William T., 76
Harte Bret, 103, 109, 124, 125, 126-27, 132, 139, 162, 164, 212, 214
Hartshorne, S. W., 32
Hauptmann, Gerhardt, 186
Hawthorne, Nathaniel, 3, 5, 67, 73, 77-83, 89, 92, 93, 100, 110, 112, 114, 157, 166, 174, 175, 178, 223, 226, 235
Hay, John 130, 136, 153, 154
Heine, Heinrich, 88, 89
Hemingway, Ernest, 146, 185, 190, 213, 221, 231, 237
Henry, O., (William Sidney Porter), 180, 188-89, 197, 206
Henry, Patrick, 26
Herford, Oliver, 179
Herrick, Robert, 181, 196
Hickok, William, ("Wild Bill"), 128
Hicks, Elias, 204
Higginson, Thomas Wentworth, 9, 136, 151, 172, 173
Hitler, Adolph, 223
Hoffman, 3
Hogarth, William, 116
Holmes, Oliver Wendell, Dr., 3, 45, 92, 93, 94-97, 98, 99, 100, 179
Homer, 68, 115, 184, 185
Homer, Winslow, 118, 136, 184
Hoppe, E. O., 167
Horace, (Q. H. Flaccus), 20
Howe, E. W., 130, 131
Howe, Julia Ward, 92, 178
Howells, William Dean, 120, 130, 146, 151, 153, 158-62, 163, 165, 176, 177, 178, 181, 183, 185, 189, 200, 207, 213
Hugo, Victor, 89
Hulme, T. E., 227
Huneker, James, 222, 223

Ibsen, Henrik, 186, 196, 230
Irving, Washington, 2, 8, 9, 10-16, 20, 29, 39, 40, 49, 52, 102, 103, 107, 110, 143
Irving, William, 10-11

Jackson, Helen Hunt, ("H. H."), 174
Jacobi, 61
James, Henry, 5, 21, 133, 138, 151, 153, 157, 164, 165, 166-70, 176, 177, 181
James, Henry, The elder, 95, 166
James, Jesse, 128

# Index

James, William, 151, 157, 166, 167, 170, 220
Jay, John, 16
Jeffers, Robinson, 236
Jefferson, Thomas, 26, 48, 216, 237
Jewett, Sarah Orne, 89, 175, 176, 209
Jogues, Father, 53
John of Barneveld, 52
Johnson, Eastman, 136
Johnson, Samuel, Dr., 60
Johnston, Richard Malcolm, 134

Kane, Elisha Kent, 109
Kant, Immanuel, 73
Karolick, Philip Harry, 42
Keats, John, 5, 90, 227
Kemble, Gouverneur, 10
Kennedy, John P., 3, 27, 28, 29, 32
Kendall, G. W., 3
Kenton, Simon, 118
King, Clarence, 154
Kinglake, 154
Kipling, Rudyard, 213, 214, 230
Kirkland, 3, 44, 45
Krutch, Joseph W., 237

La Farge, John, 153, 154, 167
Lafayette, Marquis de, 49
Lanier, Sidney, 134-36
La Salle, Cavelier de, 53
Lawrence, D. H., 41, 219
Lear, Edward, 221
Leland, Charles Godfrey, 164
Lenin, Nikolai, 215
Leopold I, (of Belgium), 56
Lewis, Grace (Hegger), (Mrs. Sinclair), 225
Lewis, Sinclair, 207, 224-26, 230, 237
Longstreet, Augustus, 29
Lincoln, Abraham, 22, 26, 103, 118-19, 144, 153, 199, 226, 237
Lindsay, Vachel, 198-99, 209, 237
Linnæus, Carolus, 37
Livy, 51
London, Jack, 187, 199, 214-15, 230, 231
Longfellow, Henry Wadsworth, 2, 24, 54-58, 88, 90, 92, 93, 103, 131, 133
Longfellow, Samuel, 45
Lope de Vega, 49
Lowell, Amy, 177, 229, 232
Lowell, James Russell, 3, 90-91, 177, 178

Lowell, John, 44
Luhan, Antonio, 219
Luhan, Mabel, (see Dodge, Mabel), 218-220

Macaulay, Thomas B., 88, 223
Mac Leish, Archibald, 237
Madison, James, 49
Maeterlinck, Maurice, 230
Mahomet, 63
Mallarmé, Stéphane, 228
Mann, Horace, 60
Marinetti, 227
Marion, Francis, 4
Marsh, Reginald, 203
Marshall, John, 26
Marx, Karl, 96, 215
Masters, Edgar Lee, 198-99
Mather, Cotton, 6
Matisse, Henri, 220
Mazzini, Giuseppe, 116
McClure, S. S., 188
Melbourne, Lord, 27
Melville, Herman, 102, 103, 107, 110-14, 133, 210, 236
Mencken, Henry L., 222-23, 224, 227, 237
Michael Angelo, 118
Millay, Edna St. Vincent, 227, 233, 234
Miller, Joaquin, 124, 126
Milton, John, 85, 227
Mitchell, 3
Molière, 179
Monckton, Henry Lewis, viii
Monk, Hank, 144
Montaigne, Michel, Siegneur de, 63
Montezuma, 51
Moody, Dwight L., 151
Moore, Thomas, 10
Morris, 3
Motley, John Lothrop, 3, 45, 52, 92, 98, 150, 157
Mount, William Sidney, 115
Mozart, Wolfgang Amadeus, 4, 83
Muir, John, 211
Mumford, Lewis, 237
Murfree, Mary, ("Charles Edward Craddock"), 139
Mussolini, Benito, 227

Nagel, L., 123
Napoleon III, (of France), 176

# Index

Nathan, George Jean, 223
Newton, Isaac, 46, 63
Nietzsche, Freidrich, 63, 215, 222, 223
Norris, Frank, 181, 186, 188, 202, 213, 214, 215, 230, 231
Norton, Charles Eliot, 98, 99, 151
Novalis, (Freidrich von Hardenberg), 134
Now, Herbert, 64

O'Neill, Eugene, 227, 230-31, 236

Paine, Thomas, 7, 236
Parke, 3
Parker, Theodore, 60, 174
Parkman, Francis, 45, 52, 53, 151, 179
Parrington, Vernon, ix
Pascal, 62
Paul, Jean, 61
Paulding, James K., 10, 11, 20, 21, 39
Peabody, Elizabeth, 71, 74, 79
Peabody, Sophia, (Mrs. Nathaniel Hawthorne), 79, 80
Peale, Charles Wilson, 5
Pearsall, 121
Peirce, Benjamin, 98, 99
Peter the Great, 52, 53
Petrarch, 49
Phidias, 58
Phillips, Wendell, 85, 133
Picasso, Pablo, 220, 221
Plato, 62, 63, 64, 74
Plutarch, 157
Poe, Edgar Allan, viii, 3, 5, 31-36, 39, 90, 91, 100, 212
Poe, Elizabeth, 31
Polack, Max, 201
Pontiac, 53
Poor, Henry V., 68
Pope, Alexander, 8
Porter, William Sidney, (see also Henry, O.), 180, 188
Pound, Ezra, 227-28, 229, 232, 236
Powell, Major, 128, 129
Prentice, 3
Prescott, William Hickling, 3, 50, 51, 52, 88, 109
Proust, Marcel, 236
Pym, John, 84

Rabelais, François, 23
Randolph, John, 27

Raphael, 145
Reed, John, 190
Remington, Frederic, 210
Rice, ("Daddy"), 131
Richardson, 5
Richter, Jean Paul, 134
Richardson, H. H., 153
Ricketson, D., 64
Riis, Jacob A., 182
Riley, James Whitcomb, 132, 133, 200, 201
Ripley, George, 72, 73, 80
Ritchie, Mowatt, Mrs., 3
Robinson, Edward Arlington, 232, 236
Rogers, Samuel, 58
Rolland, Romain, 226
Rölvaag, Ole, viii, 208
Roosevelt, Theodore, 137, 211, 214
Rousseau, Jean Jacques, 5
Rossetti, Dante G., 99
Rowson, Susanna, 6
Rubens, Peter Paul, 118
Ruskin, John, 99
Russell, Irwin, 136
Ryder, Albert, 164

Saint-Gaudens, Augustus, 154
Sainte-Beuve, Charles Augustin, 114
Saltus, Edgar, 189
Sand, George, 61, 88
Sandberg, Carl, 197, 198-99, 237
Sandoz, Jules, 208
Sargent, John Singer, 165
Saxe, 3
Schleiermacher, Friedrich, 61
Schnitzler, Arthur, 230
Schoolcraft, Henry Rowe, 24, 57
Scott, Sir Walter, 10, 12, 13, 27, 52, 62, 88, 89, 131, 134, 147
Sedgwick, Catherine M., 2
Seton, Ernest Thompson, 218
Shakespeare, William, 8, 75, 112, 115, 128, 219
Shelley, Percy Bysshe, 5, 227
Sienkiewicz, Henry, 181
Sigourney, Lydia H., 2
Shaw, Bernard, 186, 196, 222, 224, 226, 230
Sheean, Vincent, 190
Silliman, Benjamin, 7
Simms, William Gilmore, 3, 28

# Index

Sinclair, Upton, 187
Sloan, John, 204
Socrates, 74
Sorony, 121
Southey, Robert, 5
Southworth, Mrs., 2
Sparks, Jared, 50, 54
Spencer, Herbert, 158, 215
Spengler, Oswald, 40, 41
Spinoza, Baruch, 73
Stannard, Mrs., 31
Steffens, Lincoln, 182, 183, 186
Steichen, Edward, 199
Stein, Gertrude, viii, 206, 220-21, 236
Stein, Leo, 220, 221
Steinbeck, John, 231, 237
Stendhal, 227
Stephens, John Lloyd, 109, 110
Stevenson, Robert Louis, 181
Stieglitz, Alfred, 186, 204
Stoddard, Charles Warren, 124, 144
Stoddard, Richard H., 3
Stowe, Calvin, 88
Stowe, Harriet Beecher, 3, 88-89, 92, 93
Stravinsky, Igor, viii
Strindberg, Johan A., 186, 230
Stuyvesant, Peter, 9
Sumner, Charles, 85
Swift, Jonathan, 212
Swinburne, Algernon C., 227

Tarbell, Ida, 186
Tarkington, Booth, 207, 224
Taylor, Bayard, 3, 108
Taylor, Edward Thompson, 113
Taine, Hippolyte, 132
Tennyson, Alfred, 56, 90, 159, 177
Thackeray, William Makepeace, 98
Thompson, Dorothy, 226
Thoreau, Henry, 45, 61, 66-70, 75, 100, 101, 102, 108, 110, 118, 157, 219
Ticknor & Fields, 93
Ticknor, George, 48, 54, 93, 158
Ticknor, William D., 93
Toklas, Alice B., 221
Turgenev, Ivan, 167, 183
Tolstoy, Leo, 89, 162, 163, 182, 183, 204, 235
Trollope, Mrs. 108

Trumbull, John, 6
Tuckerman, Henry T., 3
Twain, Mark, (see also Clemens, Samuel), 103, 124, 125, 126, 133, 141, 142-149, 162, 163, 165, 177, 181, 185, 210, 226

Uncle Remus, 136

Van Corlaer, Anthony, 9
Veblen, Thorstein, 162, 226
Verlaine, Paul, 228
Victoria, (of England), 89
Virgil, 234
Voltaire, François, 212

Wallace, Lew, 129, 132
Warner, Charles Dudley, 147
Washington, George, 4, 52, 85
Ward, Artemus, (see also Browne, Charles Farrar), 130, 131
Webster, Daniel, 47
Webster, Noah, 46
Wedekind, Frank, 230
Weems, (Parson), Mason Locke, Rev., 4
Welby, Amelia, 3
Wells, H. G., 163, 179, 184, 224, 226
Wendell, Barrett, 178
Wharton, Edith, 190-91
Whistler, James A. McN., 164, 165, 227
White, Maria, (Mrs. James Russell Lowell), 90, 91
Whitman, George, 118
Whitman, Walt, viii, 23, 26, 100, 102, 107, 110, 114-21, 128, 145, 184, 185, 199, 202, 219, 236, 237
Whitman, Sarah Helen, 33
Whittier John Greenleaf, 3, 85, 86-87, 92, 93, 100, 103, 133, 179
William the Silent, 52
Willis, Nathaniel Parker, 3, 21, 39, 90
Wirt, William, 32
Wister, Owen, 210
Wolfe, James, 53
Wolfe, Thomas, 138, 216, 237
Woolson, Constance Fenimore, 138-39
Wordsworth, William, 90, 227, 228
Worcester, Joseph, 54

Zeno, 66
Zoroaster, 64
Zola, Émile, 167, 182, 213